WOMEN AS
NATIONAL LEADERS

OTHER RECENT VOLUMES IN THE
SAGE FOCUS EDITIONS

WOMEN AS NATIONAL LEADERS

Michael A. Genovese

editor

SAGE PUBLICATIONS
International Educational and Professional Publisher
Newbury Park   London   New Delhi

For information address:

 SAGE Publications, Inc.
2455 Teller Road
Newbury Park, California 91320

SAGE Publications Ltd.
6 Bonhill Street
London EC2A 4PU
United Kingdom

SAGE Publications India Pvt. Ltd.
M-32 Market
Greater Kailash I
New Delhi 110 048 India

Printed in the United States of America

Library of Congress Cataloging-in-Publication Data

Main entry under title:

Women as national leaders / edited by Michael A. Genovese.
      p. cm. —(Sage focus editions ; 153)
    Includes bibliographical references and index.
    ISBN 0-8039-4337-7 (cl.). —ISBN 0-8039-4338-5 (pb.)
    1. Women heads of state—Case studies. 2. Women in politics—Case studies. I. Genovese, Michael A.
    HQ1236.W6376 1993
    351.003'082—dc20   92-33064
                                                            CIP

93 94 95 96   10 9 8 7 6 5 4 3 2 1

Sage Production Editor: Judith L. Hunter

To my mother and father—
two giving people
who show grace under pressure,
love in the midst of adversity,
care and support in all things.

Contents

Preface

Studies of political leadership have been remarkably non-gender specific. This is due primarily to a tacit assumption, usually made by male scholars, that leaders are men! Historically, there is of course a good deal of validity to this assumption—almost all political leaders *have been* men. To refer to a generic of head of state as "him" may thus be understandable, if inaccurate.

Recently, however, the number of women who have served or are serving as heads of governments has risen to the point where the word *leader* is losing its gender reference. In the post-World War II period, the resurgence of the women's movement and the emergence of women as heads of national governments have given us the opportunity to examine the performance of women as political leaders, and to ask, Does gender matter? Do men exercise power in a manner different from women? Is *gender, institutional structure, role, environment,* or some other variable key to understanding executive performance?

This study is an attempt to grapple with the difficult and controversial questions relating to gender and leadership. The contributors to this volume focus on seven women leaders: Golda Meir of Israel (1969-1974), Indira Gandhi of India (1966-1977 and 1980-1984), Margaret Thatcher of England (1979-1990), Isabel Perón of Argentina (1974-1976), Corazon Aquino of the Philippines (1986-1992), Benazir Bhutto of Pakistan (1988-1990), and Violeta Chamorro of Nicaragua (1990-). While this universe of women leaders is relatively small, we can begin to explore a variety of important questions relating to gender and leadership in the political arena.

This work is not all-inclusive. Some women who have served as heads of governments are not included. The selection here is designed to be representative, and to serve as theory-building (or pretheoretical) steps in our understanding of the impact of gender on political leadership at the national level.

In an effort to develop a truly comparative study of women leaders, all authors were asked to focus their case studies on common questions: What was the *context*—the political, social, and economic situation—at that point in time? What *biographical* factors were important to this leader's rise? What *path to power* did the leader take? What *leadership style* was employed? How well or poorly did the leader *perform*, and why? And finally, to what extent, and how, did *gender* matter in this leader's rise and performance? It is my hope that, by answering these questions, this collection of cases can avoid the common criticism that case studies are "idiosyncratic" and thus "lack . . . utility for theory-building" (Thomas, 1983, p. 50).

Betty Glad (1990-1991), in defending the use of case studies, argues, "Detailed case studies . . . enable the researcher to explore a wide variety of complex relationships. From such studies, one can begin to delineate those factors which transcend the case at hand, as well as those which are specific to the particular decision or outcome being studied" (p. 13). My goal, and that of the contributors, is to use these case studies as a preliminary step in theory building on gender and leadership issues.

It is customary for authors and editors to preface their books with mournful claims that the work was more arduous and difficult than first imagined, or that the research and writing of a book were grueling and painful (I confess to having done so myself—in my youth). But I must say that, in many respects, putting this book together was a real joy ("Blasphemy!" my fellow authors are screaming). How is this possible? No doubt I can attribute this to the good fortune of choosing chapter authors who were remarkably courteous and generous, and extremely punctual. From discussions with others who have assembled edited works with original pieces, I know how unusual this sounds, and I deeply thank all the authors in this book for their professionalism and their care.

Allow me also to thank my research assistants, Valerie Barreiro, Audry Chesel, and Marija Tenzera, for their tireless efforts, and typists Margaret Edwards, Bernadette Bernard, and Edna Hastings for their outstanding work (and for their patience). I very much appreciate their contributions.

Michael A. Genovese

References

Glad, B. (1990-1991). The idiosyncratic presidency: Contingency and the use of case studies and synthetic proofs in scientific analysis. *Presidency Research Group Newsletter, 13*(1), 6-20.

Thomas, N. (1983). Case studies. In G. C. Edwards & S. J. Wayne (Eds.), *Studying the presidency* (pp. 50-78). Knoxville: University of Tennessee Press.

1

Women as Chief Executives

Does Gender Matter?

MICHAEL A. GENOVESE
SETH THOMPSON

> Her wings are clipped and it is found deplorable she does not fly.
> (Simone de Beauvoir; quoted in Darcy, Welch, & Clark, 1987, p. 3)

The study of political leadership, while widely recognized as being of great importance, is a much-neglected subject in political science (but see Burns, 1978; Jones, 1989). There are individual studies of particular leaders, but precious little that bring together this idiosyncratic material in a pre-theoretical way. Even more rare is the study of political leadership that focuses on gender issues (Adams & Yoder, 1985). Because of the dearth of women political executives, the field of leadership studies has all but ignored the role of gender in leadership (Conway, Bourke, & Scott, 1989).

As used here, the term *leadership* refers to more than mere officeholding. Leadership is a complex phenomenon revolving around *influence*—the ability to move others in desired directions. Successful leaders are those who can take full advantage of their opportunities and their skills. Institutional structures, the immediate situation, the season of power, the political culture, regime type, and the dynamics of followership define the opportunities for the exercise of leadership. The leader's style, political acumen, character traits, and personal attributes provide a behavioral repertoire, a set of skills. Opportunities and skills interact to determine the success or failure of attempts to lead and influence.

Women in Politics

Few women rise to positions of political leadership; it is the last political taboo. In a cross-cultural comparison of political leaders, Jean Blondel (1987) concludes that leaders "are overwhelmingly male" (p. 25). In Blondel's study of world leaders, less than .005% of all leaders were women (pp. 116-117). As Linda K. Richter (1990-1991) writes, "Male dominance has been legitimated in law and custom. Politics or the public life of the polity has been presumed to be a natural sphere for men while for women, to the extent they had a space or turf to call their own, the 'natural' sphere was presumed to be private" (p. 525).

In general, scholars cite three factors that lead to underrepresentation of women in public office: political socialization, situational/structural factors, and active discrimination against women (Hedblom, 1987, pp. 14-15). These, and perhaps other factors, have kept women at the margins of political power.

Even in relatively more developed and open parliamentary systems, women remain dramatically underrepresented. For example, women make up only 5% of the U.S. House of Representatives and 2% of the Senate, 7% of the British Parliament, and 10% of German parliamentarians. But Norway may offer a glimpse of the future, with the largest proportion of women in government in the West. In addition to the prime ministership and half the cabinet portfolios, women occupy 36% of the parliamentary seats in Norway.

Women as Leaders

The above statistics notwithstanding, some women have risen to become the chief executives of their countries in the post-World War II era. The number of such cases and the fact that they have occurred in diverse systems and societies under varying political conditions lead, we believe, to two conclusions. The first is that despite the persistence of enormous barriers at individual and national levels, women will continue to emerge as chief executives in a growing number of countries and types of systems. That political fact leads to the second conclusion, that the rise of women to positions of power, their performance in office, and their impact on their societies is ripe for scholarly analysis and deserves careful attention from political scientists.

The study of women in leadership positions, particularly at the very highest levels of public decision making in a society, promises to contribute to our understanding of both *gender* as a politically defined and politically relevant variable and the politics of the dynamics of *leadership*. The potential for contributions to multiple realms of inquiry is typical of the general field of women and politics (Sapiro, 1983).

When the person who achieves a top leadership role is female, the political and personal biography both allow and force attention to the interplay of perceptions, expectations, interpretations of life experiences, and myths that make up the social definition of reality and "appropriate" gender roles (Baxter & Lansing, 1983; Conway et al., 1989). The lives and careers of those women who have headed nations offer a unique vantage point on the role of gender in political life. The prevalence of gender distinctions becomes clearer as one recounts the challenges and opportunities that future leaders have faced in their climb to the top. The depth and tenacity of gender stereotypes become clear when they continue to affect individuals even after they have achieved the ultimate political position.

The ascent of any person to power within a society is, almost by definition, a rare and extraordinary event. The political leader's biography and career can help identify and highlight key features of a political system. When a leader is sharply different in an important and obvious way from her predecessors, it allows an instructive test of propositions about the truly enduring features of a particular political system and about the necessary conditions for leadership in general. The emergence of a woman head of government may be both effect and cause of social change and fundamental shifts in the distribution of political power between men and women.

A focus on the impact of a person's gender on a political career can help clarify and refine the potential contribution of gender to understanding political behavior within a system. The story of a woman's rise to power traces her encounters with the obstacles, restrictions, and deterrents that face any ambitious person in her society as well as the resources that may be available and skills that may be acquired to circumvent them. But her life will also illuminate the distinctive barriers that she faced because of marginality (Githens & Prestage, 1977, pp. 6-7) and, perhaps, her skill at developing gender-specific resources or strategies to overcome them (LeVeness & Sweeney, 1987). Every political system limits opportunity and access to elite roles by, tacitly or overtly, erecting a set of initial hurdles based on background or demographic traits. The careers of successful women can illustrate the extent to which gender itself, directly or indirectly, is a limiting condition in a particular society. To the extent that these ascriptive traits serve a gatekeeper function and discriminate against everyone who shares them, they are gender neutral. Any aspirant for a leadership position must develop a strategy to overcome them. And some of the preconditions for political success in a system are relatively gender neutral. There are, for example, class, ethnic, religious, and regional biases operative in many societies that restrict access to political power and careers.

Some of the preconditions for success in a system may appear applicable to all aspirants, but have differential effects on men and women. For example, in the U.S. political system, voters show a clear preference for candidates with presentable spouses and one or more children. This is a consideration for both male and female candidates, and thus can be seen as a systemic factor. At the same time, given the still-prevailing expectation that women have the major responsibility for child rearing and family maintenance, the bias in favor of "good family people" as candidates imposes an additional, gender-based, constraint on the politically ambitious woman. She is likely to find that she has less time and energy to devote to her career than her male competitors have.

Those aspects of a society that discriminate directly on the basis of gender are often thrown into clear relief by the experiences of those women who face them. The most obvious cases involve overtly sexist attitudes that disparage women as leaders or decision makers. Other social institutions have similar effects. For example, there are still some ostensibly private clubs in major U.S. cities in which high-level politics are conducted and women are excluded. Only a few years ago, there were many such organizations. Women's political careers may also be affected by such factors as differential access to elite educational, social, and economic institutions (Gertzog, 1984, chap. 3).

If the implicit rule in a culture is that politics is "really" a man's world, or the experience of other ambitious women suggests that there is a glass ceiling allowing a woman to rise so far but no further, any woman who aspires to the top is potentially subversive of the established order. The woman who does arrive must have found a way around or over the exclusionary bias and thus potentially undermines it.

The impact of the successful woman's career on beliefs and expectations about gender will vary directly with the extent to which it resembles that of her male predecessors in power. If a woman is already at or near the top of the elite as she begins her political career because she inherited position and status from her parental family or because she has acquired it through close association with her husband, then observers with a conscious or unconscious interest in preserving gender bias in the political system can discount her as an anomaly unlikely to be repeated or attribute her success to family or spouse rather than her own skills or efforts. But the more closely the woman leader's career resembles those of her male colleagues, the more difficult it is for observers to avoid interpretations that challenge exclusionary assumptions.

The career of a woman who becomes a head of government will thus be affected by and have an effect upon her contemporaries' expectations and stereotypes. A politically ambitious woman cannot escape the consequences of social beliefs that gender differences are politically relevant. She must come to some understanding of herself as a person and as a political figure that resolves, manages, or represses the tensions between her emerging self-view as capable of functioning effectively at the highest political levels and the generalized social view that neither she nor any other woman has that competence. Regardless of how she handles the internal impact of limiting gender roles, she must also develop strategies for dealing with them as strategic aspects of her career, because others will often react to her in terms of gender. At times that will mean overcoming or circumventing restrictions. If one hallmark of the ultimately successful political leader is the ability to transform apparent liabilities into assets, then we might expect to see her manipulate traditional stereotypes of women to outflank or disarm opponents.

Successful women political leaders are not a recent phenomenon. Throughout history, even when women in general have been excluded from political power, some individuals have exercised great influence. Several queens are central figures in the histories of their countries, there has been a handful of extraordinary women warriors (Fraser, 1988), and there have been consorts who wielded immense power through their relationships to kings or emperors. But those women experienced success by using well the opportunities and resources offered by socially defined and sanctioned gender roles, or could be defined by contemporaries as unique individuals in extraordinary times.

In contrast, the careers of those women who have occupied the highest positions in their respective political systems in the twentieth century, with few exceptions, represent a distinctive phenomenon: Their achievement of power challenges, to a greater or lesser extent, existing definitions of gender roles. This has enhanced their political visibility and, arguably, salience to students of politics. Lovenduski (1986, p. 1) argues that increased scholarly attention to women is a direct result of their growing political successes.

Elizabeth I, for instance, was an important and influential figure in British history because she capitalized on the resources inherent in her position and her considerable political skills as she presided over a profound transformation of Britain's world role and domestic economy. But her presence on the throne was fully consonant with traditional values and assumptions and did not represent an extraordinary or even particularly unusual event. She came to power in the usual way, fully in keeping with both the explicit and the tacit rules of the game. Her success did not call any basic social assumptions into question.

Margaret Thatcher's residence at 10 Downing Street, on the other hand, makes her an extraordinary figure. During the rule and reign of Elizabeth I, access to the apex of the system, the throne, was a function of birth order; chromosomes and socially defined roles were irrelevant. By the reign of Elizabeth II, access to the apex of the system had long since become the ultimate prize in a much more open competition. But that competition had been explicitly restricted to males, and at the highest levels was still tacitly exclusive. Margaret Thatcher did not come to power in quite the usual way, and her success necessarily has implications for the future of some salient aspects of the British political system.

Understanding Gender and Leadership

Developing an understanding of how social definitions of gender affect a political career will ultimately lead to two sets of conclusions: one concerning the barriers impeding politically ambitious women, and one concerning the strategies some women use to neutralize them.

Trying to disentangle systemic, situational, and personal variables in explaining the behavior of any political actor is daunting; it is even more so when the actor occupies one of the central positions in a system.

A simplistic model that casts gender as *the* independent variable and a particular decision-making style or issue position as the dependent variable is not likely to be useful (Kelly & Burgess, 1989). However, gender can be expected to have a significant impact on performance in two ways.

Gender will have an effect on the leader's performance in office to the extent that others, both allies and adversaries, perceive it as salient and change their own behavior accordingly (Sapiro, 1983). The impact of gender on the 1971 Indo-Pakistan war may be a particularly prominent example. The fact that Indira Gandhi was prime minister of India seems to have had a significant impact on President Yahya Khan of Pakistan. It is likely that Pakistan would have been less bellicose and rigid if the Indian government been headed by a male (Stoessinger, 1990, pp. 135-136). The more common effects may be more subtle, but they are nonetheless important. Anyone who rises to the top of a political system will have developed a set of strategies and a repertoire of behaviors for dealing with both challenges and opportunities. For the successful woman, the strategies she has developed and her style will inevitably be shaped and influenced by her society's definitions and expectations of gender. She will have learned, consciously or not, how to cope effectively with, and even turn to her advantage, the fact that she is a woman in "a man's world." The results of her interaction with her gender will not show in each decision she makes, or even necessarily be evident in any particular case. But a review of a range of decisions or her entire tenure in office should illustrate the relevance of gender to this leader at this point in her country's history.

The focus on women at the highest levels of officeholding provides a useful vantage point for isolating some variables. For example, there is a generally held belief, and some ambiguous evidence, that the mode for women on some dimensions of management style and decision making differs from the mode for males. One difficulty in evaluating such studies is the existence of potential confounding effects of role definitions and institutional constraints. For example, some studies suggest that women managers are more concerned with interpersonal relationships than are their male counterparts (Bass, 1990, p. 724). But if women who are managers are disproportionately clustered in positions whose occupants are expected to be responsible for maintaining group dynamics or are concentrated in firms or industries with institutional cultures that place greater emphasis on group unity and cohesion, the apparent link between gender and management style is spurious, and the useful explanation is gender bias.

Studies of the behavior of individual women as political leaders cannot directly test these hypotheses. But those roles that are at or near the top of a structure are the least constrained by expectations or institutional culture and most likely to allow for the play of variables such as personality or gender (Greenstein, 1967). If gender itself has a causal relationship to style or substance in decision making, it is most likely to be evident in the study of those women who occupy the highest positions.

A Focus on Political Leaders Who Are Women: Generalized and Idiosyncratic Variables

The study of political leaders must ultimately be comparative. Whether one is attempting to rank American presidents along the "greatness" continuum or identifying the central components of a model of leadership, understanding the role and contribution of one leader requires understanding others. One comparative question is, Which factors or variables affect all leaders and which are specific to a particular leader, a particular point in time, or a particular political system? Studies of women who achieve leadership roles in various political systems can contribute important clues that may help us to answer this question.

Comparing political executives in a single system over time can help elucidate the relatively permanent features of the system. A key issue in studies of the executive institution in a particular political system is identifying those variables that can be used to explain the performance and impact of any incumbent and differentiating them from accidental conditions or constraints. The arrival in office of a person whose background or career is sharply discontinuous with the immediate past creates a quasi-experimental situation. One salient factor that had been a constant for all preceding officeholders can now be understood as a variable, and one can ask what else has also changed and what has continued to remain constant. Given the importance of gender roles in a wide range of social interactions, their apparent persistence over time and across social groups, and the role they play in establishing both personal and social identity, when a woman becomes prime minister it clearly represents a significant departure from the past. Her relationship to, and impact upon, various elements of the government and broader political system provides evidence about the extent to which some systemic features are institutionalized and constant and others vary with the identities of the players. As long as the American presidency, for example, continues to be a male preserve, one cannot be certain that observations about the relationship between the presidency and other institutions or actors are relatively permanent features of the system that transcend the particulars of the occupant of the White House. When a woman sits in the Oval Office, her experience will provide an instructive test.

One can also compare political leaders across national and cultural boundaries. At some level, beneath the vagaries of time and place, there are constants in the fundamental political relationships between leaders and followers. Those few cases of women who have made it to the top of contemporary political systems come from advanced capitalist societies and Third World countries at different stages of development, and from established parliamentary systems, nascent democracies, authoritarian regimes, and the turmoil of revolutionary or postrevolutionary situations. They have been career politicians and inheritors of political roles relatively late in life. They have enjoyed long tenures and they have presided over short-lived regimes.

One thing they do have in common is that they have made it to the top despite significant gender bias. Their success suggests that social constraints are not absolute and may well be changing. The presence of a woman as chief executive may be an indicator that some social change has occurred. At the same time, the performance of the leader during her tenure in office and the ways in which she is evaluated by contemporaries have implications for other women, not only in politics but in a broad range of social roles. The woman leader who is perceived as highly effective undermines negative stereotypes; the woman leader who is deemed to have failed may reinforce them. One dimension for evaluating the legacy of the woman who has led her country is what effect her tenure in office had on definitions of gender in her society.

All women who have come to political power have arrived in societies where the fundamental political relationship has been between a male leader and his followers. Case studies of women in power can help to isolate the dynamics of the relationship between the leader and the followers and those aspects that may be unique to a male or female leader's relationship to followers. Case studies of women in power may indicate whether it is fruitful to think about examining four possible relationships: female or male leader and male or female followers. Does, for example, a social bias against women in leadership positions in general translate into a specific political liability for a woman chief executive? Will she receive some level of generalized support from the egalitarian or feminist sectors of society, irrespective of her political philosophy or program?

Women remain a marginal majority in societies. By focusing on women who have served in leadership roles, we may, as Richter (1990-1991) notes, also come to a deeper understanding of leadership in general: "The experience of . . . politically prominent women offers empirical 'reality checks' on theories of leadership derived almost exclusively from the experiences of men" (p. 527).

Do men and women lead differently? Is the dominant, assertive, competitive approach a male style, and a relationship-oriented approach to leading a feminine style? Virginia E. Schein (1989) notes the implications of these potential differences:

> That women would lead or govern differently is not new. Women's leadership has been linked with enhancing world peace, reducing corruption, and improving opportunities for the downtrodden. If women, as keepers of the values of social justice, nurturance, and honesty, are put in charge, then the conflicts, corruption and greed around us will go away—or so say proponents of this view. The maximalist perspective within the now fragmented feminist movement supports this idea. It argues for innate or highly socialized gender differences and views women as more likely to exhibit cooperative, compassionate, and humane types of behaviors than men. (p. 154)

Male-centered theories of leadership may indeed need to be reexamined in light of the rise of women in leadership positions, perhaps in a search for an "androgynous" style, blending the best of traditionally male and female characteristics. On the other hand, Bernard Bass (1990) notes:

> Because situational changes are rapidly occurring for women in leadership roles, earlier research may need to be discounted. Despite the many continuing handicaps to movement into positions of leadership owing to socialization, status conflicts, and stereotyping, progress is being made. Some consistent differences remain between boys and girls and less so, among adult men and women managers and leaders. Characteristics that are usually linked to masculinity are still demanded for effective management. Nevertheless, most differences in male and female leaders tend to be accounted for by other controllable or modifiable factors, although women will continue to face

conflicts in their decisions to play the roles of wives and mothers as well as of managers and leaders. (p. 737)

In this volume, we attempt to gain a clearer understanding of the impact of gender on political leadership by examining the lives and careers of women who became heads of government: Corazon Aquino of the Philippines, Benazir Bhutto of Pakistan, Violeta Chamorro of Nicaragua, Indira Gandhi of India, Golda Meir of Israel, Isabel Perón of Argentina, and Margaret Thatcher of Great Britain. These women are not the universe of women heads of government in the past 40 years, but were selected because they illustrate a variety of paths to power, offer examples of both very short and very long tenure in office, are drawn from countries with greatly differing levels of economic and political development, and experienced varying degrees of success in office. Analysis and comparison of their careers should contribute to identifying the central questions to be addressed as research continues.

References

Adams, J., & Yoder, J. D. (1985). *Effective leadership for women and men.* Norwood, NJ: Ablex.

Bass, B. M. (Ed.). (1990). *Bass & Stogdill's handbook of leadership: Theory, research, and managerial applications* (3rd ed.). New York: Free Press.

Baxter, S., & Lansing, M. (1983). *Women and politics: The visible majority.* Ann Arbor: University of Michigan Press.

Blondel, J. (1987). *Political leadership: Towards a general analysis.* London: Sage.

Burns, J. M. (1978). *Leadership.* New York: Harper & Row.

Conway, J. K., Bourke, S. C., & Scott, J. W. (1989). *Learning about women.* Ann Arbor: University of Michigan Press.

Darcy, R., Welch, S., & Clark, J. (1987). *Women, elections, and representation.* New York: Longman.

Fraser, A. (1988). *The warrior queens.* New York: Vintage.

Gertzog, I. (1984). *Congressional women.* New York: Praeger.

Githens, M., & Prestage, J. L. (1977). *A portrait of marginality.* New York: D. McKay.

Greenstein, F. I. (1967). The impact of personality on politics: An attempt to clear away underbrush. *American Political Science Review, 61,* 629-641.

Hedblom, M. K. (1987). *Women and power in American politics.* Washington, DC: American Political Science Association.

Jones, B. D. (Ed.). (1989). *Leadership and politics.* Lawrence: University Press of Kansas.

Kelly, R. M., & Burgess, J. (1989). Gender and the meaning of power and politics. *Women and Politics, 9*(1), 1-43.

LeVeness, F. P., & Sweeney, J. P. (1987). *Women leaders in contemporary U.S. politics.* Boulder, CO: Lynne Reiner.

Lovenduski, J. (1986). *Women and European politics: Contemporary feminism and public policy.* Amherst: University of Massachusetts Press.

Richter, L. K. (1990-1991). Exploring theories of female leadership in South and Southeast Asia. *Pacific Affairs, 63,* 524-540.

Sapiro, V. (1983). *The political integration of women.* Urbana: University of Illinois Press.

Schein, V. E. (1989). Would women lead differently? In W. Rosenbach & R. Taylor (Eds.), *Contemporary issues in leadership* (pp. 134-160). Boulder, CO: Westview.

Stoessinger, J. (1990). *Why nations go to war.* New York: St. Martin's.

2

Managing Softly in Turbulent Times

Corazon C. Aquino,
President of the Philippines

JEANNE-MARIE COL

The media reported that an ordinary housewife was challenging a 20-year dictator for the presidency of the Philippines. They were engaging in the kind of hyperbole that attracts readers and viewers, but may distort the truth. This ordinary housewife had been tutored in politics from an early age, first in a "politically oriented" family and later by a husband with considerable political instinct, ambition, and accomplishment. While appearing to be a shy, silent student and partner, this housewife gradually developed the perspectives and skills befitting a presidential candidate, if not also a president. What a surprise to her opponent, who suggested that she more properly belonged in a bedroom than in the chief executive's office. Perhaps Corazon Aquino herself was surprised at the extent to which she asserted herself effectively in the political arena. In her decision to focus on redemocratization as her presidential priority, Corazon Aquino made a significant contribution to welfare of the Filipino people, many of whom expressed the need for a new and genuine model of participatory governance.

Aquino assumed the presidency in 1986 in a bloodless "people power" revolution in which a diverse group of Filipinos emerged in massive nonviolent rallies to defend the election results, as reported by the "quick count" poll watchers, and as defended by key military leaders

who refused to assist incumbent President Ferdinand Marcos in sup-
pressing the demonstrators. Aquino and her advisers pursued a nonviolent strategy to mobilize popular support and to isolate Marcos. The
contrast between Marcos and Aquino was striking. Marcos denigrated
his woman opponent as appropriate only for the bedroom, and threatened to use military force, as he had often in the past, to put down any
popular uprising. Aquino accused her male opponent of a track record
of martial law, repression, cronyism, and corruption. The military
joined the people in manifesting popular impatience with old-style
politics and governance. Forces external to the Philippines supported
the prodemocracy, anti-Marcos movement. Aquino was handed the
victory by the military and the demonstrators that she had apparently
won in the popular election. The tasks of redemocratization and rebuild-
ing were hers.

Aquino is serving as both head of state and chief executive of the
government: president, prime minister, and queen combined. And she
has developed a style in marked contrast to her predecessors. Has
Aquino set an example for women and girls? Has she established a new
pattern of democratic government for future presidents? As the first
female president of the Philippines, and one of the few women presidents in modern history, has she contributed to our understanding of the
performance of female presidents and prime ministers?

The Philippines is a complex, plural society with democratic roots,
often modified by authoritarian tendencies during several colonial and
nationalist periods. While colonial and independence governments
have sought to instill national unity, this process has been frustrated by
the immense diversity and even fragmentation emanating from factors
such as religion, urbanization, isolation, ethnicity, linguism, and re-
gionalism. It is a society buffeted by natural disasters—not the least of
which have been a recent volcanic eruption, an equally devastating
earthquake, and a normal complement of typhoons. With the populace
looking to the government to ameliorate the disastrous consequences of
these problems, as well as the everyday social and economic issues of
a developing society, any leadership would be under considerable
pressure. The Aquino government is especially pressured by the enormous popular expectations emanating from 14 years of repressive
martial law. With these issues and expectations, has the simple housewife served as an effective president?

Although women have always played an active role in Philippine
society, their participation in politics is "most concealed" (Tancango,

1990, p. 323). Marcos's sentiment that Aquino could best participate in the bedroom might have been shared by a wide spectrum of Filipinos. Women, who constitute 49.83% of the Philippine population, are expected to be involved in the nurturing tasks of education and service, while men are expected to be in the forefront of leadership and decision making in politics ("The Status of Women," n.d., p. 15). According to several academic studies, precolonial Filipino culture supports an equal and partnership model of male-female relationships, in which women had equal roles not only in the family and the economy but also in decision making in the important social processes of the bigger community (Rodriguez, 1990, p. 18). The influence of the Spanish and American regimes relegated women to a more "Victorian" confinement to family and home (Estrada-Claudio, 1990-1991; Tapales, 1988). Based on centuries of mixed traditions and encouraged by current global trends, tension between the gender equality and female limitation models continues in all institutions in the Philippines. This tension is reflected in Aquino's actions as president as well as in the ambivalent interpretations of her performance.

The Philippines at a Crossroads

When Corazon ("Cory") Aquino assumed the position of president of the Philippines, the country had been subjected to an accumulation of natural and devised disasters. From earthquakes, volcanoes, and typhoons to the authoritarian dictatorship of Ferdinand Marcos, the Philippines has had more than a few distractions from steady economic growth and increasing social and political harmony and maturity.

Inhabiting an archipelago of 7,107 islands scattered across 500,000 square miles, with a land area of 114,672 square miles and extending almost 1,150 miles from north to south (Steinberg, 1990, p. 12), the 60 million Filipinos are mostly Malay in origin, later mixing extensively with Chinese immigrants and Spanish conquerors, creating the largest current group of Filipinos, which is the racially mixed mestizos. Later, the Chinese and Spanish legacy was mixed with American political and educational culture based on 48 years of American colonial rule and a strong emphasis on education as a means of achieving equality and democratization, thereby creating the now-large category of the *ilustrado elite,* who have university degrees. According to Steinberg (1990), "The Philippines has, in effect, an aristocracy based on economic and education criteria—a privileged upper class and a gap between the entitled few and the masses that is comparable to that in eighteenth-century France" (p. 50).

Anthropologists claim there are 111 different cultural and racial groups in the Philippines, speaking some 70 different languages, from Muslim Malays in the southern islands of Sulu to Episcopalian Igorots in the Cordillera mountains of Luzon ("The Philippines," 1988). The most significant cleavages are religious, with respect to the Muslim south, and cultural, involving upland tribes (Komisar, 1987, p. 19). Filipinos are family oriented in their personal relations, and family-style relations are represented in politics by patron-client relations.

Political culture in the Philippines is situated on an axis of democracy and authoritarianism. It has been contended that

> Filipino political culture has a superstructure of attitudes and values of Western origin, resting on a definitely indigenous infrastructure. From the West comes individualism and a high respect for achievement and for the rule of law, whereas indigenous values stress primary-group (i.e., family) loyalty and a particularistic view of public affairs. (Wurfel, 1988, p. 43)

According to Corpuz (1969), "The consultative decision making of the ancient barangay, the pragmatic bargaining of interpersonal relationships, and the ability to acquire political status through achievement are traditional traits that provide underpinning for modern democracy" (p. 15). And Arcellana (1969) has stated that "child rearing in the Philippines teaches very forcefully that elders, and others in positions of power and authority, must be respected and followed, not challenged" (p. 38).

The use of authoritarian and democratic styles in the presidency creates dilemmas for other politicians, the bureaucracy, and the public. Expectations are necessarily confused, and a particular style might need to be stated or modeled very explicitly in order to create understanding and appropriate learning and response. There is a question as to whether Aquino expressed her "soft," democratic style of leadership in as clear a manner as necessary to communicate to citizens how they could assume full responsibility for their lives, their development, and their government. Perhaps such clarity of expression could not have been achieved because of the ambivalence of her cabinet and bureaucratic colleagues, who shared her views in differing degrees. Cariño (1987a) has noted that "the contradictions in the society were reproduced in the bureaucracy: it was authoritarian and participatory, developmentalist and nationalistic, corrupt and committed" (p. 272).

The democratic, open, and more participatory style of government championed by Aquino is consistent with and of benefit to women seeking to overcome the inherited role of being generally relegated to a family-oriented and less public role. Although Filipinas have been influential in their homes and often important in the economy, they have been largely excluded from politics. The few early examples of women leaders are striking, and their legacy continues. In the late 1700s, Gabriela Silang, for whom a current women's umbrella group is named, carried on the leadership of a rebellion led by her husband, who was assassinated by Spanish authorities (Tancango, 1990, p. 326).

Since the 1890s, many women's organizations have emerged in anticolonial struggles, in humanitarian work, and in the promotion of women to local governments. Prominent among these is the Associacion Feminista Filipina (Feminist Association of the Philippines), the first women's volunteer organization, founded in 1905 and dedicated to both humanitarian objectives and the advancement of women in society (Tancango, 1990, p. 326). A year later the Associacion Feminista Ilonga (Association of Ilonga Feminists) was formed to work for women's suffrage (Tancango, 1990, p. 327). During pre- and postindependence periods, women formed many organizations for social, religious, civil, business, and political objectives. The Malayang Kilusan ng Bagong Kababaihan (Free Movement of Women), known as MAKIBAKA (struggle), was formed in the 1960s in order to organize both urban and rural women, but was banned during the martial law period that began in 1972. A National Commission on the Role of Filipino Women (NCRFW), formed by the Marcos regime during the United Nations International Decade for Women, confined its activities to studying legal inequities and providing income-generating and welfare projects for women.

After the removal of martial law, many more women's organizations were formed, and in 1984, many coalesced into the alliance known as GABRIELA, after the eighteenth-century heroine. Other women's groups included, for example, Women for the Ouster of Marcos (WOMB); STOP, an organization that aims to counter sex trafficking; and KALAYAAN, which exposes sexism within the family, the educational and political systems, and other institutions (Tancango, 1990, p. 329). In December 1985, 250 women who were either relatives or friends of Aquino met with her to assure her of their votes and to signify their intention to help her in the presidential campaign. These women then signed up both professionals and the masses, launching an organization, known as Cory's Crusaders, that eventually became a people's movement (Tancango, 1990, p. 345). They raised money, produced campaign materials, and participated in rallies and other activities. Cory's Crusaders were revitalized during the later senatorial campaign to assist in electing Leticia Ramos-Shahani (Tancango, 1990, p. 360). Although Filipina women are known historically to participate actively in political affairs during revolutionary times, fighting side by side with Filipino men, only to retreat to their homes during peace, the current record of Cory's Crusaders and other women's organizations indicates that gender stereotypes might be increasingly shifted to reflect a more consistently active and influential role for women.

Evolution in the political role of women in the Philippines is taking place in the context of wider sociocultural and economic patterns. For instance, income distribution is skewed in favor of a definable elite. The top one-fifth of the population receives half the country's income, with famous family names—Lopez, Laurel, Romulo, Soriano, Zobel, Cojuangco, Ayala, Aquino—ever present in political and economic arenas ("The Philippines," 1988). This elite evolved from various immigrations. Chinese traders visited the Philippines centuries before either Islam or Christianity, subsequently establishing substantial business interests. Muslims established sultanates in Sulu and on Mindanao by the mid-fifteenth century.

The Spanish arrived in 1571 and left a legacy of Catholicism and indirect rule through the Filipino elite. Building upon the Spanish colonial base, Americans exerted considerable cultural, economic, and political influence since 1946, continuing into the 1990s with the presence of U.S. military installations. After the 1869 opening of the Suez Canal and the subsequent increase in travel to Europe, ideas of nationalism and liberalism began to permeate the society.

Rebellion against the Spanish continued through the Spanish-American War in 1898, in which the Philippines were ostensibly sold to the United States for $20 million (Komisar, 1987, p. 19). Like the Spanish, the Americans ruled through the Filipino elite until partial independence in 1935. Foreshadowing future political fragmentation, national political rivalries delayed acceptance of a national constitution and partial independence for five years (Komisar, 1987, p. 21). Full independence from the United States occurred in 1946, after the Japanese occupation from 1941 to 1945.

Independence politics has been characterized as "guns, goons and gold," indicating the mobilization of political power through private armies for personal gain through patronage and largess (Komisar, 1987, p. 21). These localized political machines connected to the landed elite and paramilitary groups defended an increasingly unequal accumulation of land and other resources. Peasant uprisings in the 1920s and 1930s led to militant tenant unions and eventually to the People's Anti-Japanese Army, *Hukbulahap,* better known as the Huks (Komisar, 1987, p. 21). Both the Catholic church and U.S. officials discouraged these and other peasant movements, solidifying polarization between the educated, city-based elites and the poor, landless cultivators. From the 1920s, the tenant farmers had been demanding not land reform, but only a larger share of the harvest; during the 1940s, their demands escalated to redistribution of land. From 1946, when the Philippines achieved complete independence, the "Huk rebellion" emerged into a serious guerrilla war, with thousands of Huk troops (Komisar, 1987, p. 23). By the 1950s, Communists began to dominate the Huks in some areas, thereby exploiting the extreme income disparities to gain political support in a context of already fragmented political fiefdoms.

During the 1950s, the Philippines was recognized as the most developed nation in Southeast Asia ("The Philippines," 1988). Possessing vast natural resources such as timber, coconut, sugar, bananas, rubber, and minerals, and even oil lately being discovered, the Philippines developed an economy based on export of raw agricultural materials while establishing industries for import substitution. During the oil crisis, and with rising population and increasingly militant insurgencies, these economic strategies could not sustain economic development. The Philippines failed to create export-oriented industries and failed to develop agricultural productivity ("The Philippines," 1988). Nepotism and "crony capitalism" resulted in large foreign debt and much personal profit invested outside the country.

The political and economic situation in the Philippines worsened in the 1980s, characterized by capital flight, factory closings, rising unemployment, bank closings, devaluation of the peso by 38%, rising prices, and the collapse of world prices for sugar and coconut oil (Komisar, 1987, p. 51). Following the assassination of Ninoy Aquino, Cory's husband, rallies and disruptions were held not only by peasant/worker movements but also by clergy and Makati businesspersons. Cory was in great demand as a speaker, and was increasingly consulted during negotiations among opposition leaders. The period from 1983 to

1986 was characterized as the "parliament of the streets," in which interests were articulated in popular modalities. Aquino found herself joining, but not, at this point, leading (Gonzales-Zap, 1987, p. 78). In the 1984 elections, the opposition gained 56 out of 183 seats in the National Assembly, despite massive vote rigging ("The Philippines," 1988). Momentum for change was building.

While Marcos delayed in announcing elections, 11 potential presidential candidates struggled among themselves for prominence, with Aquino at the sidelines, repeating that she hoped that they would agree on a candidate and that she did not want to be considered.

> Although Aquino quickly became the symbol of the struggle, no one in those early days thought of her as a potential leader. Nor did she envision such a role for herself. She was never the political neophyte that some of the pros took her for—at their peril. However, she lacked such leadership qualities as experience, ambition, and confidence, which other opposition personalities possessed in excess. (Burton, 1989, p. 138)

A convener group composed of Lorenzo Tanada, Jaime Ongpin, and Aquino and a national unification council composed of Salvador Laurel, Homobono Aelaza, and Cecilia Muñoz-Palma attempted to bring together different opposition groups in order to forge an agreement about candidates and platforms, under the so-called umbrella of the Bayan or National Democratic Alliance. This conciliatory strategy floundered for months under the continuing arguments and competition between groups as varied as leftists closely allied with Communists and guerrillas and conservatives including Salvador Laurel, who had worked with Marcos as recently as 1982.

On November 3, 1985, Marcos called "snap elections" for February 7, 1986. Political pressure for increased democracy mounted, and foreign allies, including the United States, sent envoys to urge speedy elections. Unemployment stood at 20%, underemployment at 40%, and inflation was approaching 25% (Komisar, 1987, p. 81). Believing in Aquino's potential to mobilize the electorate, some opposition leaders continued to press her to contest the presidency. Aquino insisted that she preferred not to be a candidate, but would relent in the face of popular demand. She set a seemingly difficult condition: the collection of a million signatures on petitions requesting her to run for the presidency (Gonzales-Zap, 1987, p. 99). When more than a million signatures were obtained, Aquino considered her decision. As was her practice when needing to make difficult decisions, she made a one-day retreat at a Manila convent. On December 3, Aquino declared her candidacy, with Laurel reluctantly agreeing to serve as her running mate, after having been a contender for the nomination himself. Aquino agreed to lead the challenge to Marcos, and support from all strata and sectors joined the anti-Marcos movement.

Cory "Prepares" for Politics

Corazon Aquino had a long political apprenticeship. She grew up in a political family and married into another political family. After years of contentment on the sidelines, she was thrown into the political arena when her husband Benigno Aquino was imprisoned by President Ferdinand Marcos. During that imprisonment, her husband literally tutored her in politics as she served as a link between his ideas and experiences and the outside world. The tutoring continued in family discussions during exile. Later, after Benigno's assassination, Corazon Aquino evolved into a political actor and was drawn in by circumstances to compete for the presidency. Her initial shyness and dislike of politics were overcome by her increasingly sophisticated political skills and her strong commitment to save her country from the dictator she believed had been responsible for the assassination of her husband and severe political oppression.

Born Maria Corazon Simulong Cojuangco on January 25, 1933, Cory, as she was nicknamed, was the fourth of five children in a large, landed, well-educated, and political family. On her father's side, she descended from ethnic Chinese immigrants who made their fortune in trading and land (Komisar, 1987, p. 13). Her father, "Don Pepe," became a congressman, and his father was a senator. In her mother's family, her grandfather was a senator, a vice presidential candidate, and a member of the U.S.-sponsored Philippine Commission, which exercised both executive and legislative powers for the islands (Brunstetter, 1989, p. 31).

In her nuclear family, Don Pepe was patient, considerate, soft-spoken, and introverted, while her mother Demetria, known as "Doña Metring," was a strong disciplinarian. Doña Metring enthusiastically supported the political efforts of her family through monetary contributions and campaigning (Crisostomo, 1986, p. 12). Apparently, Cory was a quiet child and did not participate in any family political campaigns (Komisar, 1987, p. 13).

Education was highly valued in Cory's household. Especially significant was that her mother had earned a bachelor's degree in pharmacy.
Education of girls is correlated with the education of fathers, but
especially highly correlated with education of mothers. Cory followed
this tendency, attending St. Scholastica's, a private girls' elementary
school run by Benedictine nuns for the children of the wealthy, where
she excelled in mathematics and English and graduated first in her class.

Cory's postprimary education continued at religious-based schools
and with considerable academic success. Begun at Assumption Convent
high school in Manila, her secondary education was interrupted by the
Japanese invasion, during which her family moved to the United States,
where she attended Raven Hill Academy in Philadelphia and eventually
Notre Dame Convent School in New York. At the College of Mount St.
Vincent in New York, Cory majored in French and math, and was known
as very religious, attending mass often and participating in the Sodality
of Our Lady, a religious society that studied liturgy. This religious
school focused on imparting traditional values, including the responsibility of wives to support their husbands' wishes at the expense of their
own (Brunstetter, 1989, p. 32). According to a friend of Cory's, they
were told "that you must never do anything where your husband would
lose face. If there was an argument, you gave in, because it's much more
difficult for a man to back down than a woman, you never spoke against
your husband publicly; you never did anything that would embarrass
him" (Komisar, 1987, p. 14).

Although Cory entered law school at Far Eastern University in
Manila after graduating from college in the United States, she left after
only one term in order to marry Benigno ("Ninoy") Aquino. They were
married on October 11, 1954, after a long courtship but a short engage-
ment. Since the time when they were both 9 years old, they had met
periodically at gatherings of their families, who were friends. On her
return to Manila, they began to date regularly, and were married when
they were 21.

Moving his new family to his home town of Concepción, in Tarlac,
Ninoy immediately became both a political and a business success,
laying the foundation for future activities. He became the youngest
elected mayor at 21, then the youngest elected provincial governor at
28, and eventually the youngest elected senator. During each of these
campaigns, Cory was an uncomfortable bystander, appearing in public
only when absolutely necessary. During this early political period, Cory
was concentrating on bearing and raising children. Indeed:

Ninoy the politician never demanded much from Cory but made it clear from the start of their marriage that her first priority would be their children. Her primary role as his wife would be that of a mother of their children—and a housewife. . . . Thus, throughout her husband's political career she would stay in the background, never making any public utterance or political statement. She preferred to stay away from the limelight and deliberately tried to avoid close scrutiny by the public. At political rallies, whenever she had to be present, she would decline a seat on the stage, [and] stay at the back of the audience, incognito, and listen to what her husband told [her] non-stop far into the night. (Crisostomo, 1986, p. 14)

During her presidency, when reflecting on her role, her husband, and her marriage, Cory was quoted as saying:

My husband, well, he was a male chauvinist. He never wanted it said that I was influencing him in anything. I didn't mind, really, because mine was a very private role. And I figured, "Look, you can do what you like in public life; I'm going to make sure that these children of ours will turn out to be good and responsible citizens." And so we managed very well. . . . If you think your husband is really worthwhile, then you just have to accept. (Sheehy, 1986, p. 5)

With these words, Cory seemed to be revealing that the counsel of the nuns at college had been extremely influential in defining her relationships within her family. Only later, when her family was shaken by assassination and she was no longer overshadowed by a charismatic husband-leader, did she finally move into a more public role.

Ninoy used each of his visible, political positions as a forum for exposing weaknesses of political situations. During years of increasing political activity, Ninoy worked with the Huks and even sold the farm in Concepción to the tenants (Komisar, 1987, p. 34), thereby establishing radical political credentials. By 1972, then-President Ferdinand Marcos had declared martial law—under false pretenses, it is now known ("The Philippines," 1988)—and was able to arrest and detain vocal "critics" such as Ninoy. Even while in prison, Ninoy contested elections and developed the slogan "*Laban,*" meaning "Fight." Tortured and traumatized, Ninoy experienced a religious awakening that sustained him during his incarceration of seven and a half years, during which Cory was forced into an assertive, public role that increasingly encompassed political dimensions. According to *Time* correspondent Sandra Burton (1989):

While Ninoy was experiencing his epiphany, his wife was undergoing a crash course in realpolitik. Martial law had forced shy, sheltered Cory to shed the comfortable anonymity of housewife and mother and assume the sensitive role of liaison between her jailed husband and the outside world. For the first time since their marriage, she had become an integral part of the political milieu he inhabited. As she and Nena Diokno canvassed the military bureaucracy for news of their husbands and petitioned the Supreme Court to produce them, she encountered firsthand the arbitrary power wielded by those who administered the vast martial law apparatus. (p. 92)

During this difficult period, Cory developed confidence in her ability to analyze politics and to speak for a political agenda. Her sustenance came from tutoring sessions with her husband and her close relationship with the Catholic church. She was especially affected during his hunger strike and the time when he was sentenced to death. Eventually, Marcos offered him freedom if he would leave the country, an offer that he did not take up until he needed triple bypass surgery. During their exile from 1980 to 1983, while living with their children in the United States, Ninoy and Cory continued their "study" of politics. Deciding to contest the parliamentary elections declared by Marcos in 1984, Ninoy returned to the Philippines on August 21, 1983, to be met by an assassin's bullet. Cory would now begin her personal political odyssey, driven by her commitment to represent the ideals and perspectives that she shared with her husband.

When organizing Ninoy's funeral and the events surrounding it, Cory illustrated considerable political acumen by suggesting that "she would refuse to accept [Marcos's condolences] unless he released all political prisoners as proof of his sincerity" (Burton, 1989, p. 139). This was the strategy of a savvy politician, which, no doubt, by now she had become.

The First Woman Becomes President

However much Aquino had been prepared for a "background" role in the political arena, she was catapulted into the limelight during her campaign and presidency. Based on a feudal political culture in which there is a "cult of personality" (Abinales, n.d.) surrounding a leader, Aquino groomed herself to present an image that was compatible with her personality and her perceived need of the people. During the presidential campaign, Aquino was seen in the Catholic Philippines as "almost a Madonna, a saint in contrast to the wily, corrupt Marcos" (Richter, 1990-1991). In terms of imaging herself, she was charged by some detractors with wanting only to be "mother" of her nation, but she did, from time to time, take positions on strategic policy issues (Cariño, 1987b, p. 1). According to U.S. Representative Stephen Solarz, Aquino is a "woman who has a steel fist inside a velvet glove" (quoted in Gonzales-Zap, 1987, p. 223).

During the campaign, Aquino emphasized her commitment to such values as democracy, equity, fairness, and efficiency, but Marcos replied by saying that "women should confine their preaching to the bedroom" ("The Philippines," 1988). Marcos often accused her of having no experience in running a government. Aquino replied with statements such as, "I admit that I have no experience in lying, cheating, stealing, killing political opponents" (Gonzales-Zap, 1987, p. 107).

> Cory electrified the populace. It is said that even the famous campaign of Ramon Magsaysay paled in contrast to hers. In a country obsessed with stars, she became the country's newest superstar. Her simplicity, forthrightness and inner strength turned out to be her biggest assets. Cory is adored because she is the antithesis of the infamous family. (Lallana, in press)

During the campaign she emphasized general issues of justice and fairness, but also mentioned specific positions, including amnesty for guerrillas, dismantling of monopolies controlled by Marcos and his friends, release of political prisoners, negotiations with the Communists, a cease-fire with rebels, and "true land reform" (Komisar, 1987, p. 80).

In addition to the issues differences, the process of her campaign was in strong contrast to that of Marcos. Aquino personally visited 68 of 73 provinces and held more than a thousand rallies, but used no television commercials. Marcos visited only 22 provinces and held only 34 rallies, but made extensive use of television. It is also reported that the Catholic bishops told their poor parishioners to take money offered by the Marcos politicians, but to vote their consciences in the actual balloting (Komisar, 1987, p. 92).

During the elections themselves, NAMFREL, the National Citizens' Movement for Free Elections, which was backed by the Catholic church, business organizations, and labor and civil groups, organized poll watching and a "quick count" process. Although the official Election Commission announced Marcos the winner, its computer officials walked out, saying that the announced tallies did not reflect the computer totals (Gonzales-Zap, 1987, p. 114). After NAMFREL announced Aquino as the winner but Marcos declared himself the president, widespread political reactions occurred. Boycotts and strikes were followed by large rallies of up to 2 million people each. The Marcos regime had been under pressure before, and had always been able to suppress dissent. What made this situation escalate into a successful "revolution"?

Both external and internal factors, in addition to the character and image of the standard-bearer, Cory Aquino, led to the eventual exile of Marcos and the installation of Aquino as president. Global visibility of persistent problems and lack of popular political participation in the Philippines encouraged allies to bring pressure for change, as well as strengthened national forces for change. In particular, the United States, formerly an unwavering ally of Marcos, sent signals that Marcos might be assisted in gracefully leaving. Internally, it was apparent that Aquino was not just another politician wanting power, but an innocent and injured party within a rambunctious political scene, seeking the presidency for popular purposes and with a style and message that depended less on money than on genuine popularity, representing personal appeal as well as resonance with the felt needs of the people.

The now-famous "people power" revolution included diverse participants. Fittingly, Aquino described the February epic as "a revolution where the nun and the soldier have equal place" (Gonzales-Zap, 1987, p. 198). The EDSA (Epifanio de los Santos Avenue) demonstrations, which took place along three kilometers between two army camps, lasted four nights and days. Three recorded testimonials indicate a middle-class bias to the EDSA events:

> (1) If we clearly analyze the people who've been there, we can clearly tell that they were not farmers or fishermen; they were students, teachers, religious people, businesspersons, employees, etc. . . . people from the lower stratum of our society were not there and were not represented. . . .
>
> (2) The poor couldn't be very "active" because they have their own lives to support. They do not have extra money to spend for rallies and food to keep them overnight in the streets. When I interviewed vendors, they said that they were there for the business. . . .
>
> (3) The revolution entailed costs like sandwiches, flowers, etc. to be given away and that is something the masses do not have. Second, the leadership of Mrs. Cory Aquino is identified mainly as middle class because of her degree of intellectual growth, wealth and social position. (Cruz, 1989, pp. 246-248)

Thus factors greater than Aquino assisted in her victory, but her character, her platform, and her ability to mobilize people made her an ideal standard-bearer for a renewal of Philippine politics.

The "Cory Agenda":
From People Power to People's Power

During her presidency, Aquino emphasized process, not policy. Specifically, she sought to present a dramatically different model of the exercise of presidential power from that of President Marcos. By developing a "soft" leadership process based on reconciliation and representation, Aquino articulated in word and deed a sharp contrast to the confrontational and personal regime of Marcos. Within a few months of her victory, commentators noted that her program seemed to be "against dictatorship," rather than "for developing the country" (De Dios, 1986, p. 1). Enhancing democratic process would likely lead to some types of positive development. Aquino designated three priorities for the beginning of her administration: the constitution, the military and the insurgencies, and political democratization (Komisar, 1987, p. 136). Other matters were delegated to her ministers. Throughout her presidency, Aquino articulated policy goals but seemed to lack skills to work effectively with technical people to forge plans of action. Many studies and elegant concepts were not sufficiently transformed into practical programs for development. Aquino's three priorities were chosen in order to establish a framework for development based on rule of law, peace, and participation.

During Aquino's presidency, especially because of the dramatic political shifts that led to her election, there were opportunities not only to establish a new style of leadership but also to create a new political and policy agenda. There were many government committees, commissions, and reports. It is unclear to what extent Aquino exercised control or influence over these agenda-setting exercises. A comparison of her expressed values and her public pronouncements with the recommendations of these reports indicates that she exercised considerable influence, though not complete control, over these reports. This assessment supports the concept of a "soft" leadership style.

Early in her presidency, Aquino had to deal with the complex problem of holdovers from the Marcos era in the legislature, the judiciary, and the bureaucracy. Although some interpreted her desire for "reconciliation, not revenge" as a "soft" inability to move swiftly and decisively, she dismissed and requested resignations from key people at all levels of government, appointing transitional caretakers until elections could be held under the soon-to-be formulated and ratified constitution. The "wholesale firing of more than 70 provincial governors, 1,600 mayors and more than 10,000 council members set off a storm of bitter protests" (Komisar, 1987, p. 132) that continued nearly a year.

Although during the campaign Aquino promised, in a long letter to the bureaucracy, "I will uphold the security of tenure of the civil service. Those of you who have performed your duties competently will be protected" (Cariño, 1987a, p. 271), she gave her government full authority to purge all elected and appointed officials under the authority of the transitional Freedom Constitution. This purge, lasting for one year and until ratification of the new constitution, resulted in severe morale problems for two reasons: Not every removal was justified, and removals went beyond and below positions of authority (Cariño, 1987a, p. 273). Although Aquino cultivated the personal image of being understanding and conciliatory, she armed her ministers with powerful weapons of arbitrary power, which they apparently used unevenly. "More than one-third of career executive service officials (CESOs), the highest civil service level, lost their positions" (Cariño, 1987a, p. 274).

The first Report of the Presidential Commission on Government Reorganization (PCGR) emphasizes five guiding principles that deal primarily with process issues, with strong emphasis on wide political participation:

(1) promotion of private sector initiatives
(2) decentralization of authority and responsibility to local governments
(3) cost-effectiveness through elimination of gaps and overlapping functions among government organizations
(4) popular participation in government, especially in increased efficiency in delivery of public services
(5) public accountability (Iglesias, 1988)

In the following six years, these principles, in fact, did serve as guidelines for public policy decision making. Unfortunately, application of principles sometimes went awry, as in one case when four agencies were abolished, but nine created (Cariño, 1987a, p. 277). Aquino relied heavily on private sector executives for advice on government policy, sometimes including them as volunteers in government without pay, but claiming expenses far beyond civil servant salaries. Popular participation was reflected in a renewed emphasis on local governments, including elections at the local level, encouragement of regionalization, and government cooperation with nongovernmental organizations (NGOs) in service delivery and even sponsorship of the development of grass-roots organizations, such as the Kabisig or Link-ing Arms Movement, designed to stimulate local democracy, economic development, and probably methods to circumvent regular politics and government ("Congressmen Agree," 1990).

For a substantive agenda, Aquino emphasized economic development and peaceful resolution of long-standing internal conflicts, the latter oriented toward improvement of both process and outcomes in politics. Although neither economic development nor peaceful resolution of rebellions can be viewed as fully successful, there have been both progress and reversals in both economic and political arenas, largely dependent upon occurrence of expensive disaster relief programs and of periodic coup attempts and increases in insurgency activities.

In the area of peace, Aquino did grant amnesty to guerrillas, and some took advantage of it, leaving the hinterlands, giving up their arms, and becoming part of the normal populations in their areas. She also repeat-edly declared cease-fires with the rebels and attempted reconciliation. While this strategy was often at odds with the advice of her military leaders, she persisted in believing that a peaceful solution could be possible. She released political prisoners, some of whom were absorbed into normal society and some of whom were later rearrested for subver-sive activity. These conciliatory actions created a sense of healing among the people, but this feeling could not be maintained without significant economic progress. When economic prosperity was not forthcoming, rebels and guerrillas were able to continue their localized rebellions, especially on Mindanao, where the people diverge from the national norms ethnically, linguistically, and religiously. And, of course, generating economic development under these tense and distant conditions was especially difficult.

In the economic arena, Aquino encountered strong resistance from the economic elite, as well as from the bureaucracy. Her economic advisers were largely from the ranks of activist businesspersons who joined the opposition in the last years of the dictatorship (Tolosa, 1987, p. 38). Their preference for economic liberalization was consonant with the self-interest of many Aquino allies, including Aquino-related fam-ilies. But privatization extended to only a few sectors. The swift dis-mantling of the sugar and coconut trading monopolies stands as one of the few decisive economic policies of the Aquino presidency (Komisar, 1987, p. 175). Further efforts to privatize hundreds of government corporations, including banks, resorts, and industries, were blocked by the bureaucracy, perhaps seeking to preserve their jobs. Aquino actively sought foreign investment, but issues of debt repudiation delayed actions to improve foreign trade and investment relationships.

Aquino's presidency has resembled an uneasy coalition, reflecting the hodgepodge collection of political forces that came together to oust Marcos. After the euphoria of victory, these groups, as well as the "people's revolution" allies, reverted to deep divisions among themselves, based not only on personalities but also on policies. For instance, the military, led by Juan Ponce Enrile, was considered, by and large, loyal to him and to prefer a militant stance against the Communists and rebels. Aquino stated that she wanted to stop the fighting and to reach agreement. Middle-class businesspersons wanted protection of property and investments. Encouraged by the rhetoric of the campaign, mass groups and special interest groups felt that they could express their interests openly, including by taking part in disruptive workers' strikes. Tension evolved between the goals of improving the investment climate and improving social justice. Aquino provided inspiration to many groups, including workers, businesspersons, military, and students, but she has not been able to create productive working relationships among them. Temporary electoral coalitions are typical of Philippine politics, often resulting in a conglomeration of strange bedfellows in a coalition government.

The plight of rural farmers has been particularly problematic. With fewer than 20% of farmers owning their own land, land reform or redistribution is a perennial social and economic issue. Since the Huk rebellion beginning in the 1920s, there has been agitation for improvement of tenants' rights. Communists took advantage of the skewed ownership patterns in order to organize support in the rural areas. Marcos had started a process of distribution of land for corn and rice. Aquino continued land distribution for corn and rice, but ultimately failed to include other crops or additional land, even though the Aquino campaign led to a shift in emphasis from tenancy rights to redistribution of ownership (Komisar, 1987, p. 179). Some successes encouraged farmers. In 1986 fertilizer prices dropped by a third and prices of copra at the farm gate almost doubled ("The Philippines," 1988). The Aquino administration can claim some successes in its economic goals of ending monopolies, liberalizing trade, reforming agriculture, and promoting exports of manufactures. These are partial successes, amid controversy about moving too fast and moving too slowly, and represent typical results of coalition politics within a context of strong and vocal interest groups.

Opportunities to pursue social justice goals were limited by pressure from unexpected budgetary needs. For example, an avalanche of natural disasters—the Baguio earthquake, the Mt. Pinatubo volcanic eruption, and repeated typhoons—unduly taxed the capacity of the national budget to provide economic development opportunities. These natural disasters required mobilization of government bureaucracies, reallocation of funds allocated for other purposes to relief funds, and attention to emergency management rather than long-term economic reform and development. Continuing political uprisings or rebellions in the south also caused attention to be diverted from economic development concerns.

An assessment after the first 1,000 days, or what can now be viewed as the midterm, of her presidency gave Aquino a mixed review. While economic elites continue to find opportunities for income and wealth generation, the poor and landless are little better off. A survey released by the Philippine *Inquirer* of Manila residents "gave Aquino an overall grade of 73%, with failing grades for her efforts in law enforcement, political stability, counterinsurgency, government services and her administration's anti-corruption drive. Her best score, a 77, was awarded for her efforts to revive the economy" (Lerner, 1988).

On the positive side, in just two years,

> a freedom constitution was proclaimed so that Aquino could rule by decree and sweep away the corrupted constitution and political institutions of the Marcos era; a national plebiscite overwhelmingly approved a new, transparently democratic constitution; a new Senate and House of Representatives were chosen in the first truly free elections since before martial law; and towns throughout the country elected their own local governments. ("The Philippines," 1988)

On the other hand, internal "leftist" critics accused Aquino of ignoring human rights abuses in order to placate the military, and of abandoning genuine land reform by signing a watered-down bill to appease the big landowners. Critics on the right faulted her for lack of determination to defeat the Communist insurgency and to end rampant graft and corruption (Lerner, 1988). With the large number of unresolved problems and the relatively disruptive transition from Marcos cronyism, it is remarkable that Aquino achieved even a small measure of progress.

Agenda Priority: Democratic Leadership Style

During the campaign, it was alleged that in response to an army offer to take over militarily and install Aquino as president, Aquino said, "I am not here for the power. I want to know if the people really support me, so we must go through with this election" (Burton, 1989, p. 381). Repeatedly, Aquino asserted that she did not seek absolute and arbitrary power, but rather hoped to create a framework for institutional sharing of legitimate power. Her goal of redemocratization and her style of leadership reflect this viewpoint.

The Filipino political structures and bureaucracy historically have been centralized, a tendency that was exacerbated by Marcos. For instance, during martial law, Marcos decreed an integrated reorganization plan, including the creation of the National Economic and Development Authority (NEDA), which consolidated central planning, resource allocation, and implementation functions that had been performed or shared by different agencies. Although Marcos chose to chair this body (Endriga, 1989, p. 313), which continues as a key coordinating body in Filipino government, Aquino took a more hands-off approach, leaving operational leadership to her ministers.

> Centralization in a person who does not enjoy exercising power can immobilize government. When everyone wants the personal attention of Cory Aquino, she may postpone decisions indefinitely, unless forced by oncoming events. The May 1st (1986) proclamations on labor waited practically up to the end of the year before they were substantiated by executive order. (Cariño, 1987a, p. 281)

Although Aquino tried to model a "softer" version of executive leadership, it is uncertain whether she fully communicated the potential efficacy of a more limited presidential role. Did she give strong enough direction to government and to the people?

During the transition-to-constitution period, Aquino had access to wide-ranging powers as president, but she exercised those powers in favor of redemocratization, through reestablishing freedom of the press and access to information and releasing all political prisoners. The 1987 constitution, representing the third Filipino experience in redemocratization after 1899 and 1935, guaranteed local autonomy, separation of powers, and public accountability. It drastically restricted the powers of the presidency in matters of monetary policy, treaty making, appointments, nepotism, and conflict of interest, and included a provision limiting the president to one term of six years, without possibility of reelection (De Guzman, 1988, pp. 278-280).

Aquino's emphasis on process over policy resulted in great importance being placed on leadership style. Attempting to encourage the development of a new political culture, one characterized by rule of law, tolerance, and participation, and in sharp contrast to that of Marcos, Aquino deliberately made decisions slowly and only after elaborate and lengthy consultations with as many people and groups as feasible. Although accused of weakness and delay, Aquino did not waiver from her decision that the most important legacy of her presidency would be her presidential leadership style. This commitment often led to situations in which the content of policy decisions took a subordinate role to the process of achieving those decisions.

For example, within her newly formed cabinet, Aquino established an open style of discussion and

> encouraged debate so that she could hear different views before making her own decisions. She did not pretend to know everything, but could not be easily swayed or forced to come up with a quick answer. She would sit and listen. When she reached a decision and said, "This is what I feel," the discussion would stop. (Komisar, 1987, p. 129)

Most policy-making was delegated to the ministries involved, and Aquino did not like to become involved in policy debates among ministers, preferring for them to develop compromises or decisions among themselves. On the other hand, she "would get involved immediately when there was a question of personalities rather than issues and try to smooth over the conflicts" (Komisar, 1987, p. 129). With a cabinet of diverse and often conflicting ministers, each of whom had considerable expertise and experience, this strategy, which appeared to be akin to that of settling disputes among children, might have been successful. On the other hand, this style of conflict management may have given undue emphasis to a congenial familylike atmosphere in the cabinet, over needed arguments and decisive stands on controversial policy issues.

Although Aquino encouraged debate, she was occasionally exasperated by the fractiousness of the cabinet. It has been reported that during one particularly heated turf battle, Aquino said, "I'm the one who makes the decisions. . . . I've had it, I just have to remind you I'm the president, and if you cannot respect me, there's no way we can work together" (Komisar, 1987, pp. 129-130). Apparently she was neither authoritarian nor entirely carefree about running meetings, and perhaps cabinet ministers had difficulty associating the authority of her position with her nonauthoritarian style, occasionally requiring her to remind them. Critics have charged that, rather than building or strengthening a real coalition of political forces in the cabinet, she relied on close family members for counsel.

Aquino's style as president evolved from her sense that the country needed assurance and the continued symbol of freedom. She gave frequent speeches and made appearances before civic and professional organizations, as well as traveling to the other islands often to "meet with local labour, church, farm and business leaders in well stage-managed and publicized 'consultations' " (Komisar, 1987, p. 135). Because the presidency was virtually the only national political institution during the year of transition to constitution, Aquino was determined to use her visibility to reassure the Filipino people concerning stability, reconciliation, and democracy. Although her frantic travel and speaking pace left her relatively less time to work on policy development, she placed peace and democratization above substantive policy as her higher goals.

The unique relation between Aquino and the Filipino public could have been exploited more thoroughly through an early and planned program of citizen mobilization. Although she need not have mobilized them in favor of a particular issue, she could have mobilized them just to discuss issues. People were looking to her for cues, but she did not lead adequately (Lallana, in press). Later, in 1990, in a last-ditch effort to capitalize on her popularity, she launched the Kabisig movement for development efforts based on local NGOs and movement-style organizations. It is likely that the real power of the "people power revolution" will eventually be realized by workers, religious activists, and the urban and rural poor, who might be mobilized for action in the future (Doronila, 1988) through something like Kabisig, the Linking Arms Movement ("The Philippines," 1990), organized from the top, or modeling a bottom-up movement from the historical precedent of February 1986.

Early in Aquino's presidency, her office was criticized for delay in issuance of executive orders, which, at that time, during the interim Freedom Constitution, had the force of law (Iglesias, 1988). For instance, at a time when officials and the people at large were eager for direction, the Presidential Commission on Government Reorganization, which was given 90 days (from March 12 to June 12), submitted its report on June 27, securing cabinet approval on August 13. Given the magnitude of the task, additional days of consultation seem reasonable

(Iglesias, 1988). Within nine months, the PCGR produced two reports, 45 executive orders, and 13 administrative orders.

But 18 months after the "revolution," Aquino was still beset by delays and somewhat defensive, but honest, about the problem. Addressing a group of businesspersons, Aquino confronted the audience, saying: "The issue that really brought you here. The question you all really want to ask, is: Can she hack it? Isn't she weak?" (Clad, 1987, p. 22). She said further:

> These are the questions that were asked by all those who have openly challenged my power, authority and resolve, and who have suffered for it. I speak of the shame-faced officers who have abandoned their follow-ers . . . and the failed politicians who made the last places in the last elections and are now trying to find a backdoor to power. . . . Well, they can forget it. Although I am a woman and physically small, I have blocked all doors to power except elections in 1992. ("The Philippines," 1988)

Another indication of Aquino's fluctuating strength and decisiveness is in relation to the cabinet, which originally was filled with people to whom she owed political debts from the campaign and before. Tensions between the right and the left, between the ideologues and the tech-nocrats, and between those with and without a Marcos-era history generated much discussion, few decisions, and often public confusion concerning the direction of government. From November 1986 to Sep-tember 1987, Aquino engineered several cabinet shuffles and depar-tures, ending up with a team that "makes pretensions to cohesion and efficiency, and is therefore reasonably acceptable to the two groups, the military and business, who had grown most exasperated with Aquino's indecisiveness" ("The Philippines," 1988). Two years later, and more than three years after assuming the presidency, Aquino continued in a similar vein, "I hope that you will be patient with us because we are in a transition period. . . . I promise that this day we will unite and do a better job in serving you" (Brunstetter, 1989, p. 44).

Aquino was also accused of weak substantive leadership. Some policies appeared to be applied inconsistently because some cabinet members deliberately followed strategies opposite to her stated poli-cies. For instance, while she was on a trip abroad, Enrile, apparently with cooperation from Laurel, organized a massive military initiative against the Communists. Although such actions caused Aquino consid-erable embarrassment both internally and externally, she did not dis-cipline the two men. The ability to endure "many tongues" and even real insubordination might be a sign of humble tolerance, but in a president to whom people look for guidance and leadership, it can appear to be weakness and indecision (Komisar, 1987, pp. 193-195).

Aquino's emphasis on developing a "soft" managerial style based on commitment to democratic participation and openness both with the Filipino people and with her cabinet and senior government officials presented a definite contrast to Marcos's style of authoritarian secrecy and repression. On the other hand, some situations and issues, especially land reform, begged for greater decisiveness, which was not always forthcoming.

Success Is Leaving the Presidency to Others

By her own count, Aquino made 93 denials concerning her possible interest in running for the presidency again (*Economist,* February 1, 1992). But she waited months before finally endorsing a candidate, namely, Fidel Ramos, her army chief of staff, and the eventual winner, on January 25, 1992, less than three months before the scheduled election. Even after this announcement and her repeated denials, speculation continued that she would enter the contest. Apparently presuming that a woman incumbent would want to or need to run in order to defeat a "famous and female" Marcos, commentators increased pressure on her after Imelda Marcos declared her candidacy. In fact, Eduardo ("Dandling") Cojuangco, Aquino's estranged cousin, ably represented the Marcos faction and outpolled Imelda Marcos.

It is significant that Aquino decided to support a limited six-year term for president in the 1987 constitution and to abide by that provision when her term was nearing completion. Unlike many other national leaders, she yielded neither to party nor to popular pressure. This decision reflects her commitment to democratic processes and her belief in sharing power, rather than holding on to it tenaciously. While she assumed the "umbrella" candidacy for president reluctantly, she campaigned enthusiastically, and with considerable political interest and acumen. Once president, she governed thoughtfully and deliberately, but avoided developing the perspective that she was all-powerful or indispensable. Her respect for sharing power and the rule of law must be considered a major legacy to the redemocratization of the Philippines.

In describing her postpresidency plans, Aquino stated that she will work with nongovernmental organizations, which she believes are able to deliver services to the people in a more cost-effective and more personal manner than government organizations (*Economist,* February 1, 1992). Although Aquino is certainly financially comfortable and has a large and supportive family, she is ably setting an example of how a former president can look forward to contributing to her country and its development. Examples of peaceful transitions between presidents should not be taken for granted; they have been relatively rare and must be valued by those interested in promoting democratic ideals.

Gender Issues in the Aquino Presidency

On balance, Aquino has made an important contribution to the experience of women leaders, not so much in the policies that she pursued as in the style of governance that she modeled. She did not follow a traditional feminist or prowoman substantive agenda. She did not champion issues of divorce, birth control, or reproductive freedom. Her personal and political relationship to the Catholic church seems to have prevented her from pursuing policies in support of such issues. The church assisted in the struggle against Marcos and in the settling of issues of candidacy for president (Youngblood, 1987). Although her personal opinions are not easily disentangled from the views of her church, Aquino is clearly not antiwoman. In the end, however, she did not actively pursue any courses of action that focused on modern women's issues.

On the other hand, many of the proclaimed policy priorities of her government are likely to have had a positive impact on women, considering that she attempted to focus attention on the poor, and the empowerment of the poor, through her campaign and her development of the Kabisig movement to bring power and resources to local NGOs and movements. Land reform, loans to small enterprises, and social services all benefited women, as they are among the poorest of the poor.

Aquino's biggest contributions are found in the open and democratic style of government that she insisted upon in the 1987 constitution, in her own behavior with her cabinet and with the public, and, as often as possible, in her appointed and elected government colleagues. This style of open and democratic governance has two important meanings for women. First, in more open and democratic systems, those previously denied access to public decision making, such as women, are more able to gain positions and influence. In fact, in the 1992 elections, two candidates for the presidency were women and one of them, Miriam Santiago, achieved a relatively close second place to the eventual winner.

Second, a "softer" style of leadership is more typical of that learned by women in their families and often practiced by women in institutions in which they work, thereby encouraging women to be more comfortable in government positions of power and influence. Aquino appointed many women to executive positions in her government. Many, though not all, of them have assisted in empowering other women and in democratizing the bureaucratic culture in which they worked. The chair of the Civil Service Commission, Patricia Santo Tomas, is one executive who worked to promote qualified women and to open up decision-making processes to workers of all levels in the bureaucracy. Santo Tomas encouraged her staff to develop organizationwide strategic and operational planning, to pioneer on-site child care, and to develop positions of "equality advocates" to monitor and deal with gender-related grievances at centers and in regional offices. When Aquino's political appointees, both male and female, pursued policies that were prowoman, Aquino did not object. She had delegated authority to her appointees.

The legacy of "softly" managing a government for six years during periods of insurgency, coups, natural disasters, difficult economic times, and often chaotic politics is one that may leave a lasting impression and strong expectations for democracy in the future.

In her final "state of the nation" address on July 22, 1991, Aquino recalled the trauma of Ninoy's murder and the martial law and corruption of the Marcos regime. She chronicled the economic difficulties and natural disasters that had befallen the country during her six-year presidency. But most of all, she emphasized her effort to redemocratize the country, to bring openness and cooperation to the political arena, at both central and local levels. In the face of difficult circumstances, she persisted in her commitment to democratic methods of governance. In spite of slowness and compromises that were often criticized by political opponents, neutral observers, and even staunch sympathizers, she persisted in her pattern of open consultation and deliberate delegation and decentralization. For Aquino's unwavering commitment to democracy for the country and openness and consultation in government, her presidency will be remembered.

References

Abinales, P. N. (n.d.). *The post Marcos regime, the non-bourgeois opposition and the prospects of a Philippine "October."* Unpublished manuscript.

Arcellana, E. Y. (1969). Indigenous political institutions. In J. V. Abueva & R. De Guzman (Eds.), *Foundations and dynamics of Filipino government and politics* (pp. 38-42). Manila: Bookmark.

Brunstetter, M. P. (1989). *Women in power: Meir, Thatcher and Aquino.* Paper presented at the annual meeting of the American Political Science Association, Washington, DC.

Burton, S. (1989). *Impossible dream: The Marcoses, the Aquinos, and the unfinished revolution.* New York: Warner.

Cariño, L. (1987a). *The Aquino government and the civil service: Lessons for future regime-bureaucracy interaction. A Filipino agenda for the 21st century: Solidarity conference.* Manila: Solidaridad.

Cariño, L. (1987b). *A year after the people power revolution: The shotgun marriage between the Aquino government and the bureaucracy.* Paper presented at the Asian and Pacific Development Centre, Kuala Lumpur, Malaysia.

Clad, J. (1987, November 5). Cory comes out fighting. *Far Eastern Economic Review.*

Congressmen agree to shun Kabisig. (1990, June 28). *Daily Globe* (Manila).

Corpuz, O. D. (1969). The cultural foundations of Filipino politics. In J. V. Abueva & R. De Guzman (Eds.), *Foundations and dynamics of Filipino government and politics* (pp. 15-17). Manila: Bookmark.

Crisostomo, I. T. (1986). *Cory: Profile of a president.* Manila: J. Kriz.

Cruz, I. R. (1989). People power Kuno. In W. V. Villacorta, I. R. Cruz, & M. L. Brillantes (Eds.), *Manila.* Manila: De La Salle University Press.

De Dios, E. S. (1986, August 28). *Can there be recovery without reforms?* Paper presented at the Mid-Year Economic Review.

De Guzman, R. P. (1988). Towards redemocratization of the political system. In R. P. De Guzman & M. A. Reforma (Eds.), *Government and politics of the Philippines* (pp. 267-282). Singapore: Oxford University Press.

Doronila, A. (1988, November 13). Understanding what people power can and can't do. *Manila Chronicle.*

Endriga, J. N. (1989). Bureaucracy in an authoritarian political system: The case of the Philippines. In R. B. Jain (Ed.), *Bureaucratic politics in the Third World.* New Delhi: Gitanjali.

Estrada-Claudio, S. (1990-1991). The psychology of the Filipino woman. *Review of Women's Studies, 1*(2), 1-9.

Gonzales-Zap, M. (1987). *The making of Cory.* Quezon City: New Day.

Iglesias, G. U. (1988). *Government reorganization under Aquino: Issues and problems.* Paper presented at the Northern Luzon Conference on Public Administration, Baguio City, Philippines.

Komisar, L. (1987). *Corazon Aquino: The story of a revolution.* New York: George Brazillar.

Lallana, E. C. (in press). *Rethinking the February revolution.* Quezon City: Kalitran.

Lerner, M. (1988, November 22). After first 1,000 days, Aquino gets mixed grades. *Washington (D.C.) Times.*

Richter, L. K. (1990-1991). Exploring theories of female leadership in South and Southeast Asia. *Pacific Affairs, 63,* 524-540.

Rodriguez, L. L. (1990). Patriarchy and women's subordination in the Philippines. *Review of Women's Studies, 1*(1), 15-25.

Sheehy, G. (1986). The passage of Corazon Aquino. *Springfield Journal-Register,* "Parade."

Steinberg, D. J. (1990). *The Philippines: A singular and plural place.* Boulder, CO: Westview.

Tancango, L. G. (1990). Women and politics in contemporary Philippines. *Philippine Journal of Public Administration, 34,* 323-364.

Tapales, P. (1988). *The role of women in public administration in the Philippines.* Unpublished doctoral dissertation, Northern Illinois University.

The Philippines. (1990, July 5). *Far Eastern Economic Review.*

The Philippines: A question of faith. (1988, May 7). *Economist.*

The status of women in the Philippines. (n.d.). *Philippine Values Digest, 3*(2).

Tolosa, B. T., Jr. (1987). Constraints on democratic consolidation and the economic ideology of the Aquino government. In R. J. Bonoan, A. C. Condon, & S. S. Reyes (Eds.), *The Aquino government and the question of ideology.* Quezon City: Phoenix.

Wurfel, D. (1988). *Filipino politics: Development and decay.* Manila: Ateneo de Manila University Press.

Youngblood, R. L. (1987). The Corazon Aquino miracle and the Philippine churches. *Asian Survey, 27,* 1240-1255.

3

Benazir Bhutto
and Dynastic Politics

Her Father's Daughter,
Her People's Sister

NANCY FIX ANDERSON

When Benazir Bhutto was elected prime minister of Pakistan in December 1988, she became the first woman to head a modern Muslim state (Jack, 1986, p. 135). She was also the youngest head of a democratic government, and, when she had her second child in January 1990, she became the first elected chief executive to give birth while in office (L. K. Richter, 1990-1991, p. 530). All of this is especially remarkable in that the history of Pakistan has been characterized by the dominance of the military and of conservative Muslims. Bhutto was able to achieve power as the daughter of Zulfikar Bhutto, the civilian prime minister from 1971 to 1977, who was deposed and executed by General Mohammed Zia ul-Haq. When Zia, after ruling under martial law for the next 11 years, allowed the return of parliamentary government and free elections, Benazir Bhutto campaigned on the appeal of the memory of her martyred father and as the caring sister of her oppressed people. These appeals, successful at the polls, did not lead to success in office, and her tenure as prime minister lasted less than two years.

Background

The country over which Benazir Bhutto ruled was a relatively new nation, created in 1947 when the British granted independence to the Indian subcontinent and partitioned it along religious lines between Muslims and Hindus. Pakistan was composed of five provinces with diverse ethnic identities: Punjab, Sind, Baluchistan, the North-West Frontier, and, until 1971, East Pakistan, which was separated by 1,000 miles from the western provinces. Each province has its own language (or languages), and many Pakistani do not speak the national language of Urdu. The one unifying force in Pakistan, and indeed its raison d'être, is Islam. At least 95% of all Pakistani are Muslim. The founding father of Pakistan, Mohammed Ali Jinnah, sensitive to the many sects and interpretations of Islam and influenced by his Western education, wanted Pakistan to be a secular state, with clear distinction between political and religious authority. After Jinnah's death, however, and especially since the rise of Islamic fundamentalism in the late 1970s, the power of the Islamic mullahs (religious teachers) has increased, and attempts to make state law conform with Islamic law have achieved some success (Ali, 1991, p. 20).

Pakistani political history has been characterized by repeated overthrows of civilian governments and the establishment of military dictatorships. Founded as a dominion in the British Commonwealth, Pakistan became a constitutional republic in 1956. In 1958, martial law was declared, with Field Marshal Mohammed Ayab Khan, the army commander in chief, assuming full authority, just as General Zia later would do in a similar situation in 1977. Military dictators have been able to seize power in Pakistan in part because of the concern about national security. In conflict with India over the disputed ownership of Kashmir, a province with a Muslim majority that nevertheless was given to India at the time of independence, Pakistan has waged three wars with India. It has also felt threatened by India's ally, the Soviet Union, and therefore historically aligned itself, in the age of Cold War diplomacy, with the United States.

Military rule has additionally been seen as an effective means of dealing with internal ethnic conflict, but it was unable to quell the secessionist struggle of the Bengalis in East Pakistan. With Indian assistance, East Pakistan successfully rebelled in 1971 and established independence as Bangladesh. The Pakistani army was discredited in this humiliating defeat, which facilitated a return to civilian government, with Zulfikar Bhutto as president. Bhutto had a new democratic constitution drawn up in 1973, which created a bicameral parliamentary system, with the president as constitutional head and the prime minister as chief executive. Bhutto then resigned as president to become prime minister.

Zulfikar Bhutto came from a wealthy, politically prominent Sindhi landowning family, with his father having served as prime minister of an Indian state before the partition. Educated at Berkeley and Oxford, Zulfikar Bhutto was foreign minister under Ayab Khan, but resigned in 1967 to form the Pakistan People's Party (PPP). Despite Bhutto's enormous wealth, the PPP was committed to improving the lives of the poor. He introduced socialist reform, including the nationalization of industries and the redistribution of land. Educational programs were established to try to improve the dismal literacy rate, which even by 1985 was estimated to be only 26% (Paxton, 1990-1991, p. 978). Bhutto's Westernized life-style, which included such practices as drinking alcohol, angered orthodox Muslims, but his answer was that, although he had a drink occasionally, "unlike other politicians, I do not drink the blood of the people" (Bhutto, 1989, p. 20).[1] He also alienated fundamentalists with his measures to eliminate discrimination against women.

Bhutto's adoring daughter Benazir praised him as "the first to bring democracy" to Pakistan: "The six years of his government had brought light to a country steeped in stagnant darkness" (Bhutto, 1989, pp. 16-17). While espousing democratic principles, however, Bhutto ruled in as authoritarian a manner as any of his predecessors. Intolerant of dissent, he outlawed opposition parties and jailed their leaders. He exercised strict censorship of the press by closing down newspapers critical of his government and by retaining the National Press Trust, through which the government ran a group of newspapers and censored others. He established the Federal Security Force, which was used against political opponents (McDonald, 1988b). Described as an "arrogant, charismatic, brooding, and suspicious politician who governed with great flair and ruthlessness" (Weisman, 1986b, p. 41), he was a populist demagogue who established a personality cult that became known simply as "Bhuttoism" (Kaushik, 1984, p. 169; see also Burki, 1980; Kaushik, 1985).

Befitting his demagogic leadership, Bhutto was a strong nationalist intent on strengthening Pakistan's prestige and power. He is especially credited with restoring national pride after the Bangladesh war, when Pakistan was treated as "a pariah nation" (Burki, 1980, p. 74). At a historic meeting with Indira Gandhi at Simla in 1972, he negotiated the return of prisoners and West Pakistani territory seized by India in the 1971 war in exchange for the promise of a peaceful and bilateral solution to the Kashmir question. Steering a more independent anti-American foreign policy, he cultivated instead relations with other Islamic nations (Jack, 1986, p. 72). He wanted Pakistan to achieve nuclear capability, and remarked, with strange words for a populist leader, that the Pakistani "would eat grass if that was the price of building a nuclear weapon" (Palling, 1989, p. 6).

Zulfikar Bhutto was overthrown in July 1977 in a military coup led by General Zia, whom Bhutto himself had elevated to the position of army chief of staff. Bhutto was done in, as some of his contemporaries who were not sympathetic to Zia said, by his own greed for power and his uncompromising attitude (Weisman, 1986b, p. 86). Accused of complicity in the murder of an opponent, he was tried and convicted, and, after two years of imprisonment, was executed in April 1979. Zia reestablished martial law and, through his treatment of Zulfikar Bhutto and his own repressive policies, helped create the mystique of the martyred "man of the people." Thinking that he had eliminated Bhuttoism by executing Bhutto (Kaushik, 1984, p. 178), Zia found an equally formidable adversary in the person of Zulfikar's oldest daughter, Benazir. She took up his cause and dedicated herself to revenging her father by seeking the overthrow of Zia and the restoration of the PPP to power.

The Making of a Muslim Woman Leader

Benazir Bhutto, who was 25 years old when her father was executed, was born in 1953 in Karachi, the capital of Sind and Pakistan's largest port. Her privileged background as part of a wealthy, powerful family gave her a sense of confidence and entitlement that both enhanced and undermined her later attempt at leadership. Benazir's mother, Nuscat Bhutto, was an Iranian Shiite Muslim who was raised in Bombay. When their first child, Benazir, was born, Zulfikar Bhutto was delighted. He said she looked just like him (Bhutto, 1989, p. 204). He apparently did not share the prevailing Pakistani sentiment of disappointment over the birth of a daughter. (As an example of this common patriarchal attitude, when Benazir accompanied her father to the 1972 conference in Simla, his aides said they would signal her by saying it was a boy if the conference was a success, and a girl if it was a failure. "How chauvinistic," commented the Westernized, modernized Benazir. See Bhutto, 1989, p. 74.)

There was, according to Benazir Bhutto (1989), "no question" that she and her sister would have the same opportunities as their brothers (p. 42). Rather than discrimination, Benazir experienced privilege as the firstborn, even though two sons as well as another daughter followed. She has stated that, indeed, she received the most attention in her family (p. 42). Her father's favorite, she in turn idolized him as a saint (Jack, 1986, p. 73).

Nuscat Bhutto, college educated and raised in relative social freedom, entered the traditional Muslim woman's life in secluded *purdah* with her husband's sisters when she married, although eventually, with her husband's encouragement and especially after his death, she assumed an activist role. When Benazir reached puberty her mother wanted her to wear a *burqa*, a tentlike covering, when she traveled, but her father said it was not necessary, and she became "the first Bhutto woman to be released from a life spent in perpetual twilight" (Bhutto, 1989, p. 47). She did, however, later use the *burqa* effectively as a disguise when she was struggling against the Zia regime (p. 212). Her father did warn her that when she campaigned in rural areas she should always wear the *dupatta,* or scarf, over her head so as not to offend traditional sensibilities (p. 154). As an adult she has extended this advice, and almost as a trademark always covers her head with a *dupatta.*

Benazir had a Western education, first with an English governess and later in convent schools. English was spoken in her family as much as Sindhi, and she learned the Pakistani national language of Urdu only for political purposes (Bhutto, 1989, p. 112). Her parents were away during much of her childhood, with her father serving as foreign minister and then as head of Pakistan's United Nations delegation. She later said that she saw her father as often in the newspapers as in person (Bhutto, 1989, p. 43). He kept in touch with her, however, through lengthy letters of advice and encouragement. Even when he resigned from the Ayab Khan government and was briefly imprisoned for his opposition, he wrote to her that he was proud to "have a daughter who is so bright that she is doing O-levels at the young age of 15, three years before I did them. At this rate, you might become the president." Although he was in solitary confinement, "my father led me to believe that his major concern continued to be my education," Benazir (1989, p. 52) has said.

In 1969, Benazir was sent to study in the United States at Radcliffe College, which integrated with Harvard University in the early 1970s.

She experienced severe culture shock: "I cried and cried and cried because I had never walked to classes in my life before. I'd always been driven to school in a car and picked up in a car" (quoted in Jack, 1986, p. 71). She was also shocked by the easy heterosexual mixing. Although tall, slender, and of striking appearance, she claimed that she never even danced for fear her father would find out. He may have been a Westernized liberal, but there were limits to what he would tolerate in his daughter. And she obeyed him, even at long distance. "I respected him so much. I didn't want to fall in his eyes" (quoted in Jack, 1986, p. 73).

Benazir soon adapted to American university life in the heyday of the radical 1960s and early 1970s. She marched in antiwar rallies, despite the danger that such activity could cause her deportation. She was not a pacifist, but believed that the United States should not engage in military action in Asia. She also came in contact with the nascent women's rights movement, and delighted in being with other women who refused to be hampered by their gender: "My fledgling confidence soared and I got over the shyness that had plagued my earlier years" (Bhutto, 1989, p. 60).

Benazir's first political speech was in a Harvard class in response to a professor's criticism of Pakistan for trying, he said, to crush the nationalist movement of the Bengalis of East Pakistan. She retorted that the Bengalis exercised the right to self-determination when they chose to join Pakistan in 1947 (Bhutto, 1989, p. 63). Her father wrote long letters to her, explaining the war, which he then published as a book, *The Great Tragedy*. When he, as the new president of Pakistan, came to the United Nations in 1971 to plead his country's cause, she joined him there and acted as his assistant. She also accompanied him during her summer vacation to the Simla meeting with Indira Gandhi in 1972.

After graduating cum laude from Harvard in 1973 with a degree in government, Benazir wanted to stay in Boston to do graduate work at the Fletcher School of Law and Diplomacy at Tufts University, to prepare for a career in foreign service. She felt comfortable in Boston, and had made good friends there, friends who later were influential in helping her during her struggles against Zia. Her father insisted, however, that she go to his alma mater, Oxford University.

She spent three years at Oxford reading politics, philosophy, and economics, and then returned for an additional year when she was honored by being the first foreign woman elected president of the

Oxford Union, the prestigious university debating society. It was "really an 'old boy's club,'" where only ten years before women had been restricted to the upstairs gallery. . . . Even my father was surprised" (Bhutto, 1989, p. 85). In the race for president, Benazir campaigned so vigorously that official complaints were lodged. Her friends later commented that she wanted to be president so much to please her father (Jack, 1986, p. 73). And he was indeed pleased, because he himself in his Oxford years had been president of the Union. Moreover, in the previous year Oxford had denied him an honorary degree after doubts were raised about his role in the Bangladesh war. His daughter's election must have seemed a recompense. Working diligently as president, she delighted in picking such provocative debate topics as, for the final debate, the double-entendred "This house likes domineering women" (Hall, 1989, p. B11).

Completing her term as president of the Oxford Union in June 1977, Benazir returned to Pakistan ready to begin a diplomatic career. Two weeks later, however, General Zia overthrew and incarcerated her father. Benazir and her mother immediately began agitating for his release. Her brothers, studying abroad, were warned not to return. Zia might have considered them, as Bhutto males, more threatening than the wife and daughter. If so, he was mistaken, for the female Bhuttos' campaign was relentless and fearless. With her father in prison and her brothers abroad, Benazir symbolically and literally took over the male role in the family, as when she, at her father's direction, went to the family graveyard and at a nearby house received traditional visits from the villagers. She also settled village disputes, which traditionally had been officiated by the men in the family (Bhutto, 1989, p. 149). Coached by her father from jail, she made speeches in his support, experiencing no resistance to her as a woman. "The suffering in the country, the suffering of my family, of all of us, had risen above the barrier of gender" (Bhutto, 1989, p. 155).

> In a way I had transcended gender. There was not a person who did not know the circumstances that had forced me out of the pattern of landowning families, where young women were guarded zealously and rarely, if ever, allowed to leave their homes without a male relative. (p. 169)

Proud of Benazir's courage in staying in Pakistan and fighting against Zia, Zulfikar called her "his jewel" (Bhutto, 1989, p. 21). He asked her, should anything happen to him, to continue his mission. She promised she would (Bhutto, 1988, p. 62).

Challenging Zia to call an election to test his claim of popularity, Zulfikar said that Zia should run not against himself but against Benazir, and predicted that Zia would be soundly defeated (Kaushik, 1985, p. 301). Unable to tolerate such challenges, Zia in September 1977 put Benazir and her mother under house arrest, and then in prison. Benazir later said that she was able to overcome despair because "my father's imprint on me keeps me going" (Bhutto, 1989, p. 123). On the day before Zulfikar was executed, Benazir was able to see him for only half an hour, "half an hour to say goodbye to the person I love more than any other in my life" (Bhutto, 1989, p. 20).

Although her mother was allowed to leave the country for medical treatment in 1981, Benazir Bhutto remained in various degrees of detention for almost seven years. While under house arrest, she was able to write, usually condemnations of Zia and defenses of her father's domestic and foreign policies (Bhutto, 1978, 1983). Other times, she was imprisoned in jail conditions so horrible that even mere survival was a struggle.

Zia's repressive military regime was protected from official Western, especially American, criticism by the Soviet invasion of Afghanistan in December 1979, which increased U.S. reliance on Pakistan's support. Characterized by some as "Brezhnev's Christmas present to Zia" (Preston, 1988a, p. 47), the invasion caused the United States to turn a blind eye to Zia's human rights abuses. In the early 1980s the Reagan administration gave $3.2 billion in military and economic assistance to Pakistan, one of its largest foreign aid commitments (Weisman, 1986b, p. 41). Remembering the anti-Americanism of her father, U.S. officials were probably not too concerned about the incarceration of Benazir Bhutto. Finally, in January 1984, after pressure from her Harvard friend Peter Galbraith, who was on the staff of the Senate Foreign Relations Committee, and with the support of the committee chair, Senator Claiborne Pell, Benazir was released and allowed to leave Pakistan.

Zia had imprisoned Benazir Bhutto to break her spirit, but in fact the ordeal only intensified her determination to challenge his rule. Each incarceration, she said while imprisoned, "is just adding another layer of anger" (Bhutto, 1989, p. 36). Peter Galbraith said that she "was transformed by the fights in those difficult years. . . . Nothing in her background suggests that she would have had such courage to see it through" (quoted in Weisman, 1986b, p. 44). She was toughened, certainly, but as Steven Weisman (1986b) asked, did the experience strengthen her or "transform her into a distrustful imperious loner striving for vindication?" (p. 44).

Party Leader

When Benazir Bhutto arrived in London, she insisted to reporters that she was not in permanent exile, but had come only to seek medical treatment for a perforated eardrum. "I was born in Pakistan and I'm going to die in Pakistan. My grandfather is buried there. My father is buried there. I will never leave my country" (Bhutto, 1989, p. 259). In a message released in Pakistan, she explained that in London she would be able to work with exiled members of the Pakistan People's Party and in that way "your Sister hopes to play [a role in the] redemption of the lost rights of the people" (Bhutto, 1988, p. 65).

The Pakistan People's Party in London was active in agitating against the military dictatorship of General Zia and for the restoration of democracy in Pakistan. Sharing this goal, Bhutto quickly experienced conflict with the party's members, conflict that would plague her leadership. Largely because of the mystique of her family name and her own suffering under Zia, she was elected head of the party. Idealistic and single-minded, she was irritated by the factionalism and politicking of her associates (Bhutto, 1989, p. 273). They in turn had trouble accepting the leadership of a young woman whom they had known as a child (Gupta, 1986). In choosing her, they assumed, as had the Indian Congress party when it chose Nehru's daughter as their leader, that she would serve primarily as a symbol. (The Congress party, according to Benazir, called Indira "a dumb doll behind her back. But this silk-and-steel woman had outmaneuvered them all"; Bhutto, 1989, p. 72). Similarly, the PPP treated Benazir, a colleague observed, "like a little punk girl" (Weisman, 1986b, p. 48). She resented the party's patronizing attitude, and, showing the same resolve as Indira Gandhi, she readily dismissed these men she called her "uncles" from party positions and replaced them with her own followers, whose loyalty and deference to her authority was unquestioned.

There were no other Bhuttos available to rival her leadership. Her mother was elected as cochair of the party, but her role was for the most part titular. Neither her brothers nor her sister had political ambitions or abilities (Jack, 1986, p. 84). Her brothers, moreover, had compromised their appeal by founding an anti-Zia terrorist organization, the

Al-Zulfikar, which received particular notoriety when in 1981 it hijacked a Pakistan International Airlines plane. In 1985 her younger brother, Shah Nawaz Khan, was mysteriously murdered in southern France, with his Afghan wife as the chief suspect. Wanting to honor him even though "his path may have been different from mine and [the] People's Party" (Bhutto, 1988, p. 69), Bhutto courageously decided to take his body back to Pakistan for burial, demanding that the Zia government allow her the right to bury him according to proper Muslim rites. Probably bothered by the cheering crowds that greeted Bhutto's arrival, Zia had her detained briefly after the funeral, but then released her to return to London.

Under pressure from the United States, Zia in 1983 announced plans for a gradual restoration of democratic institutions and the return to civilian government. He felt confident enough in his own strength to loosen the hold of martial law and to rely on popular support. One of the major ways he had consolidated his power was by the Islamization of the government, a process by which he introduced state laws that were in accordance with the Shariah, the religious law drawn from the Koran and the other teachings of the prophet Mohammed. In so doing, he "implemented a religiously based legal code unparalleled in the modern history of Islam in south Asia" (Weiss, 1990, p. 439).

Putting aside more difficult questions, such as whether the charging of bank interest for loans was a violation of the Koranic prohibition of usury, Zia and his allies, the mullahs, concentrated on laws that regulated social and especially female behavior. Inspired by the triumph of Khomeini and Islamic fundamentalism in Iran in 1979, Zia's Shariah courts issued the Hudood ordinances, which punished crimes such as adultery (*zina*) and rape in strict accordance with Islamic law. This meant that four Muslim men were required as witnesses to prove a woman's charge of rape. Without the witnesses, a woman bringing a charge of rape could herself be accused of adultery and stoned to death if married, or receive a hundred lashes and imprisonment if unmarried. The pregnancy of an unmarried woman is considered proof of guilt under the *zina* law. The Hudood ordinances also raised *zina* (which includes not only extramarital but premarital sex) from a crime against an individual to one against the state. Of the 4,500 women in prison in Pakistan in 1989, 80% were sentenced under this law. In another codification of the Shariah, the Law of Evidence, issued in 1984, decreed that a woman's testimony would be worth only half as much as the testimony of a man (Bhutto, 1989, pp. 314-317; Preston, 1988b; Shaheed & Mumtaz, 1989, p. 129; Weiss, 1990).

As part of the restriction of women in the name of Islam, Zia's government idealized the image of woman as faithful to *chador aur char diwari* (remaining veiled and within the confines of the four walls of one's house) (Weiss, 1990, p. 438). Although many women of course did not return to *purdah,* traditional symbols of modesty reappeared. Female newscasters on television were required to cover their heads with *dupattas* or be dismissed. The requirement that all female teachers wear *dupattas* was expanded in 1982 to require them to wear the heavier opaque veil, the *chador.* Many women began wearing the full-body covering of the *burqa* again. Women's field hockey teams were required to keep their legs covered, which eliminated them from international competition. During the Seoul Olympics in 1984, the Pakistan television screens went blank every time a female swimmer did a flip-turn (Walsh, 1989, p. A1).

Zia's Islamization program was fiercely resisted, especially by women (Ahmed, 1983). He nevertheless felt he had enough popular support to hold, as part of his ostensible move toward democracy, a national referendum in December 1984 confirming his tenure as president. The referendum asked voters "whether the people of Pakistan endorse the process initiated by General Mohammed Zia ul-Haq, the president of Pakistan, for bringing the laws of Pakistan into conformity with the injunctions of Islam as laid down in the Holy Quran and Sunah of the Holy Prophet (Peace Be Upon Him.)." As Bhutto (1989) remarked, it was practically impossible for anyone in Pakistan, a country that is 95% Muslim, to vote against the referendum: "A 'no' vote was tantamount to voting against Islam" (p. 275). Zia used his predictable victory as his "election" to the presidency for the next five years.

Zia then called for national and provincial elections in February 1985. Because he banned political parties, the PPP decided to boycott the elections. Zia selected a prime minister from the newly elected National Assembly, and in December 1985 formally lifted martial law. In restoring the 1973 constitution, he protected his power with the Eighth Amendment, which specifies that acts, ordinances, and decrees passed under martial law can be undone only with a two-thirds majority of both houses. The president also has the right to appoint military service chiefs, and can dissolve the National Assembly anytime he feels an appeal to the electorate is necessary (Ali, 1989b, p. 39). With these safeguards, Zia, who had once described political parties as "the instruments of Satan" (Bell, 1987), now allowed parties to once again operate openly and legally, which meant the return to Pakistan of Benazir Bhutto and the Pakistan People's Party.

Bhutto's Return to Pakistan

Benazir Bhutto arrived back in Pakistan in April 1986, greeted by huge, cheering crowds at the Lahore airport and along her route to a rally. A *New York Times* reporter who was present observed:

> Hundreds of thousands of people thronged the streets here today demanding the ouster of President Mohammed Zia ul-Haq in the biggest anti-government rally in Pakistan since General Zia seized power. . . . The immense crowd turned out peacefully to cheer their loyalty instead to Benazir Bhutto. (Weisman, 1986a)

Far more people turned out for this event than anyone—politicians, diplomats, or other analysts—had foreseen. Many people had doubted that Benazir Bhutto would find the kind of support among the people that her father had, but her triumphant return proved them wrong.

Bhutto was aware that the major source of her popularity came from the memory of her martyred father. In her campaign for the return of the PPP to power with herself as prime minister she skillfully projected the image of herself as her father's daughter, referring repeatedly to him in her speeches and always having his picture in the background of her official portraits. As she told the crowds at Lahore, "Seeing you, the people, makes me feel that Bhutto is alive before my eyes. He told me at our last meeting at Rawalpindi jail that I must sacrifice everything for my country. This is a mission I shall live or die for" (quoted in Weisman, 1986a).

In emphasizing her role as daughter of a martyr, Bhutto (1989) also played the politics of suffering by dramatizing her own experiences: "I have willingly taken the path of thorns and stepped into the valley of death" (p. 329). Histrionic though it sounds, she had and would again experience severe privations and dangers. Even returning to Pakistan was an act of great courage, as evidenced by the fact that Zia again jailed her for a brief period. Bhutto made effective use of the comparison the media were making between her and Corazon Aquino, who also that year was challenging a military dictatorship to vindicate the death of a family member and to restore democratic government (Bhutto, 1989, pp. 320-321). As Weisman (1986a) has noted, 1986 was "a bad year for dictators."

Bhutto's cultivation and use of her father's mystique was not only for political expediency. He remained, as she said, her "inspiration and hero" (Hall, 1984, p. B10). She has never acknowledged the negative aspects of his rule. When a London *Times* reporter asked her about his abuses and excesses, she retorted that "none were committed by my father," although she admitted that perhaps there were some by other individuals in his government (Thapar, 1988b). The mythical image of Zulfikar Bhutto certainly propelled his daughter into a position of power, but her adoration of him also weakened her exercise of that power. She tolerated no criticism of him, and has been accused of having as advisers only those who passed the litmus test of loyalty not only to her but also to the memory of her father (Weisman, 1986b, p. 43).

Another repeated complaint against Bhutto's leadership was that she was too imperious and domineering ("From Beyond the Grave," 1988). Certainly, as a Bhutto she does have a strong sense of personal authority and prerogative. Wholeheartedly committed to her cause, she is impatient with those with whom she disagrees. The criticism of arrogance, however, was probably also due, as she herself points out, to the fact that she is a woman with a strong personality. Margaret Thatcher, she has said, had the same problem ("Benazir," 1988). Bhutto is charismatic, but charisma is rarely honored in a woman, and some of her male colleagues had trouble working with her. The Pakistan People's Party was, as a consequence, considerably weakened in the course of her campaign for election by constant defections and dismissals, often leaving her with inexperienced and ineffective advisers (Haqqani, 1987).

Bhutto was also accused of not having a clear-cut agenda (Weisman, 1986b, p. 40), and certainly her major goal was simply the overthrow of Zia, not just as the murderer of her father but as the betrayer of his people. She cleverly targeted the areas of Zia's greatest strength. She argued that he weakened the army by politicizing it (Bhutto, 1988, p. 17) and tarnished national prestige and security by allowing the Indian army to take over an area in Kashmir that had been under Pakistan's control. Zia's policies "have clearly demonstrated that we don't have the will to defend our integrity," Bhutto (1988, p. 35) declared. In the same way, she accused him of exploiting Islam by using religious law for political gain. Moreover, in "the crimes against humanity unleashed by Zia-ul-Haq" the people he has tortured "are the sons and daughters of Pakistan. . . . This makes one wonder about it all as to what hatred he has against Pakistan, what hatred he has against Muslims that he should treat us so callously. . . . Who is he to say he is a Musalman? . . . He has acted as an enemy of Muslims and he has acted as an enemy of Pakistanis" (p. 42).

Offering an alternative to Zia, Bhutto set forth, with modifications, the populist policies of the Pakistan People's Party. Playing on the theme of national security, she affirmed that a strong professional army was necessary for external defense. But she argued that security also involved the well-being of the people. She therefore promised better schools, health care facilities, and job opportunities (Thapar, 1988a). Preaching economic and social justice, she nevertheless backed off from the socialist policies of her father, in part to win middle-class support, and urged instead a mixed economy with an active state but also private industry. With this move to the center to broaden its base, her platform was inevitably criticized by her left-wing colleagues as being too middle-of-the-road, offering "little that is different from that of any other party" (Rashid, 1988a).

Perhaps the most controversial aspect of her agenda was her opposition to Zia's Islamization programs. She repeatedly emphasized, sincerely as well as expediently, her faith as a Muslim, and made a pilgrimage to Mecca before returning to Pakistan in 1986. She nevertheless insisted, as had her father, on a secular code of laws that guaranteed equality for all. She specifically campaigned against a proposed Ninth Amendment that would empower the Federal Shariah Court, Pakistan's highest religious court, to examine the validity of all existing laws in light of the teachings of Islam. The amendment would have ominous consequences for the remaining rights of women, and so was vigorously opposed by women's groups. Although declaring that she was not a "militant feminist," Bhutto opposed the amendment and urged the repeal of the Hudood ordinances and the Law of Evidence, and all "cruel and inhuman laws that degrade women and make us second-class citizens" (Jaffe, 1989). She made women's rights and the improvement of women's lives a major theme in her campaign (Bhutto, 1988, pp. 256-264; Preston, 1988a, p. 47; Weiss, 1990, pp. 444-445).

When Zulfikar Bhutto argued for sexual equality, it was not as controversial as when his daughter took a similar stand, in part because of the rise of Islamic fundamentalism since the late 1970s. Moreover, as a woman Benazir Bhutto raised more suspicion and resistance among conservatives for her stance for women's rights because of their fear of female power. Indeed, throughout her tenure as party chair and as prime minister, Benazir Bhutto had contended with opposition based on her gender.

In addition to ubiquitous male resistance to female leadership, Bhutto confronted the particular challenge of seeking political power in a Muslim country whose traditions decree the subordination and seclusion of women. As Bhutto (1988) has noted, "Pakistan is a patriarchal society to the point of caricature. It is men who define the terms of women's existence, reinforce a self-image of helplessness and subordination, whether they are treated as mere cattle or as precious wards" (p. 257). Bhutto argued, however, as have other Muslim feminists (e.g., F. Rahman, 1982), that Islam itself does not discriminate against women: "The Prophet, Mohammed, said that men and women are as equal as the teeth of a comb" (Bhutto, quoted in Jack, 1986, p. 135). In the early religious instruction she received at home, she was taught that "it was men's interpretation of our religion that restricted women's opportunities, not our religion itself. Islam in fact had been quite progressive towards women from its inception" (Bhutto, 1989, p. 44). In her campaign speeches, she repeatedly emphasized the glorious history of Muslim women who had successfully performed public roles: "People think I am weak because I am a woman. Do they not know that I am a Muslim woman, and that Muslim women have a heritage to be proud of?" (Bhutto, 1989, p. 332).

Other women provided additional justifications for female leadership. One peasant woman observed, "A woman gave birth to the Prophet, so why can't a woman also rule the country?" Another asked, "How can a woman be worse than the present rulers, who have looted the people in the name of Islam?" (M. Rahman, 1988, p. 25).

The Muslim fundamentalists were more skeptical. They even questioned whether, according to Muslim law, a woman could serve as prime minister. After much debate a *fatwa* (religious pronouncement) was issued stating that as the prime minister is not the *amir,* who is head of state (i.e., the president) and who must be a man, but is rather the head of a political party, a woman can hold the office. Members of the major fundamentalist political party, the Jamaat-e Ulema-e Islami, at first accepted this decision, then later changed their minds, in resistance to Benazir Bhutto's prime ministry (Weiss, 1990, p. 3434).

Despite the ethos of male domination in Pakistan, which confined women to a familial role, it was generally not considered inappropriate for a woman to take the political role of an imprisoned or dead male family member. In so doing, she was carrying out her assigned responsibilities as caretaker of the family (L. K. Richter, 1990-1991, p. 526). As Bhutto (1989) explained when she first began campaigning:

A woman standing on a political podium was not as strange to the crowd as it felt to me. Other women on the subcontinent had picked up the political banners of their husbands, brothers, and fathers before me. The legacies of political families passing down through the women had become a South Asian tradition. (p. 125)

She was conscious of the example of Indira Gandhi. When Benazir as a college student accompanied her father to Simla to meet with Indira Gandhi, the Indian prime minister kept staring at her. Bhutto (1989) wondered, "Was she seeing herself in me, a daughter of another statesman?" (p. 72).

To achieve legitimacy, Bhutto emphasized her familial role, not only as Zulfikar's daughter, but in a larger sense as the sister of the people. It was not a big hurdle, she said while in London, being a woman in a Muslim country: "People didn't think of me as a woman. If anything, they thought of me as a sister" (quoted in Hall, 1984, p. B11). When she arrived back in Pakistan, she reminded the welcoming crowds, "I am the daughter of martyr Zulfikar Ali Bhutto, the sister of martyr Shah Nawaz Khan Bhutto, and I am your sister as well" (Bhutto, 1989, p. 333). Moreover, as M. Rahman (1988) has pointed out in *India Today*, the Pakistan People's Party "represents the spirit of sacrifice, suffering, redemption, and renewal, qualities which a woman appears to represent far more easily than a man" (p. 25).

As a woman, Bhutto did have difficulty in dealing socially with her male colleagues. "I must always maintain a certain degree of formality. For instance, I have to be accompanied by a proper chaperon, I must always be careful how I talk to people, I can't develop the kind of camaraderie that exists between men" (quoted in Jack, 1986, p. 135; see also Jaffe, 1989). Her relations with her male colleagues were especially sensitive because Bhutto was an unmarried woman in a society in which single women were considered a dangerous aberration. She was 33 years old when she returned to Pakistan; she had resisted her mother's pressure to marry, saying that she was still grieving for her father (Bhutto, 1989, p. 351). She then told curious reporters that she did not have time for marriage, because she was totally dedicated to her political mission (Jack, 1986, p. 134). Being unmarried became, however, a political liability. She did not have the advantage of Indira Gandhi and, indeed, of Corazon Aquino, who were both widows and therefore respectable without being restricted by marriage.

When asked by a reporter if she had a boyfriend, she starchily replied that Pakistani society would not take kindly to any discussion of such a subject: "I am a Muslim woman in a Muslim society and there are certain topics that Muslim women don't discuss" (quoted in Jack, 1986,

p. 134). She was nevertheless caricatured by Salman Rushdie in his 1983 novel *Shame* as "Virgin Ironpants." Such irreverent satire of a woman is considered dishonorable in Muslim society, and was a precursor of what later got him into trouble. Faithful Muslims in Zia's government, however, acted in an even more unchivalrous way by subjecting Bhutto to constant surveillance, trying to catch her with a man. The opposition parties spread rumors linking her with young PPP men. Her own colleagues were uncomfortable around her.

> The older politicians in the traditional society have never been quite sure how to treat her—as a waif, an arrogant woman who has only got where she is because of her father's name, or as a, so to speak, honorable man. At the back of everyone's mind is her single status, which to most men brought up in a feudal culture, is an embarrassment. (Rashid, 1987b, p. 52)

Bhutto (1989, p. 353) has bemoaned the fact that men can remain unmarried without being questioned, while single women are somehow "suspect" (see also Preston, 1988a).

Bhutto therefore in 1987 made the political decision to marry, to a man chosen by her family. It was, she said, "the price in personal choice I had to pay for the political path my life had taken" (Bhutto, 1989, p. 350). Although arranged marriages are the accepted norm in South Asian society, her decision shocked her Western friends. She explained, however, that in her high-profile life she had no opportunity to meet an appropriate man. Moreover, "for me as leader of a Muslim party, it would just not do to marry for love. . . . It would be detrimental to my image" (quoted in Bennett, 1987). Her mother and aunts carefully interviewed possible candidates, and chose Asif Zardari, who was also from a Sindhi landowning family. The same age as Bhutto, he was educated at the London School of Economics. Although the marriage was arranged, Bhutto did have the untraditional right of a veto. She agreed to the match, however, when, on the fourth day after she met Zardari, he insisted she go to a doctor for a bee sting. "For once I am not the one in charge. . . . I am the one being cared for," Bhutto (1989, p. 357) said; she found she liked that feeling.

Zardari's major qualifications were that he had no political ambitions for himself (although he did have economic ambitions, which would later get him and his wife into trouble) and that he would tolerate his wife's political career. Bhutto's supporters worried (and her opponents hoped) when they heard of the marriage plans that she would give up politics, not realizing that she was in fact marrying for the sake of her career. Upon her return to Pakistan, she traveled around the country to reassure the people "that I was their sister and would always be their sister, and that my marriage would have no bearing on my political career" (Bhutto, 1989, p. 358; see also Bennett, 1987). Significantly, she retained the name Bhutto.

Repeatedly taunted by her opponents as being too Western, Bhutto used her arranged marriage to emphasize her identity as an Asian woman. She pointedly titled her memoirs, published the next year to coincide with the parliamentary campaign, *Daughter of the East*. (The book was published in the United States with the modified title *Daughter of Destiny*.) The image of her as a (somewhat) traditional Muslim bride did confuse those who knew her in her radical college days. As a London *Times* writer put it, "The metamorphosis of Benazir Bhutto, impassioned sari-wearing leader of the PPP, into demure fiancee of Asif Zardari . . . is, to western eyes, one of the most impressive transformations in a career already full of contradictions" (Bennett, 1987).

The marriage brought her respectability in Pakistan, at least in the short run, and it freed her from government surveillance. As a married woman she now had a "protector," and "to intrude into a married woman's personal life is still not looked upon favorably, even by the intelligence service" (Rashid, 1987b). (In the election campaign the next year, the opposition lost support when some of its slogans speculated about Bhutto's sex life, a tactic that offended many Pakistanis. See "The Lady Tops the Men," 1988.) The marriage was greeted with joy by the people of Pakistan. The day of Bhutto's wedding, December 17, 1987, was a day of celebration throughout the country. When she arrived at the airport in Karachi for the wedding, there was a huge banner that read "Congratulations to the daughter of Pakistan from the people of Pakistan" (Thapar, 1988a, p. 68).

The 1988 Election

Once the question of her marriage was settled, Bhutto was repeatedly asked about children. She said that they would wait (Preston, 1988a, p. 47). Zia had timed local elections to coincide with her wedding, and she felt he would do the same thing with babies. And she was right. Despite her intentions, Bhutto almost immediately became pregnant. To fool Zia, she disguised her condition for a long time, which was easy to do in the loose Pakistani clothes. She finally announced that the baby was due in November 1988, and Zia immediately called the long-awaited elections for that month. It was "the first election to be timed for gynaecological considerations" (Singh, 1988, p. 45). Bhutto, however, campaigning right up to the end, gave birth to a seven-pound boy in September, and, even though she had a cesarean birth, she was back on the campaign trail in October.

Bhutto's overriding ambition ever since her father was overthrown by Zia in 1977 was to see the return of the Pakistan People's Party to power, with her as the leader of the party and therefore as prime minister. When Zia announced that the long-awaited parliamentary elections would be held in November 1988, Bhutto, despite her pregnancy, campaigned energetically. A very disciplined person, she worked long hours, making speeches and meeting with advisers. Her dedication did not, however, compensate for her political inexperience, and she confronted serious organizational and political problems in the campaign that foreshadowed those that would eventually undermine her prime ministry.

Her major difficulty was in forging an alliance with other parties to defeat the formidable coalition of conservative parties, the Islamic Democratic Alliance (IDA), that supported Zia. A loose coalition of leftist parties, known as the Movement for the Restoration of Democracy (MRD), had been formed in 1984, but by 1988 the PPP separated itself from the group. Other party leaders in the MRD had resented what they considered Bhutto's imperial leadership (Bell, 1987; Gupta, 1988, p. 24; Haqqani, 1987). Bhutto in turn did not want the PPP swallowed up in a larger organization. The MRD then disintegrated. Steering a separate course, therefore, the PPP went into the elections only with an understanding that it would not field any candidates against leaders of its former MRD allies ("From Beyond the Grave," 1988).

Focusing her campaign on the removal of Zia, Bhutto ironically was not helped when death removed her archenemy for her. On August 17, 1988, Zia was killed in a plane crash, the cause of which was undetermined. Bhutto's reaction was one of frank joy: "I can't regret Zia's death. . . . People think it's too good to be true" (quoted in Gupta, 1988, p. 13). In political terms it was not good, in that his death eliminated the major thrust of her campaign. It did allow her to shift strategy, to try to appease the powerful military now that it was no longer controlled by Zia. It was difficult, however, for the army to accept the leader of a party whose campaign slogan was "Whoever is with the army is a traitor" ("From Beyond the Grave," 1988).

Ishaq Khan, the leader of the Senate and a supporter of Zia, became the new president, and, despite fears of a military takeover, the elections proceeded peacefully as scheduled in November. The PPP won 92 and the IDA won 53 of the 203 contested seats in the National Assembly. The Senate was chosen by the four provincial legislatures, which had been elected in the 1985 election in which the PPP did not participate. It therefore was dominated by anti-PPP parties (McDonald, 1988a). Bhutto (1989, pp. 390-391) claims that her party would have won many more seats if Zia had not earlier decreed that all voters must have identity cards, which many of her supporters, especially poor women, did not have.

Although without a majority, the PPP was the largest party in the Assembly. The president delayed, however, for two weeks before appointing Bhutto as prime minister, while he consulted with other party leaders and looked for alternatives. Finally, on December 2, Benazir Bhutto made history by becoming the first woman to head a modern Muslim state.

Bhutto as Prime Minister

Benazir Bhutto's performance as prime minister has been criticized from almost every direction: by friends, opponents, feminists, mullahs, generals, and pacifists. The problems she confronted were so formidable that it is difficult to imagine how any leader could have governed successfully. Nevertheless, along with her own weaknesses of leadership, her gender was used by many as a convenient explanation for her failures.

Bhutto's efforts at leadership were first of all hamstrung by the fact that she did not have a majority in the Assembly or Senate. Moreover, Zia's Eighth Amendment gave significant power to the president, who was clearly hostile to Bhutto even though constitutionally he was supposed to be neutral. The provision of the amendment requiring a two-thirds majority in both houses for the repeal of existing laws made it virtually impossible for Bhutto's government to undo Zia's decrees, including his Islamization ordinances. She was further limited by conditions set by Ishaq Kahn when he appointed her. She had to agree not to reduce the military budget or interfere in the Afghan policy. (With the end of the Cold War and the Soviet pullout from Afghanistan, the United States was shifting away from its policy of aiding the Muslim

Afghan rebels. There was fear among the military and the fundamentalists that Bhutto would follow a similar policy. See W. Richter, 1989.) Although Bhutto received some criticism from supporters for agreeing to those conditions, others praised her pragmatism in trying to win over army support (Rashid, 1988c). Another ominous obstacle to Bhutto's exercise of leadership was the failure of the PPP to win the provincial election in the Punjab, Pakistan's most populous state. Instead it was controlled by the IDA, headed by the formidable Nawaz Sharif, who then declared a *jihad* (religious war) against Bhutto (Rashid, 1989, p. 23).

Bhutto was further handicapped by the bad economic conditions she inherited from the Zia regime. Inflation was running about 15%, and foreign exchange reserves were at a critically low level, restricting the ability to import goods. The government had to borrow money just to pay its employees. As a further complication, Bhutto could not rely as confidently as had Zia on aid from the United States, in that Pakistan was no longer so strategically important to American foreign policy.

In these circumstances some commentators in hindsight have suggested that Bhutto should not have accepted the office. Certainly she never should have raised the already high expectations of what she could achieve as prime minister. On the day after her appointment she made a speech on television in which she reiterated the PPP program for health, education, housing, and other social programs, but her government would not have the means to pay for them. She also promised to repeal all laws discriminatory against women, even though she did not have control of the legislature.

Nevertheless, her election did immediately create an atmosphere of greater freedom in Pakistan. One young girl shouted as the election broadcast started, "The PPP must have won. The announcer isn't wearing a *dupatta.*" Bhutto immediately ordered that all death sentences be commuted to life imprisonment and that all women prisoners except those convicted of murder be released (in that most had been imprisoned under the notorious *zina* law). She lifted the ban on trade unions and student organizations ("The Lady Tops the Men," 1988; Rashid, 1988d, p. 14).

The action that had the greatest impact, both positive and negative, on the public perception of her leadership was her decision to abolish the National Press Trust, the government agency that had controlled the media and that had been retained by her father. In allowing for the first time true freedom of the press, she was carrying out her commitment to civil liberties and the democratic process (L. K. Richter, 1990-1991,

p. 536). However, she was also allowing her formidable opposition to criticize her freely and to work openly to undermine her rule. Pakistanis were not accustomed to such unrestrained criticism of their government, so it was commonly interpreted that she was weak and had lost control (Weiss, 1990, p. 435). Her perceived weakness conformed easily with the expectations of those who forecast the inevitable failure of a woman prime minister (Ali, 1989d, p. 40).

Bhutto was seen as a weak and ineffective leader not only because of her gender but also because of her youth. She was 35 when she became prime minister, and she replied to comments about her age by saying that although others may think of her as such, "I am certainly not young. I have seen too much pain and repression" (quoted in Gupta, 1988, p. 21). Her knowledge about the realities of life in Pakistan was also questioned, in that she had spent most of her life either in the West or, when in Pakistan, in jail (Rashid, 1988b; Shandra, 1986).

Bhutto was also criticized as too inexperienced in the practicalities of political leadership, an accusation that the record of her administration seems to validate. She did not display good judgment about people, and was therefore unable to select and keep experienced and effective advisers. The perennial problem of her alleged arrogance and intolerance of dissent within her ranks drove away many supporters. She was accused of nepotism, and she certainly felt better with loyal family members in positions of authority. Her mother was deputy prime minister, and her husband's father headed the parliament's public accounts committee, a position that created an opportunity for extensive corruption. In a futile attempt to broaden her support, she formed a cabinet of 50 or so ministers in a parliament of 237, which further stymied efforts at effective government. After her second child was born in January 1990, the popular joke became that all she had been able to deliver as prime minister was a baby ("Miss Bhutto's Distractions," 1990).

Women's Rights Under Bhutto

Perhaps most disappointed about Bhutto's leadership were the women's rights activists. Frustrated that she was not able to repeal Zia's repressive laws, they felt the cause was not only institutional obstacles, but also Bhutto's own lack of commitment. She was accused of being more interested in politics and the exercise of power than in women's rights (Preston, 1988a, p. 45; Schork, 1990; Thomas, 1989). Bhutto had earlier said that she was a national leader and not a leader of women only (Rashid, 1987a, p. 27).

Nevertheless, despite Bhutto's inability to change laws, her prime ministry did significantly improve the lives of Pakistani women. There was much greater personal liberty for women, who were freed from "social prisons" even as Bhutto had literally freed women prisoners (Weiss, 1990, p. 435). As one woman supporter said, under Zia it was not uncommon for a woman walking in the street with her head uncovered to be slapped in the face for not wearing a *dupatta,* but "today, I am not afraid of being assaulted because my head is uncovered" (Schork, 1990). With the end of press censorship, the media could portray women in a much freer way. The state-run television could produce documentaries on women's rights and entertainment programs showing women working outside the home (Walsh, 1989, p. A15). Pakistani women once again competed in international sports (Weiss, 1990). Although unable to repeal the Hudood ordinances or the Law of Evidence, Bhutto's government was able to prevent the implementation of both the proposed Ninth Amendment, which would have made Islam the law of the land, and the Shariah bill, which would have put religious courts above civil courts (Ali, 1989e, p. 38).

Although women's groups thought that Bhutto did not go far enough for women, mullahs and other fundamentalist Muslims thought that she went too far, and they remained unremittingly opposed to her leadership. Despite her attempts to appease them by such gestures as always wearing a *dupatta* (to the dismay of her feminist compatriots) and attempting to foster a sense of pan-Islamic unity in the Middle East and South Asia, many devout Muslims never accepted the religious validity of the leadership of a woman. Bitterly resenting the social change that took place under her rule, they were important pillars of the opposition coalition, the IDA (Hussain, 1989; Rashid, 1989).

Governing Dilemmas

The generals had as much trouble as the mullahs accepting a woman, and especially Bhutto, as prime minister. They feared that she was "soft on India" because she emphasized in her campaign the importance of peace, without which she said there could be no national progress (Gupta, 1986). She also had a known rapport with Rajiv Gandhi, who had succeeded his assassinated mother as prime minister of India in

1984. They were the same age, both of the postpartition (Bhutto delighted in asserting her nationalist credentials by emphasizing that, born in independent Pakistan, she had never been an Indian), and they were both successors of powerful, martyred parents (Ali, 1989a; Bhutto, 1989, p. 72).

The Indian press, however, did not see her as a potentially weak leader. Although welcoming the conciliatory statements in her campaign, Bobb (1986) wrote in *India Today* that she "has also made some very negative statements. . . . So we are not harboring any illusions. . . . If she does seize power, we know she will be one tough customer to deal with." They were right. During Bhutto's administration the ever simmering tensions between Pakistan and India over Kashmir heated up dramatically, bringing the two countries to the brink of war. Bhutto took a hawkish stand on Kashmir, perhaps in part for pragmatic reasons, to win the confidence of the army and to deflect attention from domestic problems (Sandhu, 1990, p. 10). She was also unquestionably a strong nationalist, and very much her father's daughter, referring to his oft-quoted threat to fight India for a thousand years if necessary over Kashmir. She toured Islamic countries to solicit support for Pakistan in the struggle. Nevertheless, despite this rhetoric, Bhutto was much more reluctant to launch a war than were the generals, who wanted to go further in arming the Kashmiri rebels ("A Coup in Mufti," 1990).

War did not break out with India, but Bhutto did confront another form of violence in her own home province of Sind, which became a critical factor in her downfall. Sind was torn by ethnic strife between the Sindhi speakers, who were mainly rural and poor, and the Urdu-speaking urban *mohajirs,* who had immigrated to Sind from India after the partition. The conflict between the two groups became so violent that there was pressure on Bhutto to call in the army to quell the unrest. She refused, but was unable through civilian police authorities to end the strife, which increased the general perception that her government was ineffectual (Ali, 1989c, 1989d, 1990a).

The final blow to Bhutto's hold on office was the charge of corruption. Corruption in the form of graft and bribes had been a regular part of South Asian politics, and certainly all of the previous Pakistani governments were tainted to some extent (Ali, 1990b). These charges were devastating to Bhutto's rule, however, because she had campaigned on such a high moral ground. The most serious of the charges were leveled against her husband, and the charges against Bhutto herself concerned bribes that were probably paid by Zardari. The occasion for the alleged bribes was a parliamentary vote of no confidence that had been brought against Bhutto in November 1989. She was at that time about to give birth to her second child, a daughter, another example of the opposition attempting to take advantage of her childbirths. Zardari took charge of winning support for her in the Assembly against this vote, and he apparently did so through bribes, perhaps the only effective way to gain a majority without sufficient political support (MacFarquhar, 1990). Bhutto survived the vote, but barely.

Zardari meanwhile was creating notoriety by the way he and his family were reputedly profiting from government influence, with graft, kickbacks, bribes, and other corruptions. Bhutto must have realized this, but she seemed powerless to stop him. She had married him for political expediency, but had apparently become obsessed with him. As one commentator said after her fall, "The manner in which her infatuation with her husband Asif . . . has undermined her political career is nothing short of dramatic. . . . [It] is the subject of incredulous discussion in all circles" (Chacko, 1991, pp. 30-31). The sins of a husband tarnish a wife, who is still commonly seen as in his shadow, even if she be prime minister, much more than the sins of a wife affect the reputation of her husband. Bhutto's ministry, already weakened by domestic tensions and a strong opposition, did not survive this scandal.

On August 6, 1990, while the world was distracted with the Iraqi invasion of Kuwait, President Ishaq Khan dismissed Bhutto as prime minister on the charges of corruption, abuse of power, and ineptitude. Legal charges were also brought against her for corruption, which, if she were convicted, would mean that she could not again serve in the government. Zardari was charged not only with corruption but also kidnapping and extortion, for which he could receive the death penalty. Bhutto called all the charges spurious, and retained her pugnacious determination not to yield. Although she and her husband were reportedly offered a safe exit from the country, Bhutto was determined to stay and fight, even as she had fought for her father against Zia: "I have a legacy. My father and grandfather were both prime ministers" (quoted in Ali, 1990c, p. 20). She also felt the responsibility of her role as the first elected woman prime minister in the Muslim world, and did not want "a future Muslim woman leader taunted that like Benazir Bhutto, when the heat is on, she will quit" (Gupta, 1991, p. 23).

Although the dismissal was in accordance with the 1973 constitution, as amended by Zia's strengthening of presidential powers, this action, as the *Economist* said, "still smelt like a coup" ("A Coup in Mufti,"

1990, p. 35). Troops surrounded Bhutto's house and the television and radio stations, and the country was placed under a state of emergency. The president did, however, call for new elections in October, and the campaigns were unfettered and the election peaceful. Bhutto was one of the active participants, trying to obtain a fresh mandate for herself and the PPP. The results were devastating. Of the 207 contested seats, the PPP won only 45, down from 92 in 1988. Although Bhutto herself was reelected to a seat, almost all of her former cabinet members lost theirs. The IDA, with 105 seats, won a majority, and that group's leader, Punjabi President Nawaz Sharif, became prime minister. The vote shows the extent to which Bhutto had lost public confidence, as evidenced also in the lack of public protest at her dismissal. Nevertheless, the PPP had the second-largest number of seats in the National Assembly, and so Benazir Bhutto, still the party leader, assumed the position of leader of the opposition.

Evaluation

Benazir Bhutto's fall from power was due in part to her failure of leadership, rooted in political inexperience and poor judgment of people. She was also blinded by her sense of mission. As a close friend said, "She never made the transition from being the leader of a crusade to being a governing Prime Minister" (quoted in MacFarquhar, 1990, p. 42). Her inability to build a strong party organization prevented the PPP from receiving a majority in the National Assembly, which stymied efforts at reform legislation. She had to expend tremendous energy trying to build support, which opened her to the charge of being concerned with politics rather than policies. Attempting to appease opponents, she alienated her own constituency without winning new support.

These difficulties of her own making, along with those caused by the restrictive conditions she inherited from the Zia regime, were compounded by the fact that she is a woman in a country with deep-rooted patriarchal traditions and attitudes. She could use her sex effectively in her role as the suffering and loyal daughter and sisterly leader in order to win support and gain power; however, once in office she found that such appeal was ineffective in dealing with the realities of governing. Her opponents then used her gender as an excuse for increased condemnation of her leadership. Experiencing the bind of many women in authority, she was repeatedly subjected to the gender-based charges that she was either too weak or too arrogant. Social disapproval and suspicion of her as a single woman compelled her to marry, which then tied her fate to that of her husband. Her pregnancies only reinforced in people's minds that she was a woman, which many saw as antithetical to effective leadership.

Bhutto's failures and limitations should not overshadow, however, the significant achievements of her government. Her commitment to democracy and civil liberties served to reestablish parliamentary government in Pakistan after long years of military dictatorship. Under her leadership, Pakistan was restored to a place of respectability in the international community. A new era of social freedom liberated Pakistani women from at least some of their traditional restrictions. Moreover, the fact that she as a woman was prime minister was important, she said in retrospect, "not only to Pakistani women, but to Muslim women the world over. It has given women a role model and an example. And it also upheld something that many Muslims believe in: That men and women are equal in the eyes of God" (quoted in Crossette, 1990).

Note

1. The source of this quote, Bhutto's autobiography, *Daughter of Destiny* (1989), was first published in Pakistan as part of her 1988 parliamentary campaign, and it must be interpreted in that light. However, as substantiated by other sources, it seems to be a reliable account of her thoughts and experiences.

References

A coup in mufti. (1990, August 11). *Economist,* pp. 35-36.

Ahmed, S. (1983, October-November). In the forefront of the struggle: The Pakistani women's movement today. *Manushi.*

Ali, S. (1989a, January 12). A hint of hope. *Far Eastern Economic Review,* pp. 10-11.

Ali, S. (1989b, September 7). Constitutional bind. *Far Eastern Economic Review,* pp. 38-39.

Ali, S. (1989c, September 21). Polarized politics. *Far Eastern Economic Review,* pp. 20-21.

Ali, S. (1989d, October 5). A showdown looms. *Far Eastern Economic Review,* pp. 40-41.

Ali, S. (1989e, November 16). Breathing space. *Far Eastern Economic Review,* pp. 36-38.

Ali, S. (1990a, June 14). Home fires burning. *Far Eastern Economic Review,* pp. 22-23.

Ali, S. (1990b, August 16). Critics in glass houses. *Far Eastern Economic Review,* p. 8.

Ali, S. (1990c, September 13). Scare tactics. *Far Eastern Economic Review*, pp. 20-22.

Ali, S. (1991, May 2). Shariah strains. *Far Eastern Economic Review*, pp. 20-21.

Bell, G. (1987, July 4). Zia meets his 10 year-old devil but still calls the shots. *Times* (London), p. 9.

Benazir, volume one. (1988, May 21). *Economist*, p. 32.

Bennett, C. (1987, July 31). Ideal arrangement? *Times* (London), p. 17.

Bhutto, B. (1978). *Foreign policy in perspective.* Lahore: Classic.

Bhutto, B. (1983). *Pakistan: The gathering storm.* New Delhi: Vikas.

Bhutto, B. (1988). *The way out: Interviews, impressions, statements and messages.* Karachi: Mahmood.

Bhutto, B. (1989). *Daughter of destiny: An autobiography.* New York: Simon & Schuster.

Bobb, D. (1986, May 15). No illusions. *India Today* (International Ed.), p. 17.

Burki, S. J. (1980). *Pakistan under Bhutto, 1971-1977.* New York: St. Martin's.

Chacko, A. (1991, May 15). A fatal obsession. *India Today*, pp. 30-32.

Crossette, B. (1990, August 8). Bhutto blames the Pakistani military for her dismissal as prime minister. *New York Times*, p. A4.

From beyond the grave. (1988, August 27). *Economist*, p. 23.

Gupta, S. (1986, May 15). Interview with Benazir Bhutto. *India Today* (International Ed.), pp. 14-15.

Gupta, S. (1988, September 15). Pakistan after Zia. *India Today*, pp. 10-24.

Gupta, S. (1991, September 15). They've crossed limits even Zia didn't [Interview with Benazir Bhutto]. *India Today*, pp. 22-24.

Hall, C. (1984, April 4). The April of her freedom. *Washington Post*, pp. B1, B10-B11.

Haqqani, H. (1987, November 5). A grassroots' test. *Far Eastern Economic Review*, p. 28.

Hussain, Z. (1989, March 31). Pakistan: Religious row. *India Today*, p. 66.

Jack, I. (1986, May). The destiny of Benazir Bhutto [Interview]. *Vanity Fair*, pp. 69-73, 134-135.

Jaffe, M. (1989, January 4). A day in the life of Benazir Bhutto. *Sunday Times Magazine* (London), p. 58.

Kaushik, S. N. (1984). Political leadership in Pakistan: Aspects of Bhutto's experiment. In P. Nayak (Ed.), *Pakistan: Society and politics* (pp. 166-181). New Delhi: South Asian.

Kaushik, S. N. (1985). *Pakistan Under Bhutto's Leadership.* New Delhi: Uppal.

MacFarquhar, E. (1990, November 5). Born to rule, bred to lose. *U.S. News & World Report*, pp. 40-42.

McDonald, H. (1988a, December 1). Benazir's big moment. *Far Eastern Economic Review*, pp. 10-11.

McDonald, H. (1988b, December 1). Coming to terms with a flawed father. *Far Eastern Economic Review*, pp. 11-12.

Miss Bhutto's distractions. (1990, March 3). *Economist*, p. 31.

Palling, B. (1989, March 19). Sweet revenge in Pakistan. *New York Times Book Review*, pp. 6-7.

Paxton, J. (Ed.). (1990-1991). *Statesman's year-book* (127th ed.). New York: St. Martin's.

Preston, Y. (1988a, March). Bhutto's choice. *Ms.*, pp. 42-45, 47.

Preston, Y. (1988b, March). Women under siege. *Ms.*, p. 46.

Rahman, F. (1982). The status of women in Islam: A modernist interpretation. In H. Papanek & G. Minault (Eds.), *Separate worlds: Studies of purdah in South Asia* (pp. 285-310). Delhi: Chanakya.

Rahman, M. (1988, November 30). A turning point. *India Today,* pp. 22-27.

Rashid, A. (1987a, February 5). Feminists fight back. *Far Eastern Economic Review,* pp. 26-28.

Rashid, A. (1987b, December 3). A feudal Sindhi and his political wife. *Far Eastern Economic Review,* pp. 52-53.

Rashid, A. (1988a, October 20). Ghosts of politicians past. *Far Eastern Economic Review,* p. 42.

Rashid, A. (1988b, December 1). Bhutto on Bhutto. *Far Eastern Economic Review,* p. 56.

Rashid, A. (1988c, December 8). Keeping the generals happy. *Far Eastern Economic Review,* pp. 13-14.

Rashid, A. (1988d, December 15). The morning after. *Far Eastern Economic Review,* pp. 14-15.

Rashid, A. (1989, March 16). War of nerves. *Far Eastern Economic Review,* pp. 23-24.

Richter, L. K. (1990-1991). Exploring theories of female leadership in South and Southeast Asia. *Pacific Affairs, 63,* 524-540.

Richter, W. (1989, December). Pakistan under Benazir Bhutto. *Current History,* pp. 433-436, 449-451.

Sandhu, K. (1990, March 31). The "other" Kashmir. *India Today,* pp. 10-16.

Schork, K. (1990, August 27-September 2). Bhutto's fall, like her rise, won't change much for women. *Washington Post National Weekly,* p. 25.

Shaheed, F., & Mumtaz, K. (1989, September 28). Veils of tears. *Far Eastern Economic Review,* pp. 128-129.

Shandra, R. (1986, May 15). From exile. *India Today* (International Ed.), p. 18.

Singh, R., with Sheikh, A. (1988, June 30). A bloodless coup. *India Today,* pp. 44-46.

Thapar, K. (1988a, January 15). Taking stock. *India Today,* pp. 66-68.

Thapar, K. (1988b, August 20). Law of the land is on our side. *Times* (London), p. 8.

The lady tops the men. (1988, November 19). *Economist,* pp. 35-36.

Thomas, C. (1989, October 11). Bhutto reforms stalled. *Times* (London), p. 11.

Walsh, M. W. (1989, May 3). Pakistan women look to Bhutto to improve a harsh existence. *Wall Street Journal,* pp. A1, A15.

Weisman, S. R. (1986a, April 11). A daughter returns to Pakistan to cry for victory. *New York Times,* p. 2.

Weisman, S. R. (1986b, September 21). The return of Benazir Bhutto: Struggle in Pakistan. *New York Times Magazine,* pp. 40-48, 110-111.

Weiss, A. (1990, May). Benazir Bhutto and the future of women in Pakistan. *Asian Survey, 30,* 433-445.

4

Women in Power in Nicaragua

Myth and Reality

MICHELLE A. SAINT-GERMAIN

On February 25, 1990, Violeta Chamorro was elected president of Nicaragua and became the first woman ever directly elected to the presidency of any Central American nation. Given the prevailing Latin norm that politics is a male domain and the proper sphere of women is the home, three questions come to mind: Why did a woman become president *now*? Why did *this* woman become president? And *what does this mean* for women and leadership?

Addressing these questions requires an understanding of the context of Chamorro's election. Thus a brief review of the historical development of political culture and gender identity in Nicaragua follows, along with a short biography of Violeta Chamorro. Also provided are the details of the 1990 presidential campaign, where the political culture and the gender identity system collided head-on to produce unique electoral conditions that ultimately resulted in the election of Nicaragua's first woman president. Finally, through an analysis of her first year in office, we can explore what Chamorro's election has meant for women in power in Nicaragua: myth or reality?

70

Political Culture

Politics in Nicaragua has been marked by invasions, civil wars, and violent deaths of heads of state (Barquero, 1945). Until 1990, Nicaragua had never experienced a peaceful transfer of government between the group in power and the opposition. Lacking traditions of democratic institutions and the rule of law, politics has been "a violent business to be carried on by force, fraud, and coercion" (Close, 1988, p. 25). This political culture was shaped early on by three colonial powers. Spain and the United States were attracted to the country because it offered the shortest mostly navigable route between the Atlantic and Pacific oceans; for Britain it was part of a strategy to dominate the Caribbean. In the twentieth century, invasions and occupations by U.S. Marines and a 40-year dynastic dictatorship reinforced the tendency for Nicaraguan politics to be dominated by foreign interests.

Beginning with the fourth voyage of Columbus in 1502, colonization by the Spanish was a violent experience that greatly reduced the native population through fighting, slavery, disease, ill-treatment, and flight (Radell, 1969; cited in Close, 1988). From the Spanish, Nicaraguans inherited a "patrimonial, corporatist political structure," which emphasized military values, and the Catholic religion, which justified that structure and those values (Close, 1988, p. 7). A corporatist system is not based on checks and balances, laissez faire, or the unfettered competition of interest groups independent of the state. Rather, corporatism is a "system of national organization in which the component social and political groups are organized functionally" in sectors, with the state as the final arbiter of conflict (Wiarda, 1981, p. 90). Corporatism stands in contrast both to liberalism—in that it is not based on individual rights—and to socialism—in that it presumes that conflict between groups can be mediated. The group is seen as the natural link between the individual and society. Political parties, however, are not seen as natural groups, and such things as a "loyal opposition" have little meaning in a system where a harmony of interests is presumed and enforced.

The Spanish established two major cities in western Nicaragua, and each city developed its own political party that reflected the major economic interests of its region. The Conservatives of Granada, on the shores of Lake Nicaragua, represented the big cattle ranchers and traders, while the Liberals of Leon, closer to the Pacific Ocean, represented the rival coffee growers and urban business interests (Envío Collective, 1989b, p. 6). When the yoke of Spanish rule was overthrown in 1821, Nicaragua fell almost immediately into a series of civil wars in which each political party was supported by a rival foreign power intent on gaining control of the country in order to build a canal across it.[1] In 1823, U.S. President James Monroe proclaimed the United States' intent to consolidate its influence over Latin America and the Caribbean under the doctrine of "America for the Americans"; by 1850, under the Clayton-Bulwer Treaty, the United States had forced Britain to give up its interests in a Nicaraguan canal, greatly weakening British political power in the region and intensifying U.S. influence over Nicaraguan politics.

The discovery of gold in California in 1848 renewed international interest in Nicaragua, because the swiftest route from the eastern United States to the West was by boat through Nicaragua. Competition between different U.S. companies for control of the routes across Nicaragua was again played out through hostilities between the Liberal and Conservative parties. For example, when the Conservative government of Fruto Chamorro (a direct ancestor of Violeta's husband, Pedro Joaquín) signed a contract with U.S. businessman Cornelius Vanderbilt, the discontented Liberals—backed by Vanderbilt's rivals—hired U.S. mercenary William Walker in 1855 to overthrow Chamorro. Walker not only defeated the Conservatives but also declared himself president of Nicaragua. Within six months, however, Walker was defeated by a coalition of Nicaraguan Conservatives and other Central American forces backed by the Vanderbilt faction (Ramírez, 1989).

The pattern of conflict between the Liberal and Conservative Nicaraguan political parties as surrogates for outside interests continued in the twentieth century. When a U.S.-supported Conservative government was threatened in 1912, U.S. Marines invaded Nicaragua and remained there almost continuously until 1932. The Marines supervised the six presidential elections held during this period in Nicaragua, deciding which parties could run, counting the votes, and declaring the winners (Vargas, 1989b).

Presidential politics in Nicaragua was thus nearly always dominated by military forces, either because the president was in the military or because a military force—national or foreign—was in de facto control of the government. Thus military rather than democratic values prevailed. As in war, in the Nicaraguan political culture, to the victor go the spoils. A patronage system developed that was so extensive that the party in power had nearly total and unlimited access to resources, and the party out of power had virtually none. In addition, the winners, as far as possible, would dismantle anything that the losers had done, including programs, policies, laws, and even the constitution. As a current government official put it, "The historic error of this country is that the government of the day ran the country for itself and its people and repressed its enemies with confiscation, jail, and exile. Nicaraguans like strong governments. The temptation to punish the loser is in our blood" (Boudreaux, 1991, p. 10).

Under these conditions, it is not surprising that most Nicaraguan presidents have attempted to secure their own reelection, or, if reelection was not possible, to rig elections to favor other candidates from their own political parties. Because winning was everything, elections were often marked by massive fraud on the one hand and massive abstention on the other, as the electorate tired of single-candidate elections, dominance by the U.S.-favored candidates, and invasions by U.S. Marines when the designated favorite did not win (Vargas, 1989a). When a popular resistance movement led by Augusto César Sandino fought the U.S. occupation forces to a standstill in 1932, U.S. officials decided to withdraw the Marines and leave behind a surrogate national police force whose purpose was to safeguard U.S. interests by controlling electoral politics so that the levels of violence were reduced. This force, the National Guard, not only failed to establish the basic conditions necessary for free elections, but also ushered in a new repressive era that continued the cycle of violence for another four decades.

In 1932, Anastasio ("Tacho") Somoza García was named head of the National Guard, ostensibly a nonpartisan force that would mediate between the two major political parties. But Somoza had personal political ambitions. First, he arranged for the assassination of Sandino in order to eliminate any prominent political rival. Then he ousted President Sacasa (his uncle) in a coup, had himself appointed interim president by the National Legislature, and engineered an electoral victory for himself in 1936. The Liberal party was turned into Tacho's personal machinery, and he was continually reelected. Somoza established a type of hereditary dictatorship (Kantor, 1969), followed by sons Luis and Anastasio Jr. (Tachito), controlling the office of the presidency for more than 40 years. During this time the Somozas added another twist to the Nicaraguan political culture that would affect the 1990 elections.

Under the Somozas, only two political parties were recognized, the historic Liberals and Conservatives. Past attempts to form other political parties had been generally unsuccessful; Sandino may have been assassinated because he was working on developing a third alternative (Envío Collective, 1989b). As the Somozas rapidly consolidated political and economic power within the Liberal party, the Conservatives became increasingly dissatisfied—not so much with the regime as with their share of power. In return for tacitly acknowledging the legitimacy of the Somozas' rule, they were awarded a quota of seats in the national legislature through various pacts. There was, however, no sharing of power with anyone or any group that disagreed with the Somozas. There was so little tolerance for dissenting opinions that both parties began to splinter into various factions. Splits developed not only over ideological differences but over personality differences and disputes over control of economic resources as well. Given the Nicaraguan preoccupation with legitimacy (perhaps deriving from their history as a conquered people), each splinter group or faction claimed the true heritage of the Liberal or Conservative party. This prevented factions that actually had much in common ideologically from uniting to form alternative (third) parties, because neither Conservative nor Liberal factions would give up names tracing their historic descent from one of the two traditional parties, the only ones recognized as legitimate power centers.

It was not until 1957 that the Social Christian party emerged, but by 1975 it too had divided into two factions. Even the Sandinista National Liberation Front (FSLN), which formed in 1961, had split into three tendencies by 1975. The Somozas tightly controlled political power, skillfully manipulated economic power, and played the various factions off against one another, successfully preventing the formation of effective coalitions until a popular uprising ousted their regime in 1979. The intolerance of pluralism within political parties enforced by the Somozas, combined with the Nicaraguan insistence on purity of political heritage and reluctance to form new alternatives, has now produced an explosion in the number of political parties. Today there are more than 20 political groups, with 6 parties calling themselves Conservative, 4 Liberals, 4 Social Christians, and 5 Socialist or Communist parties. Intolerance of dissent is so high that some parties consist of little more than close family members; others are referred to as "microparties" or "merely letterhead" (Envío Collective, 1990f, p. 30).

The Somozas also carried on the Nicaraguan tendency toward government paternalism, in which citizens do not have rights, but rather concessions from an arbitrary ruler (Velazquez, 1986, p. 54). The National Legislature, election councils, and municipal governments were all merely facades for the dictator. Any other organizations that attempted political action were forcefully suppressed. Thus the development of civil political institutions was stifled in Nicaragua. Even with modernization in the 1960s, the Somozas opposed the formation of any independent associations or organizations not aligned with the dictator's political party or the officially sanctioned "opposition" party. The Somozas also retarded the political development of the private sector by playing off competing economic interests against one another (Envío Collective, 1990h, p. 25). The only political qualities rewarded by the Somozas were loyalty and servility; the reaction to disloyalty or dissent was instantaneous, cruel, and exemplary (Velazquez, 1986).

The FSLN emerged as the leader of a national uprising that overthrew the Somozas in 1979. The FSLN was the only political party to reunite its various factions during the insurrectionary period, which gave it more strength than any other political group. The FSLN faced little serious political opposition at the time of the revolution, since there were few organized groups among the private sector that had the experience necessary to take over. The Nicaraguan elite, like other Central American ruling elites, had resisted democratic forms of government that involved power sharing, and no other groups had much experience in running a country except under a strongman or a foreign power (Close, 1988). Conditioned by years of political suppression, coupled with a tradition of appeals to external authorities, the anti-Sandinista opposition turned to the United States rather than organizing internally around their strengths to gain political power under the new situation (Close, 1988, p. 108); the result was the establishment of the counterrevolutionary force known as the *Contras*.

Thus in 1979 the Sandinistas inherited a political culture in which power was authoritarian, hierarchical, and complete; where negotiation, compromise, and power sharing were either unknown or despised; and where disagreement was experienced as betrayal. Although they attempted to change politics in Nicaragua, the FSLN was to some extent also a product of that culture, and so reforms were often accompanied by politics as usual. While they made some headway, they were also constrained by the traditional pattern of domination of Nicaraguan politics by outside interests, since throughout the 1980s various Nicaraguan political groups continued to be co-opted as surrogates for the interests of either the U.S.-led Western bloc or the Soviet-led Eastern bloc.

Gender Identity

Nicaragua's desirability as a crossroads also shaped the development of its system of gender identity. The constant migration of early tribal peoples resulted, according to Pablo Cuadra (1987), in the development in Nicaraguans of a "vagabond restlessness," a psychology of transience that is "stamped by nostalgia" (p. 47). These characteristics were later exacerbated by economic developments that forced peasants off their lands and permanently turned large numbers of Nicaraguans into migrant laborers.

Spanish *conquistadores* brought with them the gender identity system called *machismo,* an exaggerated maleness, sometimes known as the cult of virility. Its characteristics include "an exaggerated aggressiveness and intransigence in male-to-male interpersonal relationships and arrogance and sexual aggression in male-to-female relationships" (Stevens, 1973, p. 90). Maleness is associated with the rapacious Spanish *conquistador* and femaleness with the native Indian men and women who were conquered. Since Nicaraguans are for the most part mestizos (part Spaniard/part Indian), they have elements of both the conqueror and the conquered. For males this is said to present a frightening bisexuality (Goldwert, 1985). *Machismo* is "built on weakness—fear of the female and dread of passivity and intimacy" (Kovel, 1988, p. 93).[2]

The female counterpart in this gender identity system, which has been called *marianismo,* is rooted in the worship of the Virgin Mary in Catholicism. *Marianismo* is described as a "cult of feminine spiritual superiority, which teaches that women are semi-divine, morally superior to and spiritually stronger than men" (Stevens, 1973, p. 91). Insofar as a woman conforms to the behaviors prescribed by this ideal—abnegation, humility, sacrifice, patience, and submissiveness to the demands of men—she enjoys social approval and veneration. Women who stray from this model are not deserving of respect; rather, they become objects of contempt. "Home is the sphere of the woman, and the ideal woman is a mother; . . . even today, the proper woman will not leave her house except to run necessary errands or to make family visits" (Levy, 1988, p. 8). Women have their separate sphere, the home, where their authority is recognized; they do not compete with men in the public (political) sphere, and are assumed to be in fact apolitical.

Every aspect of life is governed by this dual gender identity system. Girls and boys are educated in a system that promotes distrust of the other sex (Elias, 1988) and reinforces homosociality (the tendency to associate only with members of one's own sex), although some psycho-analysts have explored the specter of homosexuality raised by *machismo* as well (e.g., Goldwert, 1985). Cultural prescriptions for distinctive gender behavior result in spatial separation as well, with women found mostly in the home and men found at work, sports events, bars, or other male-oriented places (Elias, 1988). These pressures are reinforced by economic conditions that promote men's migration in search of jobs and compounded by *machista* norms of virility. It is not unusual for Nicaraguan men to maintain sexual relations with and produce children with more than one woman at a time, drifting from one home to another, leaving the majority of women as de facto heads of household.

Men and women have their clearly defined and separate spheres, but these spheres are not equal. *Marianismo* may lead women to believe that they will be rewarded in the next life for their efforts in the here and now, but the balance of power in temporal terms clearly lies with men. Under this system, women derive their identities through their male relatives—fathers, brothers, husbands, and sons—and achieve their highest fulfillment as wives and mothers. But men are often aggressive, unfaithful, and immature, and frequently absent, so women can expect to experience much suffering at the hands of men and much sadness in life. A strong sense of victimization and resignation seems to pervade women's daily lives. According to Kovel (1988), women in a self-help workshop in Managua described men as, among other things,

> slothful, womanizing, drunkards, irresponsible, traitorous, humiliators, ingrates, opportunistic, abandoners, dishonest, imbeciles, egoistic, shameless, evil, executioners, despised, jokers, offensive, lying, farcical, prideful, loafers, bossy, cowards, wolves, brutes, coarse, vicious, vain, capricious, woman-beaters, and *machista*. (p. 92)

Positive images of men were less numerous, but included "worker, useful, good father, brave, and beloved." Women's positive images of themselves contained references to their "moral qualities having to do with being responsible or caring, . . . bravery, strength, and intelligence." Negative images reflected the women's feelings of victimization:

> marginal, discriminated against, martyred, tricked, unappreciated, wretched, lack prestige, humiliated, exploited, desperate, bitter, miserable, abandoned, needing fathers for their children, tormented, disconsolate, suffering, abnegated, slaves, objects of commercialization, and sheep. (Kovel, 1988, p. 93)

At marriage (or upon forming a couple) men and women are (rather unrealistically) expected to be able to put aside these feelings and form a stable heterosexual relationship. At this time, however, men and women do not enter a new, gender-neutral world; rather, the man enters the female world of the home, without a symmetrical integration of the woman into the masculine world outside the home. Men become uncomfortable and at the first opportunity flee the female-dominated sphere of the home, while the public sphere and its values remain alien to women. The link between male values and the political culture—and their opposition to the sphere of the home—is summed up by Díaz (1966):

> A father tends to be seen as a free agent rather than as the representative of a nuclear family in reference to the outside world. As a consequence, . . . the child sees authority as power shorn of responsibility and clothed in the symbols of the male role . . . to be physically strong, careless of consequences and dangers, jealous of one's honor and able to enforce one's wishes on others. Power is seen as unpredictable, based on personal whims, shaped by will. (p. 92)

Until now the values of the public sphere—physical strength, virility, military prowess—have dominated Nicaraguan politics, with little acceptance of the values of the private sphere—capacity for caring, sacrifice, and altruism—in the public realm.

Biographical Sketch of President Chamorro

Richter (1990-1991) suggests that when exploring women's paths to political power it is important to examine variables such as social class and life-style, historical context (including imprisonment), electoral arrangements, and the prevailing gender identity system. Each of these elements played a role in Violeta Barrios de Chamorro's election. Born in 1929, she grew up as one of six children in a wealthy ranch family; she still loves horseback riding. Her childhood ambitions were to learn to type and to become a secretary (Associated Press, 1990). Her father, a graduate of MIT, insisted that she have an education that included attending schools in the United States in order to learn English. But Violeta was not interested in studying, nor was she a particularly good student. At age 19, she returned to Nicaragua after her father's death, where she met Pedro Joaquín Chamorro, whom she married a year later.

For the next 27 years she was the wife of one of the most active opposition figures in Nicaragua, until his assassination in 1978.

In historical sources, Violeta Barrios is usually mentioned only as the wife, or widow, of Pedro Joaquín Chamorro, slain owner of the newspaper *La Prensa*. Indeed, her own accounts of her life to interviewers contain little more than descriptions of the activities of her husband and children. Her work, she says "was to be his wife, to take care of my children, take care of the house, accompany him on his trips, take food to him in prison, going to drop off the food, there and back, nothing more" (Uhlig, 1990, p. 62).

The details of her personal life are sketchy; however, her class, health, and religion stand out. She has often been dismissed as "just a housewife," but her role has actually been that of a "lady of the house" who directs the smooth running of the household, supervising others who perform the mundane domestic tasks, a nontrivial difference in life-style.[3] She has experienced considerable ill health. A bout of pneumonia kept her from returning to Nicaragua for a month after her father died. An incompatibility between her own and her husband's blood complicated most of her five pregnancies; four children survived. Her osteoporosis has caused numerous broken bones. A devout Catholic, Violeta Chamorro maintains a strong, almost mystical religious faith that she shared with her husband. They were married on December 8, the major religious feast day in Nicaragua that celebrates the conception of the Virgin Mary. Pedro Joaquín experienced premonitions of his death and saw himself as a Christ-like figure sacrificing himself for his country (Edmisten, 1990). Violeta Chamorro also has strong ties to the formal Nicaraguan Catholic church, which she calls the "true" church, as opposed to the church of liberation theology or the popular church (Heyck, 1990, p. 41), and the Catholic cardinal, Miguel Obando y Bravo.

The dominant force in Violeta Chamorro's life, however, continues to be Pedro Joaquín. In Latin America, it is said, the dead do not die. It is clear that, were he alive today, Pedro Joaquín Chamorro would have been the choice to be president. The United States considered him a possible challenger to Somoza in the 1970s, but he was assassinated in 1978, an event that precipitated the 1979 armed insurrection and raised him to the status of a national martyr. His legacy is claimed by many of the political parties in Nicaragua (Edmisten, 1990). For example, Daniel Ortega's inauguration as president in 1984 took place on January 10, the date of Pedro Joaquín Chamorro's death.[4] Like her husband, Violeta appears to be a strong nationalist, and did not flee to Miami after the revolution as so many others did, although, ironically, she was in Miami on a shopping trip with one of her daughters who was about to be married when Pedro Joaquín was killed. Since then, she has relied heavily for support on her son-in-law, Antonio Lacayo.

After the 1979 revolution, Violeta Chamorro was appointed, as the widow of the slain martyr, to the five-person junta formed to run the country. She resigned a year later, publicly citing health reasons (a broken arm) but privately blaming differences of opinion with the Sandinistas. She returned to her home, which she keeps like a mausoleum to the memory of Pedro Joaquín (Edmisten, 1990). She has on display the clothes he was wearing; the car he was driving on the day he was killed is kept on the patio. Another room contains his sailboat. Photographs cover the walls. She visits his grave often, and each night at bedtime, "commends herself to Christ, to the Virgin Mary, to Pope John Paul II, and to her husband, whose spirit is alive within her" (Edmisten, 1990, p. 91).[5]

Violeta Chamorro's status in Nicaraguan society is largely ascriptive. Despite living most of her life at the center of Nicaraguan politics, she never became a politician or a member of any political party. While receiving numerous awards from international organizations as the owner of *La Prensa,* she herself was never active in the newspaper's day-to-day operations or in political or ideological decisions (Envío Collective, 1989b).[6] Yet she achieved the ultimate status that a woman can attain in Nicaraguan society by being the devout widow of a politically correct martyr. Her role is that of the grieving matriarch who can still hold her family together. Of her four children, two are Sandinistas and two oppose the Sandinistas, not unusual in war-torn Nicaragua. However, her ability to get all the family to sit down at Sunday dinner together has achieved nearly legendary status, an example par excellence of the proper woman in the proper (private) sphere.

The 1990 Elections

The question of why a woman became president of Nicaragua *now* is probably the easiest to answer. It has become a commonplace that women in Third World countries can rise to positions of leadership under conditions of change that undermine tradition (e.g., Chaney, 1973). Although women may suffer disproportionately from the violence that accompanies political change in Latin America, war and revolution are seen as creating political opportunity for women (Levy, 1988, p. 9). Violeta Chamorro's election is due in part to the electoral conditions that were a legacy of the Sandinista revolution, including the crisis situation brought on by nine years of aggression from the United States, and in part to the challenge to the political culture that was mounted by explicitly using the Nicaraguan gender identity system as a weapon in the 1990 presidential campaign.

Electoral Conditions

First, the Sandinistas deliberately changed the status of women in Nicaragua. The Sandinista National Liberation Front, unlike its Cuban counterpart 20 years before, developed at the same time as and was influenced by the international women's movement. As early as 1969, the FSLN endorsed the principle of gender equality, promising that the revolution would "abolish the odious discrimination that women have been subjected to compared with men . . . [and] establish economic, political, and cultural equality between women and men" (Molyneux, 1985, p. 238). As many as one-third of FSLN combatants were women; several reached the highest ranks.

Upon taking power in 1979 the Sandinistas substantially increased political opportunities for women. Bills were enacted outlawing prostitution and the gratuitous use of women's bodies in advertising. Laws recognized the equal obligations of both parents to support children and do housework. Other statutes provided for 90 days of paid maternity leave and stipulated equal pay for equal work. Under the Sandinistas, women's economic participation grew in a number of fields. Among organized groups, women represented 80% of the health workers' union (FETSALUD), 70% of the teachers' union (ANDEN), 40% of the farm workers' association (ATC), and 37% of the Sandinista workers' syndicate (CST) (*Barricada International,* April 21, 1990).

In the elections of 1984, 19.7% of the FSLN deputies elected to the Nicaraguan national legislature were women, the highest proportion of any party in Central America. Women held 31.4% of the leadership posts in the FSLN party. Sandinistas appointed women as minister of health and chief of police, and 15% of ambassadors and international representatives were women, including Violeta Chamorro's daughter Claudia (*Barricada International,* April 21, 1990). AMNLAE, the national women's organization founded by the Sandinistas, grew to a membership of 80,000 at its peak—in a country where before the revolution there were only a handful of women's organizations, most of them upper-class charities or gardening clubs. Women have moved into nontraditional occupations and become vocal and active in political associations at all levels. Thus on the one hand there was a much greater ability for the Nicaraguan people to accept a woman president than ever before, as 10 years of social change had improved the opportunities for women in politics. On the other hand, the Sandinistas may have tried to move too far too fast, creating a backlash, nostalgia for the past, and preference for a more traditional woman.

Second, the Sandinistas created the conditions for opposition political parties to form, raise funds,[7] campaign, and, if the people so willed, win the election. The Sandinistas guaranteed that the victory would go to whomever was chosen by secret ballot. They waged a massive campaign to register voters and to encourage people to vote on election day, although voting is not compulsory. They invited thousands of international observers to watch over the entire election process, and thousands more journalists to record the event for the entire world to see. Never before had a government in power requested observers from foreign bodies to supervise their elections.

Thus for only the second time in modern Nicaraguan political history, space was opened up for participation by multiple opposition parties (the first time was for the 1984 elections). After many years of suppression of political expression, what emerged was a wild profusion of political parties, some representing traditional political interests, but others with little or no grounding in Nicaraguan reality. In addition, many of these parties had depended for years on a military strategy (i.e., the Contras, funded by the United States) to remove the Sandinistas from power, thus neglecting to develop their political skills or to build up grass-roots support. Confronted with the fact that power would be decided in a popular election, the opposition parties scrambled to put together a coalition that would pool their strengths.

The result was the United National Opposition, or UNO, which in Spanish means "one" or "someone." However, as an old Nicaraguan proverb says, someone in general is really no one specific (*uno no es ninguno*). UNO was a loose-knit, constantly shifting coalition of more than a dozen political parties, embracing the entire political spectrum from ultraright to Communist ideology. Voters were faced with two extremes—the FSLN or the anti-FSLN coalition (UNO)—with almost no political parties occupying a middle ground.[8] The emergence of only two major forces strengthened Violeta Chamorro's chances of election significantly over what they would have been with 20 political parties competing separately.

Third, during the Sandinista administration, the economy deteriorated and there were many war deaths, due to the low-intensity war waged against Nicaragua by the United States. The United States imposed a trade embargo, so that Nicaragua could neither sell its exports to the United States nor import goods and spare parts from the United States. The United States vetoed Nicaragua's requests for credit in multinational organizations such as the World Bank and the International Monetary Fund. And the United States trained and financed the Contras, the counterrevolutionary guerrilla army that waged war—in direct violation of U.S. and international law—on the Nicaraguan people for more than nine years. Popular discontent with the economy, the war, and the Sandinista administration in general were at high levels. By maintaining their anti-U.S. government stance, however, the Sandinistas appeared to do nothing but further antagonize the Bush administration. Nicaraguans understood that to vote for the Sandinistas was to vote for more of the same.

In contrast, Violeta Chamorro was associated with factions that were pro-United States. For example, her newspaper, *La Prensa,* had received money from U.S. foundations opposed to the Sandinistas (Sharkey, 1986, p. 36). In May 1989, Chamorro was invited to the White House. During her visit she was reportedly asked by Bernard Aronson, U.S. undersecretary of state for inter-American affairs, whether she would consider being an opposition candidate for president. Shortly after, in October, Marlon Fitzwater stated that she "is our candidate, and the candidate of the opposition forces." In November, U.S. President George Bush declared that if UNO won he would lift the embargo against Nicaragua (Envío Collective, 1990a).

At the close of 1989, the Nicaraguan people were searching for a way to put an end to the Contra war, reunite their divided country, and begin to rebuild their economy. To do this they had to seek relief from the wrath of the United States. The two political candidates offered quite different ways to do this, which became clear in the use of the symbols of the Nicaraguan gender identity system in the battle for the presidency.

Gender Symbolism

If the electoral conditions made it more possible for *any* woman to be elected president, the political culture and gender identity system almost ensured that it would be *this* particular woman who was elected. At first Violeta Chamorro seemed an unlikely choice for a presidential candidate. She was described in the *Miami Herald* as "politically illiterate" (quoted in Taylor, 1989). During her year in government after the revolution she had been called the "flower" of the junta, but was not known for making decisions (Envío Collective, 1989b). An article in her own newspaper reinforced this perception of Violeta Chamorro as apolitical, describing her as "a beautiful and noble woman, without vanity, without pride, without ambition, a homeloving woman" (*La Prensa,* September 4, 1989).

But symbolism is enormously important in bitterly polarized Nicaragua (Boudreaux, 1991). As the UNO coalition searched for a presidential candidate for the 1990 elections, what seemed to be Violeta Chamorro's political liabilities were turned into political strengths. The multiparty UNO coalition realized that only a political outsider could hold their divisive factions together,[9] and possibly hold together the nation as well. Violeta Chamorro was a symbol of the sacrifices that had been made in Nicaragua's bloody political history. She was associated with a popular independence movement as the widow of a respected voice of moderation in Nicaraguan politics. She was a matriarch who held together a divided family, a family that symbolized the divided country. As one of her brothers-in-law said, "We are not looking for someone to run the country. We are looking for someone who represents the ideal [of democracy]" (Boudreaux, 1991, p. 13). Even Chamorro described herself as "a symbol, a proud symbol that we Nicaraguans have dignity, a symbol that nobody can snatch away from one what one has by right" (*La Prensa,* September 4, 1989). Any person strongly identified with an existing political faction would have had too many political liabilities, no matter what their strengths. A strategist for Violeta Chamorro's campaign said bluntly, "Violeta wasn't chosen for her abilities as president. Violeta was chosen to win" (Uhlig, 1990, p. 72).

Violeta Chamorro, who was reportedly at home listening to the radio when she learned she had been selected, did not actively campaign for the nomination, as that would have appeared unseemly; but her newspaper, *La Prensa,* did so on her behalf. Chamorro was not the UNO coalition's only candidate for president. In fact, it took days of heated debate before a presidential nominee was selected. For some of the factions, Chamorro's demonstrated acceptability to the United States was decisive because it would be translated into the cash needed to conduct a media campaign. This expectation proved correct: In October, after Chamorro's nomination, the U.S. Congress approved an additional $9 million for the UNO campaign (Envío Collective, 1990a).[10] One observer concludes that UNO realistically had a choice only over whom to propose as candidate for vice president (Cortez, 1990). The reaction to her nomination was mixed. A dominant business coalition publicly doubted Violeta's abilities, and her vice presidential running mate at one point called her "a useless old bag of bones" (Cortez, 1990, p. 207). Popular reactions were more positive than expected. At her first campaign appearance, when thousands of people unexpectedly turned up to greet her, she became flustered and "ran away" (Preston, 1990). However, she soon became accustomed to the cheers and affection of large crowds. Often during her campaign Violeta said, "I am not a politician, but I believe this is my destiny. I am doing this for Pedro and for my country" (Boudreaux, 1991, p. 13); Chamorro stated that she had accepted the nomination "after consulting with God and my dead husband" (*Barricada International,* September 30, 1989). Even Chamorro's daughter Claudia, an FSLN supporter who openly opposed her mother's candidacy, expressed "not the slightest doubt as to [Violeta's] democratic convictions nor as to her genuine desire for Nicaragua's wellbeing . . . less still do I doubt her integrity and personal honesty" (Chamorro Barrios, 1989).

Once the candidates were selected, the campaign swung into high gear. If politics is the conscious and unconscious manipulation of symbols (Kretzer, 1988, p. 2), the 1990 Nicaraguan elections provided a stunning example. As one writer has expressed, in typical poetic style, "Politics [in Nicaragua] breathes with the heart and is expressed in symbols" (Mendoza, 1990, p. 26). With a nontraditional presidential candidate, UNO had no hope of winning the election through a show of strength, military prowess, or any of the other male-associated values. Instead, the coalition fell upon the idea of stressing the opposite qualities, for the first time interjecting the female-associated values of the private sphere into the public arena of politics.

During the campaign, Violeta's image was modeled after that of the Virgin Mary. She was dressed all in white, with a simple gold crucifix to symbolize her almost mystical Catholicism. Chamorro was introduced at political rallies as Nicaragua's "María," the "white dove of peace" (O'Kane, 1990, p. 29). She was paraded around in the back of a pickup truck under a white canopy, much as a patron saint is displayed at festival time. The fact that she had broken her leg in a fall on New Year's Day and was confined to a wheelchair only increased her image as the valiant and suffering mother, perhaps "the most important image in Nicaraguan myth" (Kovel, 1988, p. 102). "Chamorro's maternal and reconciliatory image . . . seemed to exist on a higher plane than traditional politics" (Envío Collective, 1991a, p. 4). It was not necessary for her to speak much, since the Virgin Mary is only an image. As one European diplomat remarked, "She is not really a political figure, she is an emotional and a visual figure—an icon" (Preston, 1990).

The symbolism embraced by UNO and its candidate Violeta Chamorro stood in stark contrast to that adopted by the FSLN and its candidate, Daniel Ortega. The FSLN played to the traditional male-oriented values of Nicaraguan political culture: aggression, intransigence, military might, and virility. The FSLN platform contained mostly business as usual, refusing to end the military draft, to change its confrontational attitude toward Washington, or to tone down its strongly nationalistic rhetoric. No new economic reforms were outlined. U.S. officials implied that if the FSLN won, there would be a possibility of more aid to the Contras and continuation of economic sanctions—in short, more of the same.

Ortega adopted as his image *el gallo ennavajado,* the fighting cock. He shed his thick, bullet-proof glasses for contact lenses and abandoned his usual green military fatigues for tight jeans and florid shirts open to the waist. In his campaign appearances he strode back and forth on a flatbed truck, accompanied by rock music and dancing girls, throwing autographed baseballs into the crowds. To counter Violeta's image of the national mother, Ortega presented himself as the national father. Gigantic billboards of Ortega with Camilla, the youngest of his 10 children, were erected all over the country. His female assistants took thousands of instant Polaroid photographs of Daniel kissing children, to the delight of proud parents. TV spots were accompanied by the Beatles song "All You Need Is Love." Despite U.S. threats, his campaign slogan promised that "everything would be better" (Cortez, 1990, p. 344).

In a campaign of symbols, neither side offered much substance. Other than promising to end the military draft and bring about better relations with the United States (and the hoped-for possibility of billions in U.S. aid), UNO campaign strategy consisted largely of praising their candidate and attacking the FSLN. At UNO rallies, speakers told the crowd that "Pedro and God were above watching" (O'Kane, 1990, p. 29). Violeta's almost complete identification with Pedro Joaquín Chamorro "reinforced the impression that she would have little else to offer" (Uhlig, 1990, p. 62). The selection of a woman candidate signaled to some that the United States considered this to be a throwaway election. However, Chamorro dismissed criticisms that she was incompetent to lead Nicaragua, on the grounds her critics were taking the wrong approach. "There's no need to study how to govern a country," she said. "I have accepted the challenge to revive this country with love and peace, according to the dictates of my conscience" (Boudreaux, 1991, p. 13). No one really expected UNO to win, least of all UNO coalition members themselves. Even Chamorro's most ardent supporters, however, were shocked when the election results became clear early on the morning of February 26: Their symbol had won. In her acceptance statement, Chamorro remembered her husband Pedro Joaquín, and promised to fulfill her commitments "with the help of God and the Blessed Virgin."

The results of the election are shown in Table 4.1. More than 1.75 million Nicaraguans were registered to vote, and—although voting is not obligatory under the law as in many other Latin American countries—86.3% voted. Nicaraguans fill out three ballots on election day: one for presidential and vice presidential candidates, one for candidates for the national assembly, and one (since 1990) for candidates for local offices. The majority of the votes for president (54.7%) and national assembly (53.9%) went to UNO; the FSLN polled 40.8% of the votes for both sets of ballots. The 90 National Assembly seats are apportioned according to the popular vote, with UNO gaining 51 seats, the FSLN 38, and the Social Christian party 1. Losing presidential candidates from the FSLN and the Revolutionary Unity Movement who polled a minimum percentage of the popular vote were also awarded seats, bringing the total number of representatives to 92. The actual party affiliations of representatives holding seats under the UNO coalition—a point of heated dispute within UNO—are shown in Table 4.1.

Evaluation of Chamorro's First Year in Office

In its 1989 report, the International Commission for the Recovery and Development of Central America (the Sanford Commission) describes Central America as trapped in a vicious circle in which, to paraphrase, violence impedes development and the poverty resulting from underdevelopment intensifies violence. The report concludes that social and economic justice, democratic participation, and international support for development are not only inseparable but indispensable for peace

Table 4.1   1990 Nicaraguan Election Results

Political Parties	Votes Received		Seats Received National Assembly
	President and Vice President (%)	National Assembly (%)	
FSLN	40.8	40.8	39[a]
UNO	54.7	53.9	51
National Conservative party			5
Popular Conservative Alliance			6
Independent Liberal party			5
Constitutionalist Liberal party			5
Neo-Liberal party			3
National Democratic Confidence party			5
National Action party			3
Nicaraguan Socialist party			3
Communist party of Nicaragua			3
Social Democratic party			5
Nicaraguan Democratic Movement			3
Central American Integrationist party			1
Conservative National Action			2
Popular Social Christian party			2
SOCIAL CHRISTIAN PARTY—YATAMA			1
REVOLUTIONARY UNITY MOVEMENT			1[a]
Total			92

[a.] This total includes a defeated presidential candidate—as provided for by Nicaraguan law—in addition to the 90 seats awarded in accordance with the popular vote.

in the region (Envío Collective, 1990h, p. 31). In the long run, the challenge facing any Nicaraguan president would be to break the circle of poverty and violence in Nicaragua. In the short run, this challenge has been complicated for Violeta Chamorro by problems that specifically arise in the case of women leaders (see Richter, 1990-1991). In addition to achieving peace, stabilizing the economy, and institutionalizing democracy, Chamorro has had to confront the problems caused by her lack of a stable power base, perceptions that she is only a temporary or stand-in president, and questions about her very legitimacy.

Upon taking office, Chamorro addressed the first group of problems, promising to demobilize and repatriate the Contras, to achieve economic stabilization within 100 days, and to consolidate the bases of democracy. Early in her term, Chamorro seemed headed toward some modest successes. By June 1990, most Contras had entered neutral zones set up for them in the Nicaraguan countryside after supposedly handing their weapons over to a special international commission. It appeared that the counterrevolutionary war begun nine years earlier was finally at an end. At the same time, a plan to achieve economic stabilization was set into motion. Bolstered by the electoral support of the Nicaraguan people and confident of receiving U.S. and other international aid, Chamorro's economic team announced its goals: stop inflation, replace the old currency with a new one tied to the dollar, get new foreign reserves, encourage exports, and privatize the state productive sector (Envío Collective, 1991c). And an unprecedented transition protocol negotiated by the incoming and outgoing administrations promised to start Nicaragua on the path to institutionalization of democratic principles in the political system.

One year later, the Contras (now dubbed *Recontras*) are rearming, foreign aid has not materialized, unemployment stands at nearly 50%, and the government has been unable to contain political struggle "within a civic framework" (Envío Collective, 1991d, p. 5). In making sense of the year's developments, we must examine how Chamorro attempted to develop a power base, combat the perception that she was only a temporary stand-in, and institutionalize the legitimacy of her presidency.

Power Base

As soon as the vote totals were announced, it was clear that there was a widespread lack of agreement on exactly what Chamorro's election meant for Nicaragua. Most conservative and right-wing groups saw Chamorro's election as their chance to put an end to the Sandinistas as a political force and to their revolutionary state, differing only with respect to the speed at which this process should take place and the means that should be used. Some of these groups have been characterized as willing to "sink even their own economic and political wellbeing . . . to say nothing of their country's" in order to bring down the FSLN (Envío Collective, 1989a, p. 6). In contrast, the Sandinistas and radical left-wing parties saw Chamorro's election as a chance to regroup and become a major opposition force with an eye to the next elections in 1996, but without giving up any of the important social and economic gains of the revolution—many of which are embedded in the 1987 constitution—or their political power. In a speech made the day after he conceded the election, President Daniel Ortega vowed that the FSLN would "rule from below."

Thus a very important short-run challenge facing Chamorro was to establish the rules of the political game, based on the principle that in a democracy there are limits on the means that may be used to pursue political ends, whatever those ends may be. To achieve this goal, Chamorro's government would have to be accepted as *the* dominant legitimate political force. But what was Chamorro's power base? Having never belonged to any political party, Chamorro relied on a tiny group of extended family members and close advisers to run the government. Chamorro's faction had no popular base, no party machinery, and no security force of its own. After her election, longtime friend Venezuelan President Carlos Andrés Pérez sent bodyguards to protect Chamorro and consultants to advise her on political and economic matters (Selser, 1990a), compounding perceptions that she is unduly beholden to outside interests. Despite being a sentimental favorite during the election, her actions since then have not won her many converts. For example, when a poor man complained that his children were dying of hunger, she responded enthusiastically, "Yes, but they will die in a democracy!" (Boudreaux, 1991, p. 13).

Her inner circle's attempt to keep her out of the mudslinging that goes on among the various UNO factions has also backfired to some extent, making her seem uncaring or disconnected from reality. Even Violeta's image as the embodiment of national reconciliation has been ridiculed by elites as only "laugh[ing] and hold[ing] her arms out" and by nonelites as "a sophisticated game of kisses and hugs at the top and billy clubs at the [bottom]" (Envío Collective, 1991d, pp. 3-6).

The situation has been complicated by the awakening in Nicaraguans of new political expectations. Many Nicaraguans have now become politically literate and politically active. They have high expectations of government accountability to their needs, more so than in any other Central American country (Jonas & Stein, 1990). As one Nicaraguan peasant woman said:

> Before [1979] we were ashamed, we couldn't even speak. The revolution untied our tongues. That infuriated those who wanted us to remain always like nesting hens. Now, if they don't fulfill their promises, they'll feel those promises around their necks like a yoke on a mule. *Doña* Violeta shouldn't

forget that people can throw her out, just like they put her in. She knows now that it's the people who rule. (quoted in Mendoza, 1990, p. 24)

Polls show that about one-third of Nicaraguans are strong FSLN supporters, with another third evenly divided between the extreme right and the extreme left. The final third is considered "in dispute." Some Nicaraguans admitted to casting sympathy votes for Violeta, "a nice lady with her leg in a cast," whom they did not want to see lose too badly (Envío Collective, 1990c, p. 35), and others "identify with the maternal image projected by Violeta Chamorro and with her project as well." For most, however, the overwhelming concern is "peace at . . . any price." This "silent majority" of Nicaraguans is largely passive and will not support anything that smacks of conflict (Envío Collective, 1990k, pp. 8-9), so it is unlikely that they can be politically mobilized to become a base of support for Chamorro.

To counter her lack of a strong popular base, Chamorro has turned to the executive branch of government, the branch over which she has the most control. During the campaign, Chamorro often criticized the executive branch as having too much power, but since her inauguration she has attempted to transfer functions to the executive from the three other branches—legislative, judicial, and electoral—or otherwise weaken the control of other political groups over these branches. Some of these efforts were not successful. For example, upon taking office, she issued a flurry of decrees, some of which were considered to be unconstitutional because they usurped the function of the Legislature (Selser, 1990a). She did succeed in decreasing FSLN control of the Supreme Court by increasing the number of justices from seven to nine and giving the position of chief justice to one of her appointees. In addition, by arranging for the resignation of two of the seven FSLN justices, Chamorro managed to thwart the right wing's plan to increase the total number of justices to 15 and pack the court with its supporters (Envío Collective, 1990j, p. 5).

Perceptions of Permanence

Another factor that complicates Chamorro's ability to act as president is the perception that she is merely a temporary leader, or stand-in. Because of her deeply religious orientation, she is perceived by some as a surrogate for Cardinal Miguel Obando y Bravo, who was reportedly approached before

Chamorro as a possible UNO presidential candidate.[11] Her lack of skills is also taken as a sign that she is only a figurehead. Upon assuming the presidency, she knew little about the government or how it worked, and her knowledge of world affairs was also limited. She forgets the names of foreign leaders (like Ronald Reagan) and struggles to remember well-known events (Preston, 1990) or the names of the colleges she attended (Heyck, 1990, p. 44). Her attention span is said to be short. She does not deliver prepared speeches well, but when she talks spontaneously she often makes slips of the tongue that later have to be "explained" by her aides. For example, she has suggested that she could fund the national educational system by winning the state lottery, and that the budget of the Ministry of Health should be slashed because its efforts could be taken over by international agencies (Envío Collective, 1990g, p. 5). Some of her pet projects seem petty—for example, a plan to change the uniform of the national police from tan to light blue, the color of the Nicaraguan flag. Staff in the presidential offices are prohibited from calling people *compañero* or *compañera,* the preferred form of address under the Sandinistas. No miniskirts, tight pants, or shorts are allowed, and women who wear sleeveless blouses must shave under their arms (S. Cuadra, 1990b). She ordered the elementary school textbooks introduced by the Sandinistas to be thrown out and replaced with texts from Honduras financed by U.S. aid (Jiménez, 1990).

Even members of her own coalition (UNO) treat her as merely temporary. When UNO representatives elected to the National Legislature caucused in April, on the eve of Chamorro's inauguration as president, to select a slate of candidates for the governing board of the Legislature, some reported being pressured by Vice President Godoy to vote for his slate rather than the Chamorro slate. One delegate reported, "Dr. Godoy threatened me . . . saying that he would be president within a year and would make those of us who did not vote for [his slate] pay" (Envío Collective, 1990d, p. 8).

Portrayed as strong-willed, President Chamorro declared upon her election that "under the Constitution, I'm going to be the one in charge. I will be the one who gives the orders" (Hockstader, 1990). She also tends to be stubborn and to divide the world into "them" and "us" (Heyck, 1990, p. 37). But in fact she is not the key decision maker in the government, although she disputes any suggestion that she is not in charge. For example, she was not involved in the development of the UNO platform and its plans for economic renewal. Her son-in-law, Antonio Lacayo, married to Violeta's daughter Cristiana (publisher of

La Prensa), is the power behind the throne, along with his brother-in-law Alfredo César (a former Sandinista *and* a former Contra, regarded by both sides as an opportunist). (Ironically, *Lacayo* translates into English as "lackey.")

The question of whether Violeta Chamorro is a stand-in, and for whom, has also complicated the problem of securing international aid. Before the election, a political cartoon showed President Bush flying a Violeta Chamorro doll over Nicaragua (*Barricada International,* September 30, 1989), signifying the switch from a costly military strategy to a cheaper political strategy to defeat the Sandinistas, and, for some, also signifying that the United States felt it could control Chamorro. For other Nicaraguans, Violeta Chamorro's claim to be the legitimate heir to all that Pedro Joaquín stood for was tarnished when she went on a preelectoral fund-raising trip among his former enemies (ex-*Somocistas*) in Miami. Throughout the campaign, rumors circulated that if Violeta Chamorro won, the United States would pour so many aid dollars into Nicaragua that no one would have to pay utility bills, bank debts, or even bus fare (Envío Collective, 1990c, p. 35). Indeed, it seemed reasonable that Nicaragua could expect to reap its own "peace dividend," with the money that had funded the Contras now funding development projects. But months after Chamorro won the election, there was still no substantial U.S. aid for Nicaragua. Chamorro's personal appeal to President Bush for $40 million in emergency aid was refused (Envío Collective, 1990e, p. 4) in a humiliating manner.

Why was U.S. aid not forthcoming? For one thing, Nicaragua is no longer unique. It is now—along with Panama—just one of many new democracies that must compete with Eastern European states, the former Soviet Union, and others for U.S. aid dollars. And the United States, itself in deep debt, has no wish or ability to expand its foreign aid program. For another, Chamorro has not complied with U.S. wishes to remove FSLN party member Humberto Ortega as head of the army. During a general strike in the summer of 1990, the U.S. ambassador reportedly pressured Chamorro to step down, ostensibly for health reasons, so that Vice President Godoy—more favorable to U.S. interests—could take over (Envío Collective, 1990j, p. 6). The United States continues to exert strong pressure on the Chamorro government to "accelerate Nicaragua's privatization process, further reduce the size of the army, and withdraw Nicaragua's case against the U.S. [for its illegal Contra war] in the International Court of Justice" (Envío Collective, 1990k, p. 9). An extremely cynical view, but one that makes sense given continued U.S. hostility toward the Sandinista party, is that aid is being withheld so that in the resulting economic and social deterioration the FSLN might commit some tactical error that would weaken popular support for the party (Envío Collective, 1990e, p. 5) or some act that could be used as a pretext for a U.S. invasion to restore order.

Nicaragua's international financial situation is also at a standstill. Until its debts with international lending institutions are paid off, no more credit will be extended to Nicaragua. Lenders are willing to renegotiate these debts, but only if strict austerity measures are imposed, such as cutting utility, transportation, food, education, health, and other subsidies, cuts that disproportionately affect the poor and working classes. But so far, pressure from labor unions and other organized groups in Nicaragua has prevented the Chamorro government from implementing these measures. No foreign government is willing to give Nicaragua the cash to pay off those debts so that it can bypass the austerity measures required for renegotiation, because at its current rate of spending it would soon be back in the same situation, and the government is perceived as lacking the clout to alter the current spending formula.

Legitimacy

Threats to Violeta Chamorro's legitimacy as president began on her first day in office. Animosity between Chamorro and Vice President Godoy exploded in a dispute over office space and ended with Chamorro banning Godoy from the presidential office building, giving him no space, staff, or support. Godoy, who leads the major group within the UNO coalition, constantly attacks Chamorro's legitimacy. He does not participate in cabinet meetings, nor does he preside over the government in the president's absence as the constitution directs, that duty being taken over by Chamorro's son-in-law Antonio Lacayo, minister of the presidency. A foreign reporter once asked him, "Dr. Godoy, are you in the government?" (Envío Collective, 1990i, p. 26). Godoy's only official assignment is to a task force investigating the revival of the Central American parliament. Godoy, who served for four years as minister of labor under the FSLN, is now seen as a "very embittered man [who] would do anything to get rid of the Sandinistas" (Envío Collective, 1990f, p. 29), apparently even seizing power from his own president if necessary.

Without foreign aid, the two apparent successes of Chamorro's early days—ending the Contra war and restarting the economy—turned to failures that also threaten her government's legitimacy. When the Sandinistas turned over control of the government to the Chamorro administration, and the army was reduced by nearly half, the Contras lost their last reason for continuing hostilities. By June, most fighters had moved into neutral zones from which all regular military and police forces had been banned.[12] The Contras entered the zones in part because the Chamorro government promised to provide "credit, housing, roads, health care, education, running water, and electricity," despite the fact that these services were largely unavailable in any existing towns and the cost would have been enormous. Not surprisingly, given the government's financial crisis, these promises were not kept (Envío Collective, 1991b, p. 20). Since then, ex-Contras have pressed their demands by taking over both private and state lands, farms, and cooperatives, blockading roads and clashing with military and police forces outside the special zones. Other than demands for land, most ex-Contras do not appear to have a larger political agenda, and most seem to be favorably disposed toward President Chamorro personally. However, they represent a potential armed force that can be tapped by factions hostile to the FSLN. For example, Vice President Godoy reportedly used ex-Contras to attack workers who occupied buildings or people who built barricades during the general strike in July 1990.[13]

The net result has been a transmutation of the nine-year conflict between the Nicaraguan Army and the counterrevolutionary forces that took place mostly in the remote countryside and border areas into an ongoing conflict between numerous armed groups in cities and towns all over Nicaragua (e.g., FSLN supporters, Godoy faction, several rival groups of ex-Contras, radical ultraleft- and right-wing supporters). The possibility that the country will break into civil war, or further destabilize into a Central American Lebanon, seems more likely than ever. To maintain order, Chamorro must depend on the Nicaraguan Army and the National Police, which remain heavily influenced by the FSLN. She is reluctant to do so because her reliance on these forces is used as an excuse by the right wing to mount their own "defense forces," since they believe the destruction of the FSLN (and the army and police) should be the primary objective of the new government and for them any sign of cooperation between Chamorro and the FSLN means that the government has lost its legitimacy because it has been taken over by the FSLN.

As observed by Richter (1990-1991) in Asia, qualities such as tolerance and willingness to compromise—qualities that are necessary for democracy—are perceived in the violent Nicaraguan political culture as signs of personal weakness or timidity that make the bearer unfit for the presidency. Violeta Chamorro's plan for national reconciliation, *concertación,* or a social pact, is perceived by some Nicaraguans as "a cry from those who lost, who need a safety net" (Tellez, 1990), while others see it as "class suicide" (Selser, 1990b). The very word *pact* "sends shivers up the spines of most honest Nicaraguans," because it has historically signified an agreement among elite national (and often international) interests on how to divide power up among themselves, at the expense of nonelites (Nuñez, 1990). Politicians on the left and right of Chamorro's middle faction accuse her of lacking legitimacy. The right wing says she has "betrayed the noble and generous people of Nicaragua by signing a secret pact with the Sandinista mafia" (Envío Collective, 1990i, p. 27), while the left wing accuses her of subverting the election by trying to undo the gains of the revolution by extralegal means. In sum, it is commonly accepted in Nicaragua that toppling the Chamorro government would be easy; what keeps most groups from trying to do so is the certain knowledge that the result would only be worse.

Implications for Women and Politics in Nicaragua

In one sense, a woman president in Nicaragua is as unexpected as Mary, the first queen of England, centuries before. Neither Mary Tudor nor Violeta Chamorro had any "examples of appropriate behavior for them, particularly in the public aspects of their rule" (Levin, 1986, p. 42). In defining her role, Chamorro has chosen for the most part to act within the boundaries established by the male-oriented values of Nicaraguan political culture and the dual gender identity system of *machismo* and *marianismo.* She has neither denied her femaleness by becoming "one of the boys" nor differentiated herself from other women by saying, "Do as I say, not as I do." During the campaign, she emphasized that "I act and speak as a woman" (O'Kane, 1990, p. 29). As a woman, mother, and widow, Violeta Chamorro challenges the stereotype of what a president should be like, but survives by conforming to the typical expectation in Latin American countries that women who become involved in politics will do so as an extension of their role in the home. It is only on their cultural authority as mothers that women can acceptably venture into the political sphere in Latin America, as, for example, in movements of mothers of the "disappeared."

Violeta Chamorro fits this mold quite well. During her campaign, she often spoke of returning women to the home, of strengthening the family, of reestablishing traditional values. In her inaugural speech, and on countless other occasions, she referred to the country as the Nicaraguan family, a family that is divided by conflict but that she will redeem through her abnegation and suffering as the national mother. Other women in politics who do not conform to this mold are treated far more harshly. For example, Miriam Argüello, a career politician who was once jailed by the Sandinistas, who openly campaigned for the UNO nomination for president, and who was elected to the National Legislature and served as its president, has been ridiculed in the popular media for being a spinster. Violeta Chamorro challenges the conception of what a president is or should be by her mere presence; paradoxically, however, her challenge may be limited by her source of moral authority. As Kovel (1988, pp. 102-104) points out, women who have historically derived their power through their identity with nature itself, or with a mother image, are identified with something seen as unchanging. Insofar as the mother image is timeless, it is also outside history, excluded from the possibility of self-transformation, mythic but passive as a force for change. Chamorro is one of a select group of women who have come to power through unique and sometimes tragic circumstances, often involving the political assassination of a male relative (see Richter, 1990-1991). As such, she does not provide a viable model for most women seeking political power, and faces the difficult challenge of converting her moral authority into a positive force for changing the culture of Nicaraguan politics.[14]

Women are more than half the electorate in Nicaragua, but Violeta Chamorro has no specific agenda for women. During the presidential campaign, she repeatedly asserted, "I'm not a feminist, nor do I want to be one. I am a woman dedicated to my home, as Pedro taught me." Further, she declared that she had been "marked with the Chamorro branding iron" (S. Cuadra, 1990a)—an image of female subjugation that was seen as excessive even in *machista* Nicaragua. Chamorro does not favor increasing the participation of women in politics, and has given few political posts to women in her government. There was little in the UNO platform of benefit to women, except indirectly, by ending the military draft and negotiating an end to the war. Rather, analysts feared that "the privatization and state budget cuts called for in UNO's overall economic plan are likely to have a disproportionate effect on the female labor force" and to affect women and children by cutting funding for child-care centers, health programs, and school milk programs (Envío Collective, 1990b, p. 25).

In this context, changes for women and political power in Nicaragua will probably be brought about by women and men identified with other forces. Besides Chamorro, there was another woman candidate for president, and another for vice president. Roughly 25% of the 1,632 candidates nominated for National Assembly and municipal council posts were women, with the FSLN nominating 35 women, the Social Christian party 28, and UNO 20 for the 90 seats in the National Assembly (S. Cuadra, 1990a). Women have increased their numbers as deputies in the national legislature and represent a wide spectrum of parties. For example, Azucena Ferrey, a former Contra, is now also in the legislature. And many women have risen to positions of power within various political parties.

Other factors, however, will have a dampening effect on women's quest for political power. Nicaragua is a poor, dependent, peripheral country, where women do not have the affluence, occupational structure, services (such as child care), or control over fertility that are seen by some as "indispensable" for advancement (Kovel, 1988, p. 107), nor is their economic situation likely to improve soon. With no unique products or services to market, Nicaragua must compete with other Third World nations to sell its few agricultural exports. Constant cycles of violence have discouraged foreign capital investment, and there is no large urban proletariat that could work in assembly plants. A chemical industry did provide employment for highly skilled technicians, but also resulted in massive pollution of the environment.

Another problem, which is also occurring in Eastern European nations, is that progressive thinking on women's issues is now associated with a party that has recently been turned out of office. While the opposition stressed conservative values and "reconstruction of the family group" (García & Gomáriz, 1989, p. 243), the FSLN championed women's issues, at least at the level of public discourse, so much so that now any concerns about child care or reproductive rights are seen as linked to its discredited ideology. It will take Nicaraguan women some time to detach major women's organizations from the FSLN party, make it clear that women's issues transcend partisan politics, and adopt new alternative strategies for putting women's issues on the agenda. A tentative plan for all women representatives in the National Assembly to form an interparty caucus is one hopeful step in this new direction.

A third complication is that Nicaraguan women, consistent with their traditional gender role, have been repeatedly called upon to sacrifice their demands in the interests of national security, national unity, reconstruction, the economic crisis, or any number of other things that are seen as having precedence. Gender consciousness has been raised a number of times—for example, in the open forums surrounding the framing of a new constitution in 1986—but many of the statutes enacted have not been fully enforced. It may be difficult to convince women to muster the necessary energy to again take up the cause of women's issues when there have been so many disappointments before, and when to do so runs counter to the prevailing standard of selflessness as appropriate behavior for women.

In conclusion, there is no immediate danger that Nicaragua will become a matriarchy. President Chamorro's task, however, is nearly as daunting: to change the political culture (Boudreaux, 1991, p. 10). Her accomplishments to date—staying alive, staying in power, and keeping the country from full-blown civil war—are by no means trivial. The longer her government lasts, the stronger the democratic tradition and institutions it is establishing will become. It remains to be seen, however, what she can accomplish in the five years that are left. As long as she remains in office, Nicaraguan President Violeta Chamorro will certainly be worth watching.

Notes

1. The canal was eventually built across Panama instead, ironically because Nicaragua was deemed too politically unstable.

2. Interestingly enough, although women are obviously *mestizos* as well, the issue of what this dual heritage means for females is almost never explored. That is, men are presumed to have to deal with both their male and female characteristics, while women are presumed to have only female characteristics.

3. She has been compared with Philippine President Corazon Aquino, who was also sometimes dismissed as "just a housewife," but in other respects the two women are quite different. On a visit to Washington, some U.S. officials hailed Violeta Chamorro as another Corazon Aquino, but Aquino, who has her own political history, reportedly declined to have her picture taken with Chamorro (Cortez, 1990, p. 223).

4. Many people who are now Sandinistas were associated with *La Prensa* when it was an opposition newspaper in Somoza's time, for example, Danilo Aguirre Solis, a Sandinista representative in the National Legislature; Sergio Ramírez, former vice president; and Rosario Murillo, companion of former President Daniel Ortega.

5. Various accounts of her visits to her husband's grave put them at twice a week, once a week, and monthly on the anniversary date of Pedro Joaquín's death.

6. Members of the Chamorro clan run all of the daily newspapers in Nicaragua: Violeta's eldest daughter manages the now progovernment *La Prensa*, her youngest son manages the official Sandinista party newspaper *Barricada*, and her brother-in-law manages the independent *El Nuevo Diario*.

7. Bowing to opposition demands, the electoral code was changed to permit foreign interests to donate money and supplies to Nicaraguan political parties—a practice that is illegal in most countries and a move that clearly favored the coalition of political parties (UNO) supported by the United States.

8. Some political parties did occupy a middle ground but were virtually unknown to voters because they neither had the money to finance their own campaigns nor would join the opposition coalition (UNO) in order to gain access to the foreign donations that flowed to the UNO campaign coffers.

9. The difficulty of building a coalition that includes extreme right- and left-wing parties became apparent when members of different factions engaged in shoving matches and fistfights during the campaign and began scrambling for power as soon as the elections were over.

10. The United States had already "spent 12.5 million for the 'promotion of democracy' and election activities, or about $7.00 per [Nicaraguan] voter" (Sharkey, 1990, p. 22); other estimates put total U.S. spending at $25 million (*New York Times,* April 27, 1990).

11. Having a religious orientation, however, is not unusual in Nicaragua. Even Francisco Mayorga, an economist and head of the Central Bank, closes his speeches with the line, "with help from God and the Holy Virgin Mary" (S. Cuadra, 1990b).

12. Ironically, it was only in defeat that the Contras were able to accomplish their objective of occupying land inside Nicaragua, a goal they were never able to attain during nine years of counterrevolutionary guerrilla warfare.

13. This is according to personal interviews I conducted in Nicaragua during the July 1990 general strike.

14. Still, Chamorro's presidency has reportedly inspired at least one other Central American woman to launch a campaign to become president—Margarita Penón de Arias, wife of former Costa Rican President Oscar Arias.

References

Associated Press. (1990, February 26). Dateline Managua, Nicaragua.

Barquero, S. L. (1945). *Gobernantes de Nicaragua: 1825-1947.* Managua: Publicaciones del Ministerio de Instrucción Pública.

Boudreaux, R. (1991, January 6). The great conciliator. *Los Angeles Times Magazine,* pp. 9-13.

Chamorro Barrios, C. (1989, October 27). UNO unites my father's enemies. *Barricada, 10,* p. 21.

Chaney, E. M. (1973). Women in Latin American politics: The case of Peru and Chile. In A. Pescatello (Ed.), *Female and male in Latin America* (pp. 103-139). Pittsburgh, PA: University of Pittsburgh Press.

Close, D. (1988). *Nicaragua: Politics, economics, and society.* London: Frances Pinter.

Cortez Dominguez, G. (1990). *La lucha por el poder.* Managua: Vanguardia.

Cuadra, P. A. (1987). The Nicaraguans. In R. S. Leiken & B. Rubin (Eds.), *The Central American crisis reader* (pp. 46-48). New York: Summit.

Cuadra, S. (1990a, January 20). A vote for equality. *Barricada International, 10,* p. 11.

Cuadra, S. (1990b, May 19). There's more to politics than meets the eye. *Barricada International, 10,* p. 6.

Díaz, M. N. (1966). *Tonalá: Conservatism, responsibility, and authority in a Mexican town.* Berkeley: University of California Press.

Edmisten, P. T. (1990). *Nicaragua divided: La Prensa and the Chamorro legacy.* Pensacola: University of West Florida Press.

Elías, A. (1988). Los hombres que creen amar a las mujeres. *FEM, 12*(69), 38-40.

Envío Collective. (1989a, June). Nicaragua's electoral process: The new name for the war. *Envío, 8,* 3-10.

Envío Collective. (1989b, October). Navigating the electoral map. *Envío, 8,* 3-14.

Envío Collective. (1990a, January). A thorn by any other name pricks the same. *Envío, 9,* 6.

Envío Collective. (1990b, March/April). UNO plans market economy. *Envío, 9,* 21-27.

Envío Collective. (1990c, March/April). After the poll wars: Explaining the upset. *Envío, 9,* 30-35.

Envío Collective. (1990d, May). On the verge of peace, or civil war? *Envío, 9,* 5-9.

Envío Collective. (1990e, June). Playing with fire. *Envío, 9,* 3-13.

Envío Collective. (1990f, June). UNO's balance of power—on a tight rope. *Envío, 9,* 26-32.

Envío Collective. (1990g, July). From military to social confrontation. *Envío, 9,* 3-8.

Envío Collective. (1990h, July). Two faces of UNO. *Envío, 9,* 24-37.

Envío Collective. (1990i, August/September). UNO politics: Thunder on the right. *Envío, 9,* 26-30.

Envío Collective. (1990j, October). Polarization and depolarization. *Envío, 9,* 3-11.

Envío Collective. (1990k, November). Who will conquer the chaos? *Envío, 9,* 3-10.

Envío Collective. (1991a, January/February). Concertación and counter-concertación. *Envío, 10,* 3-9.

Envío Collective. (1991b, January/February). Rebellion in the ranks: Challenge from the right. *Envío, 10,* 18-27.

Envío Collective. (1991c, March). A year of UNO economic policies: The rich get richer . . . *Envío, 10,* 30-49.

Envío Collective. (1991d, May). Bankers and masses square off: Economic overhaul, social breakdown? *Envío, 10,* 3-15.

García, A. I., & Gomáriz, E. *Mujeres Centroamericanas: Vol. 2. Efectos del conflicto.* San Jose, Costa Rica: FLASCO.

Goldwert, M. (1985). Mexican machismo: The flight from femininity. *Psychoanalytic Review, 72*(1), 161-169.

Heyck, D. L. (1990). *Life stories of the Nicaraguan revolution.* New York: Routledge.

Hockstader, L. (1990, March 1). Chamorro assails Ortega. *Washington Post.*

Jiménez, M. (1990, May 19). Neo-liberalism in the classroom. *Barricada International, 10,* p. 8.

Jonas, S., & Stein, N. (1990). The construction of democracy in Nicaragua. *Latin American Perspectives, 17*(3), 10-37.

Kantor, H. (1969). Nicaragua: America's only hereditary dictatorship. In H. Kantor, *Patterns of politics and political systems in Latin America* (pp. 159-184). Chicago: Rand McNally.

Kovel, J. (1988). *In Nicaragua.* London: Free Association.

Kretzer, D. I. (1988). *Ritual, politics, and power.* New Haven, CT: Yale University Press.

Levin, C. (1986). Queens and claimants: Political insecurity in sixteenth-century England. In J. Sharistanian (Ed.), *Gender, ideology, and action: Historical perspectives on women's public lives* (pp. 41-66). Westport, CT: Greenwood.

Levy, M. F. (1988). *Each in her own way: Five women leaders of the developing world.* Boulder, CO: Lynne Rienner.

Mendoza, R. (1990, October). We erred to win. *Envío, 9,* 23-50.

Molyneux, M. (1985). Mobilization without emancipation? Women's interests, the state, and revolution in Nicaragua. *Feminist Studies, 11,* 227-254.

Nuñez, O. (1990, June 30). Pacts, accords, and alliances. *Barricada International, 10,* p. 19.

O'Kane, T. (1990). The new old order. *NACLA Report on the Americas, 24*(1), 28-36.

Preston, J. (1990, February 27). Chamorro faces task of reconciling a divided nation. *Washington Post.*

Radell, D. (1988). *The historical geography of western Nicaragua.* Unpublished doctoral dissertation, University of California, Berkeley.

Ramírez, S. (1989). The kid from Niquinohomo (L. Baker, Trans.) *Latin American Perspectives, 16*(3), 48-82.

Richter, L. K. (1990-1991). Exploring theories of female leadership in South and Southeast Asia. *Pacific Affairs, 63,* 524-540.

Selser, G. (1990a, June 16). Slanted justice. *Barricada International, 10,* pp. 5-7.

Selser, G. (1990b, June 30). Social pact? What social pact? *Barricada International, 10,* p. 3.

Sharkey, J. (1986, September/October). Back in control: The CIA's secret propaganda campaign puts the agency exactly where it wants to be. *Common Cause,* pp. 28-40.

Sharkey, J. (1990, May/June). Nicaragua: Anatomy of an election. How U.S. money affected the outcome in Nicaragua. *Common Cause,* pp. 20-29.

Stevens, E. P. (1973). Marianismo: The other face of machismo in Latin America. In A. Pescatello (Ed.), *Female and male in Latin America* (pp. 89-101). Pittsburgh, PA: University of Pittsburgh Press.

Taylor, C. (1989, November 11). UNO: Throwbacks and greenbacks. *Barricada International, 9,* pp. 12-13.

Tellez, D. M. (1990, June 16). Who needs a "national Accord"? *Barricada International, 10,* p. 19.

Uhlig, M. A. (1990, February 11). Opposing Ortega. *New York Times Magazine,* pp. 34-35.

Vargas, O.-R. (1989a). *Elecciones presidenciales en Nicaragua, 1912-1932.* Managua: Fundación Manolo Morales.

Vargas, O.-R. (1989b, September 30). Elections in Nicaragua (1912-1974). *Barricada International, 9,* pp. 6-7.

Velázquez P., J. L. (1986). *Nicaragua: Sociedad civil y dictadura.* San Jose, Costa Rica: Libro Libre.

Wiarda, H. J. (1981). *Corporatism and national development in Latin America.* Boulder, CO: Westview.

5

Indira Gandhi
and the Exercise of Power

JANA EVERETT

How do we make sense of Indira Gandhi's role as the central political leader of India from 1966 when she became prime minister to 1984 when she was assassinated by her Sikh bodyguards? Did it matter that she was a woman? Her critics often used gender imagery, as in Salman Rushdie's (1980) description of a prime minister who "aspired to be Devi, the Mother-goddess in her most terrible aspect, possessor of the *shakti* [female energy] of the gods, a multi-limbed divinity with a center-parting and schizophrenic hair" (p. 522; see also Rushdie, 1985). Yet most commentators have not seen gender as significant in Mrs. Gandhi's governance. For example, *India Today*'s effort to capture her complexity used gender-neutral terms: "Dictator or democrat? Saint or tyrant? Consolidator or destroyer? Peacemaker or warmonger? She was all of these yet none of them. To the final tragic end, the Indira enigma remained intact" (Bobb, 1984, p. 94).

Among the myriad efforts to explain Mrs. Gandhi's policy decisions, leadership style, and political legacies, there are two main theoretical approaches. The first is a Marxist approach that depicts the Indian political economy as directed by a coalition of dominant classes and

AUTHOR'S NOTE: Thanks to the College of Liberal Arts and Sciences at the University of Colorado at Denver for awarding me a small grant to write this chapter, and to my brother, Jim Matson, and to Sue Ellen Charlton and Betsy Moen, my feminist academic support group, for helpful comments on an earlier draft.

characterized by structural crises of backward capitalism (Banerjee, 1984, pp. 2028-2031; Roy, 1984, pp. 1896-1897). Writers using this approach interpret Mrs. Gandhi's actions as shaped fundamentally by exacerbating crises and conflicts among the classes. The second is a psychological approach that explains her actions in terms of personality variables leading to a compulsion to dominate (Hart, 1976; Malik, 1988). Within this approach some writers focus on a sense of insecurity engendered in childhood and others focus on the amoral political culture of the 1960s. Both of these approaches are ultimately unsatisfactory. While the Marxist approach discounts the independent effect of Indira Gandhi as a leader, the psychological approach dismisses the context confronting this leader. Sudipta Kaviraj (1986) offers a more useful approach that takes into account the extent to which domestic and international constraints forced Mrs. Gandhi to work out a "logic of survival" upon becoming prime minister: "Initially, this logic of survival made her act pragmatically, but eventually, these *ad hoc* and individual initiatives altered the basic structure of Indian politics" (p. 1697). Although not addressed by Kaviraj, gender considerations appear to have played a role in Indira Gandhi's survival strategies.

Context

India may have been the "jewel in the crown" of British colonialism, but under the British, India experienced economic stagnation.[1] Urban Western-educated elites, created by the colonial system to work in its administration, began to demand economic and political reforms. The Indian National Congress, formed in 1885, created a mass movement for independence under the leadership of Mohandas Gandhi (1869-1948) and Jawaharlal Nehru (1889-1964). Independence was achieved in 1947, and with it the trauma of partition, as the Muslim majority areas in the eastern and western parts of the subcontinent became Pakistan. Nehru presided over the process of constitution making, which established a parliamentary democracy with a prime minister, a federal political system with central and state governments, guarantees of fundamental rights, a largely ceremonial presidency, a Supreme Court with powers of judicial review, and emergency governmental powers when national security was threatened. Congress transformed itself from a mass movement to a political machine, winning the first three general elections in a one-party dominant political system.

The challenges facing the Indian state were enormous. About half of the citizens were extremely poor. Rural India, constituting the vast majority of the population, was characterized by crop yields among the lowest in the world and by extreme inequalities in landowning: While the top 5% of households (owning 20 acres or more) controlled 41% of the land, 22% of households owned no land, and 39% of households (owning 2.5 acres or less) controlled 8% of the land (Frankel, 1978, pp. 96-97). India has great cultural diversity (Hardgrave & Kochanek, 1986, pp. 4-11); 12 major languages and hundreds of minor ones are spoken in India. Although Hindus make up more than 80% of the population, they are divided into high castes (the Brahmins, Kshatriyas, and Vaishyas), middle castes (the upper *shudras*), "backward castes" (the lower *shudras,* 25% of the population), "scheduled castes" (the former untouchables, 15% of the population), and tribals (mainly counted as Hindus, 7% of the population). Religious minorities include Muslims (11%), Christians (3%), and Sikhs (2%).

Nehru was committed to democratic social transformation, self-reliance, and "a third way," distinct from capitalist or communist approaches in both domestic and foreign policy. In foreign affairs Nehru was the most distinguished spokesperson for the Afro-Asian world; in advocating nonalignment, he was often at odds with U.S. policymakers who sought to build alliances to contain Communism during the Cold War era, including a 1954 mutual defense treaty with Pakistan. Indo-Pakistan relations remained tense, with wars in 1948 and in 1965 over Kashmir, which remained under Indian control. Nehru's prestige suffered in a 1962 war with China over disputed territory, when Indian defenses collapsed.

Scholar Akhil Gupta (1989) notes, "Democratic-capitalist third-world states are characterized by an internal tension because their developmental goals frequently run up against the limits imposed by the private control of productive resources" (p. 790). The coalition of dominant classes—industrial capitalists, rich farmers, and profession-als (state bureaucrats and intellectuals)—constrained the development strategies of the political elites, who were unable or unwilling to organize the peasantry to promote radical agrarian reform. Under Nehru's direction India had embarked on a policy of rapid industrial-ization, with a strong public sector. Nehru favored institutional changes in agriculture—land reform, rural cooperatives—to achieve gains in agricultural productivity necessary for industrial growth. However, state leaders resisted these changes, and the increases in productivity were not forthcoming.

By the mid-1960s, India was dependent on foreign assistance from the United States and the Soviet Union to finance development plans and on imports of food grains to feed its people. Under Prime Minister Lal Bahadur Shastri (1964-1966), national economic policy shifted toward a larger role for private investment and modern technology to increase agricultural production. Upon taking office in 1966, Mrs. Gandhi's options were severely constrained. India's military and agricultural weakness had created international dependence and domestic crises. The Congress party organization did not seem able to handle the demands of an increasingly politicized electorate. Mrs. Gandhi herself was dependent on Congress President K. Kamaraj Nadar and other party bosses.

Indira Gandhi's Early Years

Several themes can be extracted from the stories Mrs. Gandhi and her biographers tell of her childhood, youth, and early adulthood (see Bhatia, 1974; Gandhi, 1980; Hutheesing, 1969; Malhotra, 1989; Masani, 1976; Moraes, 1980). National politics permeated her family life. The public invaded the private, absorbing her father, dominating her play, eclipsing her marriage. She did not perform well in student political and academic life in England, the conventional masculine route to political leadership among the nationalist elite. Her route to power would be different, based on being the daughter of a widowed prime minister. Mrs. Gandhi's early career revealed the difficulties she had in being accepted by male political leaders as an equal. Under the shadow of her father, she was not taken seriously by the politicians and statesmen who met with Nehru, and she had to absorb her husband's hostility over her success. These difficulties would also be seen during her years as prime minister.

Indira Gandhi, the only child of Jawaharlal and Kamala Nehru, was born into the prominent nationalist family on November 19, 1917, in their family home in Allahabad. The Nehrus were Kashmiri Brahmins who had served in the administration of both Mughal and British rulers of India. Indira's paternal grandfather, Motilal Nehru (1861-1931), was a successful lawyer and leader of the moderate wing of Congress. Jawaharlal Nehru had been trained as a lawyer in England but turned to full-time work in the nationalist movement. In 1920 the Nehru family joined Mohandas Gandhi's noncooperation movement, giving up their lavish Westernized life-style for *khadi* (hand-spun and handwoven cloth), simple Indian food, and numerous terms of imprisonment.

With a constant stream of nationalist leaders coming to the Nehru home, Indira had few opportunities to play with other children. She recalled a close relationship with Gandhi: "As a very small child, I regarded him, not as a great leader but more as an elder of the family to whom I went with difficulties and problems, which he treated with the grave seriousness which was due to the large-eyed and solemn child I was" (quoted in Masani, 1976, p. 18). She was separated from her father for long periods during his jail terms. Her schooling was also frequently interrupted, and Indira was primarily taught at home through her twelfth year. She would amuse herself by playing political games: lining up her dolls to confront each other as nationalists and police, and delivering speeches to the servants. Exposed to a wide range of books, Indira developed a fascination for Joan of Arc, telling her aunt, "Some day I am going to lead my people to freedom just as Joan of Arc did" (quoted in Hutheesing, 1969, p. 45). In a 1972 interview with Oriana Fallaci, Mrs. Gandhi painted a picture of a lonely, insecure childhood that taught her self-reliance:

> If you only knew what it did to me to have lived in that house where the police were bursting in to take everyone away! I certainly didn't have a happy and serene childhood. I was a thin, sickly, nervous little girl. And after the police came, I'd be left alone for weeks, months, to get along as best I could. I learned very soon to get along by myself. (quoted in Fallaci, 1976, p. 173)

In her extended family household, conflict among the female relatives marked Indira's childhood. Kamala was deeply religious, teaching her daughter the Hindu classics and the Hindi language. The more sophisticated Nehru women, especially Motilal's wife, Swarupani, and her daughter Nan (later Vijayalaksmi Pandit), ridiculed Kamala, who they did not believe was good enough for Jawaharlal. Swarupani's other daughter, Krishna (later Hutheesing), was more supportive. Indira Gandhi later said of her mother: "I loved her deeply and when I thought she was being wronged I fought for her and quarreled with people" (quoted in Malhotra, 1989, p. 30). Kamala eagerly embraced Gandhi's cause. Indira Gandhi (1980) remembered her mother as "a convinced feminist, a position which I didn't understand then because I felt that I could do what I liked and that it didn't make any difference whether I was a boy or a girl" (p. 23). Throughout Indira's childhood, her mother's health was poor. A diagnosis of tuberculosis led Jawaharlal, accompanied by Indira, to take Kamala to Switzerland for treatment in 1926-1927.

Indira's adolescence was marked by her mother's deteriorating health and separation from her father because of his imprisonment. In 1931 Kamala too was arrested; as president of the Allahabad Congress Committee, she had organized women to picket liquor stores and foreign cloth shops. Left out of the Congress actions because of her age, Indira organized children into the Vanar Sena ("Monkey Army," from the Indian epic *Ramayana*), which served as Congress auxiliaries, bringing water to demonstrators, smuggling messages to Congress leaders, and spying on police stations. Jawaharlal, in prison, supplemented Indira's education with a series of letters later published as *Glimpses of World History*. She was sent to nationalist-oriented schools, first in Poona in 1931 and then in 1934 to Rabindranath Tagore's school in Santiniketan, Bengal. In May 1935 Indira accompanied her mother, whose condition had worsened, to Europe for treatment. Jawaharlal joined them in September after his release from prison. Kamala died in February 1936 in Lausanne, Switzerland.

After her mother's death, Indira went to England to prepare for the Oxford entrance examinations while her father returned to India to assume the Congress presidency. Her schooling was again interrupted, by trips home and to Southeast Asia and Europe with her father, and by ill health. She developed a close friendship with Feroze Gandhi, a student at the London School of Economics who had been a devoted follower of Kamala Nehru. Gaining entrance to Oxford on her second attempt, Indira joined Somerville College in February 1938 to read modern history. She did not stand out in academic work or in the politics of the Indian community in England. An 11-month recuperation in Switzerland followed an attack of pleurisy. Indira returned to India with Feroze in 1941, giving the war and her health as reasons for abandoning her studies. In 1985 a fellow student revealed that she was forced to leave Oxford because she failed a Latin examination (Malhotra, 1989, p. 44).

Against the initial objections of her father, Indira married Feroze Gandhi on March 26, 1942, in Allahabad. Nehru was more concerned by Feroze's modest economic background than by the religious differences between them—Feroze belonged to the Parsi or Zoroastrian community, while the Nehrus were high-caste Hindus. Nehru quickly came to their defense when there was a public outcry about their "mixed marriage." Both Feroze and Indira spent time in prison in conjunction with the Quit India Movement and then moved into the Nehru family home in Allahabad. Their first child, Rajiv Gandhi, was born in August 1944. At the end of the war, Jawaharlal Nehru assumed the leadership of the interim government and appointed Feroze managing director of the *National Herald,* a Lucknow newspaper founded by Nehru. Mrs. Gandhi moved to Lucknow with her husband and son, but was soon commuting to Delhi to act as hostess for her father. Her second son, Sanjay, was born in Delhi in December 1946.

On August 15, 1947, Jawaharlal Nehru became prime minister of independent India. Nehru, Mrs. Gandhi, and her sons moved to Teen Murti House in Delhi, leaving Feroze in Lucknow. According to Mrs. Gandhi (1980), the decision to help her father "wasn't really a choice"; his grief after the assassination of Mahatma Gandhi on January 30, 1948, increased her determination to stay with him (p. 69). Stressing her duty to her father also covered up marital discord brought on by Feroze's difficulties with being "son-in-law of the nation." In 1955, Mrs. Gandhi wrote, "I have been and am deeply unhappy in my domestic life. Now, the hurt and the unpleasantness don't seem to matter so much. I am sorry, though, to have missed the most wonderful thing in life, having a complete and perfect relationship with another human being" (Norman, 1985, p. 28). Her responsibilities grew as she supervised the Nehru household, traveled abroad with the prime minister and on her own, and gradually began to stand in for Nehru at meetings. She became active in the organizational wing of the Congress party, working in the Women's Department and serving on the Congress Election Committee and Working Committee. In 1959 she was elected Congress president.

Meanwhile, Feroze pursued a political career of his own as a member of Parliament from 1950 to his death in 1960. Moving to Delhi, he occupied housing provided for M.P.s and also stayed with his wife and children at Teen Murti House. He developed a reputation as an independent Congress backbencher, uncovering a corruption scandal that led to the resignation of the finance minister in 1957. In a 1966 interview, Indira Gandhi described the tensions in their relationship: "When I went into public life and became successful, he liked it and he didn't like it. Other people—friends, relatives—were the worst. They would say, 'How does it feel, being so-and-so's husband?' He would get upset, and it would take me weeks to win him over" (Hutheesing, 1969, p. 137). After Feroze suffered a slight heart attack in 1959, they reconciled, and the family went for a holiday in Kashmir. When he had a second heart attack in September 1960, Mrs. Gandhi rushed to the hospital and sat up with him all night; she was with him when he died in the early morning. In spite of their estranged relationship, Mrs. Gandhi wrote shortly after his death: "Up till now I had somebody to whom I could pour out my thoughts—even if there was a lack of attention and sympathy—and with the removal of that outlet I have to look outward" (Norman, 1985, p. 78). Four years later her father would die, and less than two years after that Mrs. Gandhi would become prime minister.

Path to Power

From the perspective of 1991, the dynastic character of Indian political leadership is apparent: Nehru family members served as prime ministers for 40 of the 44 years of independence. Indira Gandhi groomed first her son Sanjay and then her son Rajiv to succeed her, and after Rajiv Gandhi's assassination at the close of the 1991 election campaign, Congress (I) leaders tried unsuccessfully to persuade his widow, Sonia, to accept the Congress party presidency. Nevertheless, Indira Gandhi's accession to power was by no means a foregone conclusion. Her status as the only offspring of the widowed prime minister created a political career for Mrs. Gandhi, but her father took no action to indicate he wished her to succeed him in office. Only after his death did any signs of Mrs. Gandhi's ambition to be prime minister surface, and even then her accession to the office did not seem especially likely.

A constellation of factors thrust political leadership upon Indira Gandhi.[2] One factor was the Indian political context in 1966: the unexpected death of Prime Minister Shastri, a factionalized Congress party, and party leaders determined to prevent a particular individual, Morarji Desai, from becoming prime minister. Another was the "Appendage Syndrome" (Fraser, 1988, pp. 307-308). Congress President Kamaraj orchestrated Mrs. Gandhi's selection as prime minister because he perceived her to be weak enough that he and the other regional party bosses (known as the Syndicate) could control her, and yet strong enough to beat Desai in a party election because of the high regard for her father. In addition, her lack of association with any party faction meant she had fewer enemies than the other possible candidates. According to Dom Moraes (1980):

> Kamaraj felt that a woman would be an ideal tool for the Syndicate, especially Nehru's daughter. He had watched her, gentle, sedate, obedient to her father, properly courteous to her elders: her parentage would capture the public imagination, and once she was properly in power the Syndicate could switch professions: from queenmakers to puppet masters. (p. 123)

Although Prime Minister Nehru asserted publicly that he did not want to play a role in choosing his successor, a policy initiative taken by him in August 1963 weakened the prospects of Finance Minister Morarji Desai, who was too conservative in Nehru's view. Known as the Kamaraj plan, this initiative was designed ostensibly to strengthen party organization by having 12 government officials at the state and national levels resign their positions and devote themselves full-time to party work. Both Desai and Home Minister Lal Bahadur Shastri stepped down from the cabinet under the Kamaraj plan. Shastri was brought back into the cabinet in early 1964.

Some, including Desai, have argued that the Kamaraj plan was designed not only to eliminate Desai's chances of becoming prime minister, but also to ensure Mrs. Gandhi's selection (Frankel, 1978, pp. 242-243; Richter, 1990-1991). However, since Nehru neither openly advanced her candidacy nor appointed her to a cabinet office, it seems unlikely that he planned for her to succeed him. When Nehru died of a stroke in May 1964, Mrs. Gandhi was not seriously considered as a candidate for prime minister. Congress President Kamaraj and the Syndicate orchestrated a party consensus behind Shastri as his successor. The Syndicate shared Nehru's distrust of Desai, but for different reasons: They saw him as too individualistic to accept Syndicate control.

Mrs. Gandhi joined Shastri's cabinet as minister of information and broadcasting and became a member of the Rajya Sabha, the indirectly elected upper house of the Indian Parliament. According to Mrs. Gandhi (1980), Shastri insisted "he must have a Nehru in the Cabinet to maintain stability" (p. 101), and he offered her the position of foreign minister, which she refused. This seems unlikely; given her administrative inexperience, her cabinet appointment can be seen as a tribute to Nehru's memory and Shastri's attempt to neutralize her as a political force (Brecher, 1966, pp. 103, 107; Masani, 1976, p. 133; Moraes, 1980, pp. 120-121).

While Mrs. Gandhi apparently performed in a lackluster manner in the conventional parliamentary and cabinet arenas, she found other ways to develop a public following. She moved to 1 Safdarjung Road and continued the Nehru custom of the morning *durbar*—opening her home to the public, who came with petitions or simply to view Nehru's daughter. She criticized the government for drifting to the right and in two instances—during language riots in Madras and at the onset of the 1965 war with Pakistan—gained public admiration for her courage and resoluteness. Arriving in Kashmir at the same time that several thousand

Pakistani infiltrators were discovered, Mrs. Gandhi went to the military control room, communicated the seriousness of the situation to Prime Minister Shastri, and helped to maintain morale. Her actions won her the title of "the only man in a Cabinet of old women" (Masani, 1976, p. 136).

Becoming Prime Minister

On January 10, 1966, Prime Minister Shastri died suddenly of a heart attack in Tashkent, where he had signed a peace agreement formally ending the 1965 Indo-Pakistan war. Succession politics returned, and once again Congress President Kamaraj played the crucial role in the selection process. His choice of Indira Gandhi was initially opposed by the Syndicate because of her perceived leftist leanings, but she gained their support after building a coalition of state chief ministers. This time an open contest for prime minister was unavoidable, because Desai refused to step aside again "for this mere *chokri*" (slip of a girl) (Masani, 1976, p. 139). On January 19 the Congress Parliamentary Party (CPP) elected Indira Gandhi prime minister over Morarji Desai, with a vote of 355 to 169. On hearing of her election, the crowds cried not only "Long live Indira," but also "Long live Jawaharlal" (Moraes, 1980, p. 127).

Looking more broadly at the processes of political succession in India and also elsewhere in South and Southeast Asia, the means by which Indira Gandhi achieved power appear fairly typical of these political systems, which are all characterized by prominent political families and elite factionalism (Richter, 1990-1991). Widows, daughters, and sisters of male leaders have served as prime minister or president in Sri Lanka (Sirimavo Bandaranaike), Pakistan (Benazir Bhutto), Bangladesh (Khalida Zia), and the Philippines (Corazon Aquino), as well as in India. In addition, currently imprisoned Daw Aung San Suu Kyi, winner of the 1991 Nobel Peace Prize and daughter of Burmese nationalist leader U Aung San, is leader of the Burmese political party that was prevented by the military from taking power after winning elections in 1990. Under conditions of bitter political rivalries, female representatives of political dynasties have played a unifying role, but in some cases they have also raised fears in the military leadership. In India's first two successions, a small group of party leaders decided upon a candidate, but a broad array of institutional interests within the party were involved in the selection process: the Congress Working Committee, the state chief ministers, and the CPP. The contrast in the succession of Rajiv Gandhi—he was chosen by the Congress Parliamentary Board (CPP executive) and sworn in as prime minister within hours of his mother's assassination—serves as an indicator of the deinstitutionalization of Indian politics and its dynastic character by 1984.

Leadership Style

Commentators have described Mrs. Gandhi's leadership style as pragmatic, reactive, and characterized by extended periods of drift interspersed with periods of decisive action (Carras, 1979, p. 37; Tharoor, 1982, p. 74). Over the course of her tenure in office, she would fashion strategies to increase India's military and economic power as well as her own. These strategies did not constitute an overarching, deliberate design; they were not ideologically consistent, but they had elements in common. Kaviraj (1986) views Mrs. Gandhi as outwitting her adversaries by acting decisively in a manner characterized by "a disregard for institutional norms" (p. 1700). Although her initiatives increased her personal power, they limited the options available for her to solve future crises. Having eliminated political leaders with independent bases of support from Congress, and having almost destroyed the party, Mrs. Gandhi was left to rely on her own presence, state policies, and the agencies of state repression.

Several elements of Mrs. Gandhi's leadership style emerged in 1969 (Brass, 1988; Kothari, 1988; Manor, 1983; Rudolph & Rudolph, 1987, pp. 134-145). As in her college days and in her time in Shastri's cabinet, the conventions of male political behavior did not work for her, so she conceived her own. When rules of the game worked against her, she changed the rules. When the party bosses threatened her, she overthrew them and weakened the party. Using radical rhetoric and championing the needs of the poor, Mrs. Gandhi pursued a populist style to establish a personal relationship with the electorate unmediated by institutions. Elections became referenda on Mrs. Gandhi's rule. The rhetoric was not followed by the implementation of radical change. Under Mrs. Gandhi there was a centralization of power in the party and a breakdown of party organization. Intraparty elections were not held; instead, officials were appointed from the top. Mrs. Gandhi selected chief ministers and other officials on the basis of personal loyalty, not on the basis of their political standing at the local level. State politics lost autonomy through "unprincipled intervention by the center in state politics" because Mrs.

Gandhi believed her power depended on this degree of control (Brass, 1988, p. 212). The personalization of power contributed to institutional decay as Mrs. Gandhi overturned commonly accepted procedures, norms, and principles of political competition and governance to achieve political advantage.

Mrs. Gandhi's vision for India (and perhaps also of her own leadership) was articulated in a 1977 interview: "We want India to be self-reliant and to strengthen its independence so that it cannot be pressurized by anybody. . . . this cannot be done unless we solve our own problems, and the major problem is poverty and economic backwardness" (quoted in Tharoor, 1982, p. 88). This vision was pursued in isolation; Mrs. Gandhi lacked close ties with other political leaders due to her own past experiences and to additional gender considerations: A woman could not be too intimate with male politicians (Carras, 1979, p. 50). Instead, Mrs. Gandhi relied on a shifting group of personal advisers in the prime minister's secretariat and increasingly on her sons and their families. Rajiv and Sanjay lived with Mrs. Gandhi and, after their marriages, Sonia and Maneka joined the Gandhi household. Perhaps partly due to her isolation, Mrs. Gandhi developed a tendency to interpret policy failures and political opposition in terms of conspiracies against her, often with external involvement. In response, she built up the intelligence capability of her office and increasingly resorted to coercive force to put down dissent.

Mrs. Gandhi's Agenda

The Achievement of Political Survival: 1966-1971

Indira Gandhi's performance during her first few years in office underscored her weak position. She continued Shastri's economic liberalization and green revolution policies. In March 1966 Mrs. Gandhi traveled to the United States, seeking food aid and foreign exchange. She avoided criticism of U.S. policy in Vietnam and agreed to a proposal for a joint Indo-U.S. educational foundation in India. India's dependence on U.S. food aid, the World Bank, and the Aid to India Consortium was symbolized in the announcement to devalue the rupee by 36.5% made on June 6, 1966. Within 10 days, the United States resumed food aid suspended the previous year at the outbreak of the Indo-Pakistan war. These policies, especially devaluation, were extremely unpopular in India and in the short run were unsuccessful. Devaluation led to a drop in foreign exchange earnings of 8% in 1966-1967, and more generally increasing disparities accompanied economic stagnation (Frankel, 1978, pp. 322-336). Shipments of U.S. food aid were delayed and irregular; the United States put India on a "short tether." Facing the failure of a second monsoon, Mrs. Gandhi was deeply humiliated by this treatment and resolved never to be in such a position of dependence again.

Mrs. Gandhi's credibility as a national leader was seriously compromised by domestic political developments. Political protests, including riots, strikes, student "indiscipline," rural rebellions, and secessionist movements, increased dramatically after 1965 (Rudolph & Rudolph, 1987, pp. 227, 238). The 1967 elections demonstrated a dramatic decline in Congress popularity and power. The Congress share of the Lok Sabha vote declined 4%, to 41%, and, more significantly, alliances among opposition parties led to a 21% decline in Congress seats, leaving a slender majority of 25 (Frankel, 1978, p. 353).[3] Congress lost legislative elections in eight states as the Congress share of the state assembly vote fell 3%, to 42%, and opposition coalitions took office.

Within the party Mrs. Gandhi found herself generally outmaneuvered by the Syndicate and harassed in meetings of the party organization and Parliament, where she was nicknamed "the Dumb Doll" (Malhotra, 1989, p. 93). After the 1967 elections, supporters of Morarji Desai once again advanced his candidacy for prime minister, charging that government policies and the party bosses (including Kamaraj) that had put Mrs. Gandhi in office had been repudiated by the electorate. Kamaraj was able to work out a compromise, but it involved including Morarji Desai in Mrs. Gandhi's cabinet as deputy prime minister and finance minister. At the end of 1967 Mrs. Gandhi was able to prevent Kamaraj from having another term as Congress president, but the party bosses refused to let her become president, and she was forced to accept S. Nijalingappa, a Syndicate member. By early 1968, Kamaraj had decided Mrs. Gandhi should be removed as prime minister.

In what can be seen as the fashioning of a survival strategy, Mrs. Gandhi began to edge cautiously to the left in both foreign and domestic policy, a direction that offered increased autonomy internationally, greater popularity nationally, and the potential to defeat her rivals within the party. She visited the Soviet Union in July 1966 and demanded an unconditional halt to U.S. bombing of North Vietnam, and she hosted a Non-Aligned Summit for Tito and Nasser in October 1966.

In 1967 the Indian government dropped the planned Indo-American Education Foundation. The Soviet Union became India's most important arms supplier and increased development aid commitments. While shifting superpower relationships with India reflected international political considerations (primarily concerning China) over which India had little influence, closer ties with the Soviet Union replaced military and economic aid from an unreliable United States and enhanced anti-imperialist rhetoric that built popular support for Mrs. Gandhi.

Domestically, Mrs. Gandhi endorsed a reformist 10-point program adopted by the Congress Working Committee in May 1967, but made no immediate moves to implement the policies—including nationalization of general insurance, removal of the privileges of the princes, public distribution of food grains, and restriction of industrial monopolies—that were opposed by party conservatives such as Desai. Although party radicals pushed for bank nationalization, Desai was able to get the government to accept a compromise scheme for the "social control" of banking. By 1969, Mrs. Gandhi and Nijalingappa were publicly debating policy issues, with the prime minister supporting a strong public sector and the party president criticizing its inefficiencies.

The struggle over power and policy direction within Congress came to a head in the contest for president of India in 1969 (Frankel, 1978, pp. 414-425; Masani, 1976, pp. 196-204). By acting decisively, Mrs. Gandhi was able to win a power struggle and to advance her own policy agenda. The struggle pitted the Syndicate (now seeking to oust Mrs. Gandhi in favor of Morarji Desai) against Indira Gandhi, who was supported by a group of "young Turks" in the Congress Forum for Socialist Action. Mrs. Gandhi abruptly divested Desai of the finance portfolio, opposed the Syndicate choice for president, Sanjiva Reddy (the official Congress candidate), and announced her support for bank nationalization, which was signed into law on August 10. The popularity of bank nationalization was enormous; she had seized the moment with a populist program. When complimented by a friend on the strategic timing of bank nationalization, Mrs. Gandhi responded, "They drove me to the wall and left me with no other option" (quoted in Malhotra, 1989, p. 120).

Since she had lost in the party, Mrs. Gandhi sought to win in the wider national arena. She announced a free vote for president, and her candidate, V. V. Giri, the interim president running as an independent, won a narrow victory based on the support of Communists, Socialists, and regional parties, as well as from approximately one-third of Congress legislators. Mrs. Gandhi (1980) framed the conflict in the following terms:

Whether (a) the Congress should be a mass based organisation or one manipulated by a handful of party bosses, (b) it should adhere firmly to its declared
policy of secularism and socialism, and (c) in a democracy the elected head
of government could be overruled by a party organisation which is not
responsible to Parliament. (p. 133)

The Syndicate portrayed the conflict in terms of party discipline and
tried to take action against Mrs. Gandhi for voting against the official
party candidate for president. The Congress split, with two rival All
India Congress Committees holding meetings in November. Although
the Syndicate instructed the CPP to choose a new leader, a majority (310)
of the 429 members supported Mrs. Gandhi (Bhatia, 1974, p. 226). (The
president is chosen by an electoral college composed of M.P.s and state
legislators.) There were now two Congress parties—Congress (R) (Ruling)
and Congress (O) (Organization). Because Mrs. Gandhi's party had lost its
absolute majority in the Lok Sabha, Congress (R) now depended on the
support of the Communist Party of India (CPI), several regional parties,
and independents. The Congress split strengthened Mrs. Gandhi's power
immeasurably; few questioned the methods she had used.

After the split in Congress, Indira Gandhi pursued a populist program: More industries were nationalized, and the privy purses of the
former princes were terminated. Conflicts increased between an activist
Parliament and a conservative Supreme Court, which struck down much
of the legislation on the grounds of unconstitutional interference with
private property rights. In order to amend the constitution, Indira
Gandhi required a two-thirds parliamentary majority, which she
achieved in elections held in March 1971. She campaigned with the
slogan "*Garibi hatao*" (Remove poverty), which the opposition alliance
countered with "Indira *hatao*" (Remove Indira). Congress (R) won a
resounding victory in the 1971 elections, with 43% of the vote translat-
ing into the needed two-thirds majority in the Lok Sabha (Frankel, 1978,
p. 455). Congress (O) dropped from 65 to 16 seats in the Lok Sabha.
Indira Gandhi utilized her increased power base to pass two constitutional amendments to establish parliamentary supremacy over the Supreme Court in the interpretation of fundamental rights.

From the Heights to the Depths: 1971-1975

Shortly after her impressive electoral victory, an international crisis
brought on by a struggle for self-determination within East Pakistan
confronted Mrs. Gandhi (Frankel, 1978, p. 461; Kissinger, 1979,

pp. 853-897; Malhotra, 1989, pp. 134-141; Masani, 1976, pp. 237-247). Following the Awami League sweep of the December 1970 elections based on a campaign for maximum autonomy, the Pakistani army launched brutal military repression in East Pakistan on March 25, 1971. The Awami League went underground, proclaimed Bangladesh independent, and launched a resistance movement. More than 10 million refugees swarmed over the Indian border during the ensuing months, taxing Indian resources. Although the Indian public clamored for intervention, Indian leaders feared Chinese retaliation and were aware of the Nixon administration's "tilt" toward Pakistan.

Mrs. Gandhi devised a carefully constructed strategy to cope with this crisis: launching an international diplomatic initiative to explain the difficulties facing India and to pressure Pakistan to negotiate a settlement, securing support from the Soviet Union in the form of a 20-year Treaty of Friendship, supplying covert aid to the resistance, preparing Indian troops for armed conflict with Pakistan, and building a national consensus for her actions. When Pakistan mounted a surprise air attack on December 3, 1971, the Indian army launched a speedy conquest of East Pakistan; Pakistani forces surrendered on December 16. Through a quick military victory, Mrs. Gandhi was able to head off U.S. efforts to intervene on behalf of Pakistan in the United Nations, and she refused to be intimidated by units of the U.S. Seventh Fleet sent to the Bay of Bengal. Bangladesh had achieved independence, Pakistan had lost its eastern wing, and India was now clearly the predominant power in South Asia.

State legislative elections held in March 1972 continued the "Indira wave," with Congress winning 47% of the vote and 70% of the seats (Frankel, 1978, pp. 474-477). Success came at the cost of centralization of power in the party and in the government; Mrs. Gandhi replaced four chief ministers with her own nominees. Factionalism and corruption increased as weak state leaders put in office by Mrs. Gandhi were challenged by rivals. "Black" (illegal) money from corporations and organized crime played a growing role in elections. The taint of corruption touched the Gandhi family in charges against Mrs. Gandhi's son Sanjay for his unsuccessful government-financed Maruti car project. After the Supreme Court once again limited the power of Parliament to amend the constitution and the position of chief justice of the Supreme Court became vacant in April 1973, the government departed from the established convention of seniority and bypassed the three most senior judges to appoint a chief justice favorable to the government's position.

Mrs. Gandhi did not follow up her populist rhetoric with radical policy initiatives on poverty. A number of credit and rural works antipoverty schemes were initiated, but they reached less than one-tenth of the eligible small farmers and rural unemployed (Frankel, 1978, pp. 497-508). Land reform legislation, a campaign promise, was extensively watered down by the time it passed the state legislatures. The state's effort to take over trading in food grains was a complete failure and had to be abandoned.

In 1973, India was again confronted by economic crisis in the form of food shortages and inflation, partly triggered by OPEC oil price rises. Inept chief ministers, preoccupied with staying in power, were unable to cope with these problems (Kochanek, 1976). Mrs. Gandhi responded to the ensuing protests with repression; the army was deployed against civilian unrest 15 times in the period 1973-1975 (Cohen, 1988, pp. 125-126). The 1971 Maintenance of Internal Security Act (MISA) was expanded in scope; it allowed the preventive detention of individuals threatening national security, public order, or essential services. Under pressure from the International Monetary Fund and the World Bank, the government enacted anti-inflation ordinances and certain economic liberalization measures.

Popular uprisings emerged in Gujarat and Bihar against the state governments and coalesced into the nationwide J.P. movement, named after J. P. Narayan, a veteran nationalist leader. Mrs. Gandhi charged that she "had become the target of a conspiracy by 'external elements in India's affairs in collusion with some internal groups' " (Frankel, 1978, p. 527). The government invoked Defence of India Rules (DIR) and MISA to arrest the leaders of a threatened railway strike called for May 8, 1974, and then quickly crushed the strike by arresting more than 20,000 workers (Frankel, 1978, pp. 529-530).[4] Two unrelated policy initiatives during this period appear as diversions from the increasing level of political conflict. In May 1974, India carried out an underground nuclear test, and in April 1975 Sikkim was incorporated into India.

On June 12, 1975, Mrs. Gandhi experienced two serious challenges to her political leadership (Frankel, 1978, pp. 539-540; Hardgrave & Kochanek, 1986, pp. 212-213). The Allahabad High Court ruled that she had committed election code violations by using the services of government officials in her 1971 campaign. This conviction invalidated her 1971 election and barred her from elective office for six years, which meant that she would have to resign as prime minister. The ruling was stayed for 20 days in order to permit an appeal to the Supreme

Court. On the same day, state legislative elections in Gujarat resulted in a victory for the opposition coalition, Janata (People's) Front, over Congress (R), a massive assault on the prestige of Mrs. Gandhi, who had campaigned hard in the state. Opposition parties and the press called for her resignation, which was vigorously opposed by Congress politicians and especially by Sanjay Gandhi, who at that time was his mother's most influential adviser. A few years later, Mrs. Gandhi explained her thinking at the time to Dom Moraes (1980):

> After my judgment in 1975, what could I have done except stay? You know the state the country was in. What would have happened if there had been nobody to lead it? I was the only person who could, you know. It was my duty to the country to stay, though I didn't want to. (p. 220)

On June 24 the Supreme Court rejected Mrs. Gandhi's application for an absolute stay; she was allowed to continue as prime minister pending consideration of her appeal, but she could not participate in the Lok Sabha. On June 25 there was a mass rally in Delhi led by opposition leaders J. P. Narayan and Morarji Desai, who called for a nationwide movement to depose Mrs. Gandhi.

Emergency and Political Wilderness: 1975-1979

Convinced that her leadership, now gravely challenged, was indispensable to the nation, Mrs. Gandhi acted decisively to maintain her power by transforming the political process from democracy to dictatorship. In the evening of June 25 she informed the president that she planned to invoke the emergency provisions of the constitution in response to the threat to internal security posed by the opposition, and he signed the Proclamation of Emergency, which was issued the next day. Mrs. Gandhi justified the imposition of the emergency in an All-India Radio address the morning of June 26: "I am sure you are conscious of the deep and widespread conspiracy which has been brewing ever since I began to introduce certain progressive measures of benefit to the common man and woman of India" (quoted in Hardgrave & Kochanek, 1986, p. 214). Under the emergency, the central government imposed authoritarian rule over the country; the constitutional powers of the states and guarantees of fundamental rights were suspended. Opposition leaders and Congress dissidents were arrested early the morning of June 26 under MISA. Press censorship was imposed, many political organizations were banned under DIR, constitutional protections against arbitrary arrest were suspended, and more than 110,000 people were jailed without trial (Hardgrave & Kochanek, 1986, p. 215).

Mrs. Gandhi's policies during the emergency centered on constitutional changes to reduce the power of the judiciary and on her "Twenty-Point Program" and Sanjay Gandhi's "Five-Point Program" of social and economic reform. Parliament approved the emergency, and through two retroactive constitutional amendments made declaration of an emergency and electoral disputes involving the prime minister or other national officials nonjusticiable. The most important constitutional change was made by the Forty-Second Amendment, which took the power of judicial review away from the Supreme Court (Frankel, 1978, p. 570).

The accomplishments of the emergency fell short of the commitments to basic social changes for the poor because of the lack of institutional infrastructure for implementation (Frankel, 1978, pp. 551-556). The Twenty-Point Program promised to implement land ceilings for agriculture, abolish bonded labor, increase agricultural wages, lower prices, prevent tax evasion, take action against smugglers and hoarders, and many other popular policies. While more land was distributed through land ceiling legislation during the emergency than during the previous three years (1.1 million versus less than 62,000 acres), progress in the rural programs was very uneven. More was achieved in the urban areas: Direct taxes collected rose 27%, more than 2,100 smugglers were arrested, worker-days lost in strikes declined. The inflation rate declined in part due to a good monsoon and record agricultural production. There were some moves toward economic liberalization.

Sanjay, through his leadership of the Youth Congress, assumed a central role in policy-making during the emergency and brought criminal elements into the party (Frankel, 1978, pp. 562-566). His Five-Point Program urged people to plant trees, practice family planning, abolish dowry, eradicate slums, and teach illiterate people to read and write. Under his orders, slum demolitions in Delhi were carried out in a heavy-handed manner, resulting in the eviction of 700,000 people and the destruction of their homes; in one case of resistance, 6 residents were killed by the police. Sanjay concentrated on family planning after the government announcement of a new National Population Policy in April 1976. Although the new policy did not sanction forced vasectomies, pressure by Sanjay Gandhi and overzealous efforts by government officials trying to ingratiate themselves with the Congress leaders

led to coercion, sterilization quotas imposed on local government employees, nearly 2,000 deaths, and widespread rumors of abuses as the
target of 7.5 million vasectomies was surpassed (Chadney, 1988, p. 93;
Hardgrave & Kochanek, 1986; Weiner, 1978, pp. 35-39).

On January 18, 1977, Mrs. Gandhi unexpectedly called for national
elections in March; political prisoners were released, press censorship
was relaxed, and other emergency regulations were lifted. She believed
that Congress (R) would win because of a good record of economic
growth during the emergency, and she also wanted to rehabilitate her
image as a democratic leader. The election became a referendum on the
emergency; the opposition coalition, Janata party, won a resounding
victory, with 43% of the vote and 270 seats in the Lok Sabha. With 35%
of the vote and 153 seats, Congress was the chief opposition party, but
was swept from power in North India (Frankel, 1978, p. 573). The
reasons for the anti-Congress vote were the "excesses" of the emergency—forced sterilizations, slum demolitions, arbitrary arrests. Mrs.
Gandhi formally lifted the emergency and submitted her resignation.
Morarji Desai was chosen as prime minister on March 24. In January
1978, Congress (R) split with some leaders repudiating the emergency,
and Mrs. Gandhi's party became known as Congress (I) (for Indira).

Kaviraj (1986) points out that the Janata period demonstrated how
much Mrs. Gandhi dominated Indian politics because "much of its three
years in power the Janata government spent in debating what to do with
Indira Gandhi rather than what to do with the country" (p. 1706). It
appointed the Shah Commission to investigate abuses of authority
committed during the emergency, and removed many of the emergency
measures. Both Mrs. Gandhi and her son Sanjay faced numerous criminal charges. On December 20, 1977, the Lok Sabha passed a constitutional amendment restoring the Supreme Court's power to rule on the
constitutionality of state or central legislation. Mrs. Gandhi reemerged
as a political leader warmly received by the people as she traveled
across India. In November 1978, Mrs. Gandhi won a Karnataka by-
election to the Lok Sabha, but she was expelled from Parliament and
jailed during the seven-day session in December on grounds that she
had engaged in misconduct and abuse of authority. In 1979, legislation
set up special courts to try the senior government officials in charge
during the emergency. However, by the summer of 1979 the Janata
government collapsed because of infighting among its constituent parties; new elections were called for January 1980, after which all charges
against Mrs. Gandhi and Sanjay were dismissed.

Return to Office: 1980-1984

Mrs. Gandhi campaigned on the theme, "Elect a government that works," and she promised "law and order" and a restoration of stability (Hardgrave & Kochanek, 1986, pp. 223-227). Sanjay played a central role in candidate selection. Congress (I) emerged victorious, with 43% of the vote and 351 of the 525 seats in the Lok Sabha. With the disintegration of the Janata party, Congress (I) was able to win back many of the votes lost in 1977. In 1980 Janata won 19% of the vote and Lok Dal won 9%; the two parties unified in 1977 had won 43% of the vote. In February 1980, Mrs. Gandhi called for new elections in the nine opposition-controlled state legislatures, and Congress was able to win eight of those state elections.

On June 23, 1980, tragedy struck Mrs. Gandhi with the death of Sanjay, who was widely viewed as the "crown prince," in the crash of a small airplane he was piloting. After Sanjay's death Mrs. Gandhi began to rely on her elder son, Rajiv, who had been a pilot with Indian Airlines. Rajiv was elected to the Lok Sabha from Sanjay's former constituency in a by-election in 1981 and was appointed a party general secretary. Now Rajiv became the "heir apparent." This was resented by Sanjay's widow, Maneka, who felt she should inherit Sanjay's position.

Foreign affairs remained Mrs. Gandhi's sphere of greatest accomplishment. Overall, her policies reflected the response she gave to an American reporter's question about why India always tilted to the Soviet Union: "We don't tilt on either side, we walk upright" (quoted in Malhotra, 1989, p. 265). Mrs. Gandhi faced a difficult situation when the 1979 Soviet invasion of Afghanistan prompted massive U.S. arms shipments to Pakistan. Having fought three wars with Pakistan, the Indian government was extremely concerned about a Pakistani arms buildup when 19 of its 21 divisions were deployed against India (Kapur, 1988, p. 57). After initially condoning the invasion, the Indian government attempted to develop an independent position that both foreign troops and foreign interference in Afghanistan should cease (Dutt, 1990, p. 37). In response to the increased Pakistani military threat, the Indian government modernized its weapons, buying military hardware from France, West Germany, and Great Britain.

In addition, Mrs. Gandhi moved on the diplomatic front to strengthen India's position internationally and in South Asia (Andersen, 1983, p. 120; Hardgrave, 1984, pp. 216-218). Efforts, not noticeably successful, were made to normalize relations with Pakistan and China. Among her 18 trips abroad to 23 countries were trips to both the United States and the Soviet Union in 1982. A compromise was reached on conflict with the United States over supplying fuel to India's Tarapur nuclear reactor. The United States refused to honor this commitment unless India signed the nuclear nonproliferation treaty, which India viewed as "discriminatory and unfair" (Malhotra, 1989, p. 264). In 1983, the South Asian Association for Regional Cooperation (SAARC) was formed. Mrs. Gandhi served as president of the Non-Aligned Movement (NAM) and hosted the 1983 NAM New Delhi summit, where she called for a restructuring of the international economic order and a nuclear freeze.

Mrs. Gandhi continued the economic liberalization begun during the emergency, explaining to a chief ministers' meeting that her government "does not believe in doctrinaire theories" (Andersen, 1982, p. 124; Kohli, 1989, pp. 308-310). In 1981-1982, India applied for a $5.8 billion loan from the IMF. The liberalization policies that loosened government control of the economy were introduced piecemeal while Mrs. Gandhi continued to voice commitment to the poor and to formulate antipoverty schemes that were initiated with great fanfare. In the new Twenty-Point Program introduced in January 1982, Mrs. Gandhi emphasized expansion of integrated rural development and rural employment (Bhargava, 1988, p. 73).

Center-state relations deteriorated in the 1980-1984 period under conditions of increased centralization and personalization of power. In response to factionalism within governing Congress (I) parties at the state level, Mrs. Gandhi removed chief ministers in five states, selecting four chief ministers in Andhra in three years. Mrs. Gandhi and her son Rajiv campaigned actively in 1983 legislative assembly elections held in Karnataka and Andhra, which were widely viewed as a referendum on her leadership; Congress (I) lost both elections. Centrally appointed governors, acting upon Mrs. Gandhi's orders, invited Congress to form governments in Haryana and Himachal Pradesh in 1982 without ascertaining whether the party commanded a legislative majority and dismissed opposition governments in Sikkim, Kashmir, and Andhra in 1984 for partisan reasons. In one of these states, Andhra, the chief minister flew his 161 legislative majority to Delhi, and the governor had to reinstate him. Mrs. Gandhi began to appeal to Hindu chauvinist sentiments, as she anticipated the main competition to Congress (I) would come from the right-wing Bharatiya Janata party. According to one report, "In November 1983, she stated that the religion and traditions of Hinduism were under attack and ought to be defended" (Puri,

1985, p. 149; see also Banerjee, 1984, pp. 2029-2030; Manor, 1988, pp. 80-82).

Religious, caste, linguistic, and ethnic confrontations escalated over the course of Mrs. Gandhi's tenure in office, as did her tendency to respond to these confrontations with repression. The government passed the National Security Act, authorizing preventive detention, and the Essential Services Maintenance Act, banning strikes in many occupations. In 1984, more than 40 million Indians were living under military rule, and the military had been called in to suppress domestic violence 19 times in the period 1980-1984, excluding the ongoing cases of Assam and Punjab (Cohen, 1988, p. 100). These two movements for regional autonomy were perceived by Mrs. Gandhi as threatening the political stability of her government and represented intense grievances felt by both winners and losers in the development process (Kaviraj, 1986, p. 1706).

The issue in Assam, one of the poorest states, was control of resources by the Assamese, 59% of the state's population (Das Gupta, 1988). The Assamese movement demanded the expulsion from the state of all foreigners, who were mainly refugees from Bangladesh. The Assamese movement demanded that these "illegal aliens" be purged from the electoral rolls, but they were a crucial vote bank for the Congress (I), and the government went ahead with 1983 state assembly elections in the face of a massive boycott by opposition parties. Violence erupted, the most serious incident involving the massacre of almost 1,400 Bengali Muslims by Assamese tribals. Although Congress (I) won the election, it was discredited, for less than one-third of the electorate had voted, half of the 1978 voter turnout (Hardgrave, 1984, p. 210).

"Divide and conquer" tactics by Mrs. Gandhi and her advisers to ensure Congress (I) rule in the Punjab played a large role in creating a crisis in the center of the green revolution (Brass, 1988, p. 180; Tully & Jacob, 1985). During 1977-1980, while the Akali Dal, a Sikh political party, was in power in the Punjab, Sanjay Gandhi brought criminals into the Punjab Congress (I) and supported the rise of a Sikh fundamentalist, Sant Bhindranwale, in order to weaken the Akali Dal. Congress regained power in the Punjab with the 1980 state elections in a radicalized atmosphere. When the Akali Dal launched an agitation for increased state autonomy, Mrs. Gandhi's government both refused to make concessions that might undermine her support in the Hindu majority states of north India and failed to control Sikh extremists such as Bhindranwale. In a situation of escalating violence, Mrs. Gandhi imposed president's rule on the Punjab in 1983 after a number of Hindus were killed by Sikh militants. Bhindranwale directed a campaign of terrorism from the Golden Temple, the holiest shrine of the Sikhs. In June 1984, Mrs. Gandhi launched Operation Bluestar, a military assault on the Golden Temple resulting in an official death count of 576 (including Bhindranwale) and considerable damage to the temple.

On October 31, 1984, Mrs. Gandhi was assassinated by two of her security guards who were Sikhs (Hardgrave, 1985, pp. 139-141; Malhotra, 1989, pp. 15-24). Following news of the assassination there was a wave of violence against Sikhs in Delhi and other cities; research by human right groups indicated the violence was orchestrated by Congress (I) party bosses. Immediately after the assassination, the Congress Parliamentary Board nominated Rajiv Gandhi as the leader of the CPP, and he was sworn in as prime minister. This selection was validated by the Indian electorate in late December 1984, as Rajiv won a massive victory in Lok Sabha elections, winning just under 50% of the vote and 79% of the seats contested.

The Gender Factor

Gender mattered for Indira Gandhi in complex and contradictory ways. On the surface, Mrs. Gandhi did not identify herself in gender terms, and she did little to advance the cause of gender equality. She seemed to operate as an "honorary male," many times asserting that she did not feel handicapped by being a woman: "As Prime Minister, I am not a woman. I am a human being" (Carras, 1979, p. 48; Fraser, 1978, pp. 307, 318). The Indian feminist journal *Manushi* asserted, "No woman could be more alienated from her sex than she is" (Manushi Collective, 1979-1980, p. 4). Mrs. Gandhi did not appoint any women to full cabinet rank or make any special effort to encourage women leaders, and during her tenure in office the conditions of the majority of Indian women worsened, as reflected in literacy and employment rates and the declining sex ratio (Bumiller, 1990, p. 164; Manushi Collective, 1979-1980, pp. 2-5).

On another level, however, Mrs. Gandhi's career, path to power, agenda, style of leadership, and overall performance can be seen as profoundly shaped by a patriarchal political system in which women in power "are there on men's terms and for their survival they have to forget that they are women, and that as women they are unequal" (Manushi Collective, 1979-1980, p. 5). Like Mrs. Gandhi, nearly all

Indian women in political office are relatives of prominent male politicians; they are members of political families that lack male members of the appropriate age or temperament to continue the family dynasty (Bumiller, 1990, pp. 151-153; Wolkowitz, 1987). As prime minister, Mrs. Gandhi continually encountered male hostility directed at her gender. The disrespect ranged from despair among some Indians over having a woman leader to sexist overtones in the contempt expressed by her critics, as in Salman Rushdie's referring to her as "the widow" in *Midnight's Children* (1980) or Pakistani President Yahya Khan's outburst during the Bangladesh conflict, "If that woman thinks she is going to cow me down, I refuse to take it" (quoted in Malhotra, 1989, pp. 137, 190).

Manushi argued, "To survive [women political leaders] must, on the one hand, make themselves like the stereotyped male—aggressive, competitive, ruthless, authoritarian—and on the other, continue to play the "good woman" role" (Manushi Collective, 1979-1980, p. 3). The male-defined rules of the political game worked against Mrs. Gandhi. In overthrowing them, she behaved in a ruthless and authoritarian manner. Many commentators have identified the above "male" characteristics with Mrs. Gandhi, but in interviews and behavior the "good woman" surfaced as well. She stressed that motherhood was the most important part of her life:

> To a mother, her children must always come first, because they depend on her in a very special way. The main problem in my life was, therefore, how to reconcile my public obligations with my responsibility towards my home and my children. When Rajiv and Sanjay were babies I did not like the idea of anyone else attending to their needs and I tried to do as much for them as I could. Later when they began school, I was careful to have my engagements during school hours so as to be free when the boys returned home. (Gandhi, 1980, p. 55)

Mrs. Gandhi always dressed modestly, covering her head with her sari, when she traveled within India. Her husband died when she was only 42, but she neither developed any other romantic attachments nor wanted any (Malhotra, 1989, pp. 184-189). Mrs. Gandhi's fishbowl existence precluded such liaisons, but gossip persisted throughout her time in office.

One instance in which Mrs. Gandhi did not play the good woman role was when she threw Maneka, Sanjay's widow, out of her home in March

1982, accusing her of being "a willing tool of my enemies" (Malhotra, 1989, p. 241). The nation had been entertained by "first family" intrigue since Sanjay's death, and Mrs. Gandhi came across as a shrew, with press photographs of Maneka's luggage dumped outside. Maneka retaliated by comparing her mother-in-law to the goddess Kali, "who drinks blood," and by forming a political party to oppose Congress (I). Arun Shourie (1983) commented, "The Great Mother image [was] nudged by the stereotype mother-in-law image" (p. 26).

To say that gender did not matter to Mrs. Gandhi herself and that she was victimized by it does not capture the complexity of gender relations for this woman leader, for Mrs. Gandhi also used powerful gender imagery in a purposeful manner. Sometimes she identified herself as mother of her country, as in a 1967 campaign speech to villagers: "My burden is manifold because scores of my family members are poverty stricken and I have to look after them" (quoted in Malhotra, 1989, p. 104). Motherhood also became intertwined with dynastic politics as Mrs. Gandhi groomed her sons to succeed her. Rajiv explained his decision to enter politics after Sanjay's death by saying, "Someone has to help Mummy" (quoted in Bobb, 1991, p. 30). One paradox of Indian civilization is the coexistence of traditions of female power alongside extremely patriarchal beliefs and practices. There are Hindu goddesses as well as gods, and several queens ruled after their husbands died. After the Bangladesh war, Mrs. Gandhi was hailed as the Hindu goddess Durga and worshipped as the incarnation of *shakti,* images that she manipulated when needed. A reporter described Mrs. Gandhi reviewing crowds from a balcony in Cochin during her comeback campaign in 1978: "She jammed a torch [flashlight] between her knees, directing the beam upwards to light her face and arms. She rotated the arms as if perfecting the dance of Lakshmi, Goddess of Wealth. . . . 'You've no idea how tiring is to be a goddess' " (Chatwin, 1989, p. 119).

Although Mrs. Gandhi played the game of patriarchal politics only too well, her legacy for feminists was not completely negative. She used gender imagery to empower herself, but she also became an image of women's power. Ela Bhatt, leader of the Self-Employed Women's Association of Ahmedabad, expressed the feeling in the following manner: "Consciously or unconsciously, every woman, I think, feels that if Indira Gandhi could be a prime minister of this country, then we all have opportunities" (quoted in Bumiller, 1990, p. 151).

Conclusions: Mrs. Gandhi's Performance

To what extent was Mrs. Gandhi able to achieve self-reliance for India and to solve domestic problems such as poverty and economic backwardness? In what ways did the constraints and opportunities inherent in the context in which she operated shape her strategies and performance in office? What consequences did her strategies have for Indian politics? How did gender figure in?

Contemporaries offer a split verdict on Mrs. Gandhi's performance. A survival strategy approach draws attention to the enormity of the challenges facing Mrs. Gandhi throughout her career and thus to the high level of political skill she demonstrated in gaining, maintaining, and regaining political power over an 18-year period. Although Mrs. Gandhi would have denied it, a central challenge she faced was that of operating in a male-dominated political system. Sometimes her survival rested on the destruction of male-defined institutions and norms, but she failed to create replacements. A survival strategy approach also draws attention to some of the destructive political consequences of the strategies she devised—political consequences that are playing out in the problems facing India in the 1990s.

There is widespread agreement that Mrs. Gandhi's greatest achievements were in foreign policy—maintaining India's self-reliance, strengthening the military, and helping India become the predominant power in South Asia. The business-oriented *India Today* noted that "foreign policy was to prove her greatest forte and the mark she finally left on the world stage exceeded even her own high expectations" (Bobb, 1984, p. 100). The left-intellectual *Economic and Political Weekly* concurred: "A considerable part of India's current stature is directly attributable to the nimbleness and sense of self-confidence with which Indira Gandhi had directed the nation's external relations" ("Indira Gandhi's Bequest," 1984, p. 1849).

Mrs. Gandhi's economic performance elicits mixed reviews. On the plus side, the green revolution eliminated famines and dependence on food aid, and bank nationalization made banking relevant to an underdeveloped country. While many commentators criticized economic policies that zigzagged in response to political calculations, India's economy continued to grow, albeit slowly, and the growth rate rose to 5% in 1984. On the minus side was the continued misery of half of the

Indian population in abject poverty and increasing disparities among regions and between rich and poor. *India Today* emphasized the central failure "to grasp the growth opportunities presented by a period when new countries emerged on the global economic scene as forces to be reckoned with. India was not among them" (Ninan, 1984, p. 107). *Economic and Political Weekly,* in contrast, emphasized inequality and corruption: "Socio-economic pronouncements . . . do not mean a thing in actuality, the apparatus of the State is all the time being manipulated for the sake of fractional minority of the population at the top of the social hierarchy . . . for ensuring the accumulation of private hoards" ("Indira Gandhi's Bequest," 1984, p. 1849).

Mrs. Gandhi's leadership style generates the harshest criticism for her contributions to political centralization and deinstitutionalization. Inder Malhotra (1989) has described the emergency as "the body blow to Indian democracy she chose to deliver and from which the Indian system has yet to recover fully" (p. 306). Malhotra and others have also faulted Mrs. Gandhi for polarizing Indian politics, for believing she was indispensable, and, most important, for destroying the Congress party. Some commentators have expressed admiration for the relationship Mrs. Gandhi developed with the Indian people, but also have acknowledged that she lacked the ability to follow through on her commitments. Rajni Kothari (1988) points out that she "captured the attention and loyalty of the Indian masses far more than the traditional radical left." He goes on to say: "The basic contradiction in Indira Gandhi's brand of populism . . . lay in the fact that whereas her appeal was to the rural masses and the poorer strata, the power structure at the centre on which she relied so much was essentially urban, upper middle class, bureaucratic and to not a small extent capitalist" (p. 2226).

The assessments of her contemporaries seem basically accurate, but most of them tend to underestimate the constraints facing Mrs. Gandhi—an international environment hostile to the Third World, domestic poverty and inequality, polarized citizens impatient with two decades of unfulfilled promises, as well as party political bosses and, of course, sexism. The class structure in a backward capitalist political economy further constrained Mrs. Gandhi's options. The party structure she inherited was not able to meet the challenges of the 1960s. Destroying the party was hardly a creative solution, but transforming it to represent the subordinate classes was beyond her capability. Male hostility to her independent action from her husband in the 1950s and from the party bosses during her first years as prime minister led her to distrust leaders she did not control. The conventional institutions through which political recruitment occurred and political leadership was exercised—English university life, Parliament, cabinet, Congress party—did not work very well for a woman, and so they were downplayed and disregarded. With limited room to maneuver, Mrs. Gandhi survived politically through populist appeals, centralization of power, and ad hoc improvisations. These in turn created policy zigzags and deinstitutionalization, and contributed toward the polarization of politics during her time in office.

The consequences of the survival strategies devised by Mrs. Gandhi appear extremely negative from the vantage point of the early 1990s. The Indian government faces violent secessionist movements in the Punjab and Kashmir; the level of violence among religious groups, castes, and classes is extremely high; politics remains corrupt; and the violence-plagued 1991 elections took the life of Rajiv Gandhi and resulted in a minority Congress government lacking in leaders of national stature. The contributions of aspects of Mrs. Gandhi's survival strategies can be seen in each of these problems—her political interference in Punjab and Kashmir politics, her frequent use of government repression, her use of communal appeals in the last years of her life, her ridding Congress of strong leaders, and, most important, the deinstitutionalization of the Congress party and corruption of political life more generally.

It does not seem necessary to focus on childhood insecurity to explain Mrs. Gandhi's urge to dominate the national scene and her sense of indispensability. Her experiences in childhood and as a young adult revolved almost completely around duty to the nation; this cause took her father away for long periods of her childhood, and it destroyed her marriage. No wonder the boundaries between her own interests and those of the nation were so blurred. The phrase coined by party president D. K. Barooah, "Indira is India, India is Indira," resonated in her (Rudolph & Rudolph, 1987, p. 135). In Mrs. Gandhi's will, written shortly before her death, she wrote, "No hate is dark enough to overshadow the extent of my love for my people and my country; no force is strong enough to divert me from my purpose and my endeavor to take this country forward" (quoted in Malhotra, 1989, pp. 307-308). As in her childhood, the public became private and the private became public. The Indian people were her children; members of her family were the only people capable of leading them.

Notes

1. For overviews of the Indian context, see Bardhan (1984, pp. 548-549), Frankel (1978, pp. 96-97, 548-549), and Hardgrave and Kochanek (1986, pp. 4-11).

2. For a discussion of succession politics, see Brecher (1966) and Frankel (1978, pp. 228-229, 240-245, 288-292).

3. The Lok Sabha (House of the People) is the directly elected lower house of Parliament.

4. The Defence of India Rules were preventive detention regulations authorized by the 1971 external emergency declared during the Bangladesh war, which was still in effect.

References

Andersen, W. K. (1982). India in 1981: Stronger political authority and social tension. *Asian Survey, 22*(2), 119-135.

Andersen, W. K. (1983). India in 1982: Domestic challenges and foreign policy successes. *Asian Survey, 23*(2), 111-122.

Banerjee, S. (1984). Contradictions with a purpose. *Economic and Political Weekly, 19*(48), 2028-2031.

Bardhan, P. (1984). *The political economy of development in India.* Oxford: Basil Blackwell.

Bhargava, A. (1988). Indian economy during Mrs. Gandhi's regime. In Y. K. Malik & D. K. Vajpeyi (Eds.), *India: The years of Indira Gandhi* (pp. 60-83). Leiden, Netherlands: E. J. Brill.

Bhatia, K. (1974). *Indira: A biography of Prime Minister Gandhi.* New York: Praeger.

Bobb, D. (1984, November 30). The Indira enigma. *India Today,* pp. 94-103.

Bobb, D. (1991, June 15). Ordeal of Prince Charming. *India Today,* pp. 30-39..

Brass, P. (1988). The Punjab crisis and the unity of India. In A. Kohli (Ed.), *India's democracy: An analysis of changing state-society relations* (pp. 169-213). Princeton, NJ: Princeton University Press.

Brecher, M. (1966). *Succession in India: A study in decision making.* London: Oxford University Press.

Bumiller, E. (1990). *May you be the mother of a hundred sons.* New York: Fawcett Columbine.

Carras, M. (1979). *Indira Gandhi in the crucible of leadership: A political biography.* Boston: Beacon.

Chadney, J. C. (1988). Family planning: India's Achilles' heel? In Y. K. Malik & D. K. Vajpeyi (Eds.), *India: The years of Indira Gandhi* (pp. 84-97). Leiden, Netherlands: E. J. Brill.

Chatwin, B. (1989, Spring). On the road with Mrs. Gandhi. *Granta, 26,* 107-130.

Cohen, S. P. (1988). The military and Indian democracy. In A. Kohli (Ed.), *India's democracy: An analysis of changing state-society relations* (pp. 99-143). Princeton, NJ: Princeton University Press.

Das Gupta, J. (1988). Ethnicity, democracy and development in India: Assam in a general perspective. In A. Kohli (Ed.), *India's democracy: An analysis of changing state-society relations* (pp. 144-168). Princeton, NJ: Princeton University Press.

Dutt, V. P. (1990). India and the super powers. In A. K. Damodaran & U. S. Bajpai (Eds.), *Indian foreign policy: The Indira Gandhi years* (pp. 23-42). New Delhi: Radiant.

Fallaci, O. (1976). *Interview with history* (J. Shepley, Trans.). New York: Liveright.

Frankel, F. R. (1978). *India's political economy, 1947-1977: The gradual revolution.* Princeton, NJ: Princeton University Press.

Fraser, A. (1988). *The warrior queens.* New York: Vintage.

Gandhi, I. (1980). *My truth* (E. Pouchpadass, Ed.). New York: Grove.

Gupta, A. (1989). The political economy of post-independent India: A review article. *Journal of Asian Studies, 48*(4), 787-797.

Hardgrave, R. L., Jr. (1984). India in 1983: New challenges, lost opportunities. *Asian Survey, 24*(2), 209-218.

Hardgrave, R. L., Jr. (1985). India in 1984: Confrontation, assassination, and succession. *Asian Survey, 25*(2), 131-144.

Hardgrave, R. L., Jr., & Kochanek, S. A. (1986). *India government and politics in a developing nation* (4th ed.). New York: Harcourt Brace Jovanovich.

Hart, H. C. (1976). Indira Gandhi: Determined not to be hurt. In H. C. Hart (Ed.), *Indira Gandhi's India: A political system reappraised* (pp. 241-273). Boulder, CO: Westview.

Hutheesing, K. N. (1969). *Dear to behold: An intimate portrait of Indira Gandhi.* London: Macmillan.

Indira Gandhi's bequest. (1984). *Economic and Political Weekly, 19*(44), 1849-1850.

Kapur, A. (1988). Indian security and defense policies under India Gandhi. In Y. K. Malik & D. K. Vajpeyi (Eds.), *India: The years of Indira Gandhi* (pp. 42-59). Leiden, Netherlands: E. J. Brill.

Kaviraj, S. (1986). Indira Gandhi and Indian politics. *Economic and Political Weekly, 21,* 1697-1708.

Kissinger, H. (1979). *White House years.* Boston: Little, Brown.

Kochanek, S. A. (1976). Mrs. Gandhi's pyramid: The new Congress. In H. C. Hart (Ed.), *Indira Gandhi's India: A political system reappraised* (pp. 93-124). Boulder, CO: Westview.

Kohli, A. (1989). Politics of economic liberalization in India. *World Development, 17*(3), 305-328.

Kothari, R. (1988). Integration and exclusion in Indian politics. *Economic and Political Weekly, 23*(43), 2223-2287.

Malhotra, I. (1989). *Indira Gandhi: A personal and political biography.* Boston: Northeastern University Press.

Malik, Y. K. (1988). Indira Gandhi: Personality, political power and party politics. In Y. K. Malik & D. K. Vajpeyi (Eds.), *India: The years of Indira Gandhi* (pp. 7-21). Leiden, Netherlands: E. J. Brill.

Manor, J. (1983). Anomie in Indian politics. *Economic and Political Weekly, 28*(19-21), 725-734.

Manor, J. (1988). Parties and the party system. In A. Kohli (Ed.), *India's democracy: An analysis of changing state-society relations* (pp. 62-98). Princeton, NJ: Princeton University Press.

Manushi Collective. (1979-1980, December-February). Our alarming silence: Women, politics and the recent elections. *Manushi, 4,* 2-6, 76.

Masani, Z. (1976). *Indira Gandhi: A biography.* New York: Thomas Y. Crowell.

Moraes, D. (1980). *Indira Gandhi.* Boston: Little, Brown.

Ninan, T. N. (1984, November 30). The zigzag march. *India Today* (pp. 104-107).

Norman, D. (1985). *Indira Gandhi: Letters to an American friend, 1950-1984.* New York: Harcourt Brace Jovanovich.

Puri, B. (1985). Era of Indira Gandhi. *Economic and Political Weekly, 20*(4), 148-150.

Richter, L. K. (1990-1991). Exploring theories of female leadership in South and Southeast Asia. *Pacific Affairs, 63*, 524-540.

Roy, A. (1984). The failure of Indira Gandhi. *Economic and Political Weekly, 19*(45), 1896-1897.

Rudolph, L. I., & Rudolph, S. H. (1987). *In pursuit of Lakshmi: The political economy of the Indian state.* Chicago: University of Chicago Press.

Rushdie, S. (1980). *Midnight's children.* New York: Alfred A. Knopf.

Rushdie, S. (1985). Introduction. In T. Ali, *An Indian dynasty: The story of the Nehru-Gandhi family* (pp. xi-xv). New York: G. P. Putnam's Sons.

Shourie, A. (1983). *Mrs. Gandhi's second reign.* New Delhi: Vikas.

Tharoor, S. (1982). *Reasons of state: Political development and India's foreign policy under Indira Gandhi 1966-1977.* New Delhi: Vikas.

Tully, M., & Jacob, S. (1985). *Amritsar: Mrs. Gandhi's last battle.* London: Jonathan Cape.

Weiner, M. (1978). *India at the polls: The parliamentary elections of 1977.* Washington, DC: American Enterprise Institute.

Wolkowitz, C. (1987). Controlling women's access to political power: A case study in Andhra Pradesh, India. In H. Afshar (Ed.), *Women, state, and ideology: Studies from Africa and Asia* (pp. 204-224). Albany: State University of New York Press.

6

Golda Meir

A Very Public Life

SETH THOMPSON

From her birth as Golda Mabovitch in Kiev, Russia, in May 1898 to her death in Jerusalem in December 1978, three themes run through the life of Golda Meir: her sense of Jewish identity, a conscious commitment to a public, political life, and gender.

Golda Meir's sense of being Jewish began in early childhood amid poverty, pogroms, and pervasive insecurity; it matured into an unshakable commitment to Zionism and an understanding that the individual Jew's fate and future were inextricably linked to the creation and maintenance of a Jewish state.[1] It led her to leave the relative comfort of the United States in the 1920s for the challenges of pioneering in Palestine, sustained her through hardship, and animated her political career.

The desire to participate actively in public purposes and life was first clearly expressed in Golda Meir's work with the Labor Zionist movement in the United States as organizer, orator, and fund-raiser, and shortly afterward her decision not only to be a pioneer in Palestine but also to join the fledgling kibbutz movement and live in a collective. When events and personal considerations prevented her from remaining on the kibbutz, she found a way to develop a much-needed job into the first step on the ladder to a formal political and governmental career.[2] In fact, some of the most emotionally trying moments in her life were the result of a preference for the public over the private.

AUTHOR'S NOTE: Excerpts from *My Life* by Golda Meir, © 1975 by G. P. Putnam. Used with permission of The Putnam Publishing Group.

While gender is an inescapable fact of social life, its impact and salience varies with time, setting, and a person's position in the life cycle. In Golda Meir's case, as the following analysis will show, while initially of great consequence, gender issues played a decreasing role over time. This is because Golda herself refused to be bound by conventional definitions, even when that refusal carried a heavy emotional price, and because she lived most of her life in a society that was in the midst of defining itself, heavily influenced by an egalitarian ideology, and acutely aware that it had an opportunity to serve as an example.[3]

This chapter offers an understanding of Golda Meir as person and national leader by dividing her life into four relatively distinct phases and commenting on the impact of the three themes outlined above during each stage. The concluding section discusses Golda's own perception and assessment of the relevance of gender to her career and then offers some summary reflections on the impact of gender on Golda Meir, the political leader and the person.

From Kiev to Palestine

The first eight years of Golda Mabovitch's life were spent in Kiev and Pinsk at a time when anti-Semitism raged and the Czarist order began to crumble. Her own memories of the period revolved around physical threats, economic insecurity and discrimination, and nascent political activity. "That gay, heart-warming, charming *shtetl* on whose roofs fiddlers eternally play sentimental music, has almost nothing to do with anything I remember" (Meir, 1975, p. 15). What she did remember was potential violence from Gentile neighbors; mounted cossack patrols; the fact that her father, a skilled carpenter, was barely able to eke out a living and was the victim of overt discrimination when cheated out of a moderately lucrative contract; and the involvement of her older sister in clandestine political discussion groups. When she was 6 years old, her father left the family to seek a new life in the United States; two years later, he sent for his wife and three daughters (Sheyna, four years Golda's senior; Golda; and Golda's younger sister, Clara) to join him in Milwaukee, Wisconsin.

In Milwaukee the family first survived and then attained a modicum of prosperity through the joint efforts of both parents. Her father continued to ply his trade as a carpenter and her mother provided a steady income by running a small grocery store (with Golda as an unwilling clerk before and after school). Golda quickly established herself as an exceptional student in elementary school, and tagged along with her older sister to informal meetings of a group of young Russian emigrés who vigorously debated politics, revolution, Zionism, and philosophy. (Indeed, Golda titled the second chapter of her autobiography "A Political Adolescence.")

She experienced her first political success as the main organizer and keynote speaker, at age 10, of a benefit show to raise money for her classmates who could not afford the nominal charge for textbooks. In hindsight, one can see patterns that would be repeated time and again: identification of a wrong that needed to be rectified, a focus on fundraising, diligent organizing and persuading (including talking the owner of a hall into renting it on the promise of payment after the event), and delivery of a major address ad lib.[4]

The end of Golda's grammar school career also brought to a head underlying conflicts with her parents. Her relationship with her parents was rarely easy. She clearly resented having to assist her mother in the shop (Meir, 1975, p. 32), she was strongly influenced by her older sister's political interests and activities (which had led Sheyna to break with her parents and move out), and (one suspects) success in school and as a leader among her peers had led her to see possibilities beyond the traditional and conventional fate of most young women of her generation and circumstances. The battle was joined over education: Golda's passionate desire to attend high school versus her parents' belief that further education was not only unnecessary but also dangerous to a young woman's marriage prospects. Her solution was to enroll in high school anyway and get a part-time job to secure economic independence.

Golda's autonomy was underscored when she accepted an invitation from her older sister to come to Denver, Colorado, where Sheyna was recuperating from a serious bout of tuberculosis. In Denver, Golda lived with Sheyna and her husband, experienced the difficulties of making a living at unskilled labor, and became an increasingly active member of a group of young Jewish intellectuals. It was at this point that she decided that the Labor Zionist movement, a blend of utopian socialist ideals and commitment to a Jewish state in Palestine, was her philosophical and emotional home. She also met Morris Myerson, who was profoundly disinterested in politics but keenly interested in art and music, areas in which Golda felt ignorant.

The sojourn in Denver was followed by a reconciliation with her family and return to Milwaukee, where Golda finished high school (and started training as a teacher), married Morris Myerson in 1917, and became increasingly publicly active in the Zionist movement. Her political role developed; she went from being one of several organizers and sidewalk orators to being the person who was asked to accept responsibility for raising the funds to keep a struggling party newspaper going.

The fact that this meant extensive travel throughout the upper Midwest and into Canada, that only months after her wedding Golda was packing her bags and leaving for weeks or months at a time, seemed to her merely a necessary means to a good end. Her father had a more conventional reaction—fury. Golda's autobiography is unclear about her new husband's feelings in this matter; from the perspective of 50 years later, she first portrayed him as understanding that she could not turn down the movement, then recognized that there must have been some significant pain (Meir, 1975, pp. 66-67). She had also decided to leave for Palestine at the first opportunity (Meir, 1975, pp. 65-67). She would have to wait until the war ended and a tenuous civil order was established by the mandatory authorities in Palestine, but the decision was irrevocable and, she felt, inevitable. The opportunity came in 1921 and, leaving friends and most of her family behind, she joined a small band of American Jews on a difficult voyage to the Middle East.[5]

Intellectual, Political, and Social Foundations

The first 23 years of Golda Meir's life established the themes and directions that would dominate the next 57. Her social and intellectual life revolved around the Jewish communities in Russia, Milwaukee, and Denver. She felt little attachment to the Russia of her childhood and soon came to regard the United States as a way station on the route to Palestine. In her mind, the logic was as simple as it was elegant: To be Jewish is to be a Zionist and to be a Zionist is to participate in the creation of the Jewish state in Palestine. It was that sense of identity and purpose that gave meaning and direction to her life and career, and she clung to it even at the cost of physical and emotional distress.

Golda's involvement with the movement honed her political skills and gave her an arena in which to use them. She established a reputation as an effective speaker before medium-sized to large groups, and as a persuasive advocate in more intimate settings. Her success flowed in part from facility with language (initially English and Yiddish, adding Hebrew later in life); in part from a straightforward, powerfully simple logical presentation; in part from the depth and sincerity of her convictions (and their uncomplicated nature); and in part from her ability to speak extemporaneously.[6] She also demonstrated her ability to direct and organize other people. More important, she took for granted that public purposes had priority over private desires, that one's identity and fate as an individual were inseparable from the larger Zionist project of creating a setting where Jews could control their identity and fate as a people. Reflecting on the earliest days of her marriage, when she was traveling extensively, Golda wrote, "Whenever I was out of town, I wrote long letters to him, but they tended to be more about the meeting I had just addressed or the one I was about to address, the situation in Palestine or the movement than about us or our relationship" (Meir, 1975, p. 67).

The fact that she was female also had a significant impact on this first quarter of Golda's life. She grew up in a family where the father was well intentioned but somewhat distant and did not appear able to cope well with the external world. It was her mother who organized things, who opened a store only weeks after arriving in the United States and before she knew any English, let alone anything of the finer points of retailing. Golda's education was important to her, but much less so to her parents. Their resistance to her attending high school was explicitly based on beliefs about what was necessary and proper to enhance the marriage prospects of a young lady. Inevitably, given the time and place, much of what Golda did conflicted with conventional expectations: sidewalk oratory on behalf of a "radical" political movement, the grand project of emigrating to Palestine, the stint as traveling fund-raiser and salesperson for a Zionist newspaper. To some extent, political activity of this sort is unusual enough to arouse unease and opposition from many parents, regardless of the gender of the offspring. But unquestionably it was far more difficult to accept in a daughter than in a son. The struggle to establish an autonomous self and gain the freedom to do what she felt she must was harder for Golda precisely because she was female.

Pioneering in Palestine

The 12 years between her arrival in Palestine and Golda's accession to a position in the emerging Zionist political elite can be seen as laying the foundation for the rest of her life. The centrality of Jewish and Zionist identity to Golda's self-definition and self-assessment was the justification for the hardships and trials of the period. After laconically describing some of the difficulties of finding sufficient food and shelter in the first days in Tel Aviv, Golda noted:

> There were all kinds of compensations for these small hardships, like walking down the street on our first Friday in Tel Aviv and feeling that life could hold no greater joy for me than to be where I was—in the only all-Jewish town in the world. . . . only here could Jews be masters, not victims of their fate. So it was not surprising . . . I was profoundly happy. (Meir, 1975, p. 81)

It was Golda who insisted on tackling the rigors of life in a collective enterprise to carve a farming community out of wasteland. She felt compelled to prove herself to the other members, not so much because she was a woman but because she was the "American girl" and there were suspicions that she was thus too soft and too pampered to really take it (Meir, 1975, pp. 87-88). But she not only demonstrated her ability to work as hard as anyone, she also eagerly embraced the communal and collective life, living with people "who debated everything so thoroughly and with such intensity and who took social problems so seriously" (Meir, 1975, p. 93). But no matter how much she enjoyed the discussions and debates, Golda evinced an important aspect of her public career: a penchant for seeing that something should be done and doing it, without much regard for the ideological niceties.

The kibbutz movement's emphasis on equality encouraged women to tackle the work of the fields and led many to see work in the communal kitchen as retrograde. Golda had no doubts about equality. But she did not define kitchen work and the quality of the communal meals as an ideological issue. To her there were only simple practical questions: Why shouldn't even simple food be properly cooked? Why was it more virtuous to drink out of cracked and rusting enamel cups instead of clean glasses? Why shouldn't the communal table be more or less properly set? And so, in the face of objections from some of the other women, she reorganized the kitchen (Meir, 1975, p. 89). That style of leadership—directive, problem oriented, somewhat simple and unreflective—would remain throughout her career.

The kibbutz experience also brought to a head the conflict between the public and private dimensions of Golda's life. The backbreaking labor that she gladly accepted and even savored as her contribution to creating the Jewish homeland was almost unbearably tedious to her husband, who had never shared her Zionist convictions and was frequently ill. Where she relished the give and take of collective life, he felt acutely the lack of privacy. And as Golda dreamed of raising children and living her life in a Jewish socialist polity, Morris dreamed of a traditional family, in which the parents, not the entire community, were responsible for the children. After two years of increasing strain between them and serious deterioration in his health, Golda abandoned the struggle, and she and Morris left the kibbutz for Tel Aviv and then Jerusalem.

The period between 1923 and 1928 was extremely difficult. Golda and her husband, like most of the other Jewish immigrants, were poor—jobs were hard to find and tenuous—and they made do in a small, two-room apartment. Life became even more constrained with the birth of a daughter and then a son. For Golda, the physical hardships were compounded by the depressing sense that she was sitting on the sidelines and missing the struggle to create a new society. The hard life of the kibbutz had a larger political meaning; poverty in Jerusalem was strictly private (Meir, 1975, p. 102).

Entry Level for a Political Career

The physical aspects of Golda's life did not get easier in 1928 when she accepted a position as secretary of the Women's Labor Council of the Histadrut,[7] but the move restored her fundamental sense of participating in the birth of the Jewish state and creation of a new society, and revitalized her sense that the difficulties of the moment had meaning and purpose. The Histadrut position was pivotal in Golda's public and personal lives. It gave her entrée to the merging political elite; from that point on she would play a more and more prominent role in the emergence of Israel and the internal politics of the left. The position also brought the conflict between the private roles of wife and mother and her desires for a public life into stark relief. The job with the Women's Labor Council meant moving from Jerusalem to Tel Aviv, as well as substantial travel throughout Palestine and even abroad. It was difficult for Morris, who had very traditional expectations and values, to accept the fact that his wife was going back to work. It soon proved impossible for him to live with a woman whose first interest was her public life and who would be gone much of the time. The couple separated amicably, Golda and the children moving to Tel Aviv and Morris remaining in Jerusalem. He visited frequently on the weekends, and they remained friends until his death in 1951.

In Golda's mind, the marriage had failed well before she took the job; the separation was simply an admission of the fact. Her explanation is confined to the personal level:

> The tragedy was not that Morris didn't understand me, but, on the contrary, that he understood me only too well and felt that he couldn't make me over or change me. I had to be what I was, and what I was made it impossible for him to have the sort of wife he wanted and needed. So he didn't discourage me from going back to work, although he knew what it really meant. (Meir, 1975, p. 112)

Golda did not recognize that their individual differences were problematic precisely because they were contrary to expectations for gender roles. A man who felt a public career was necessary, who could not be happy with purely private pursuits, married to a woman with traditional values, would not be faced with a choice between career and relationship. This is the clearest and most dramatic instance of the impact of gender on Golda Meir's life and career.

Gender was also directly linked to her job. Given the egalitarian strain in Zionist ideology (and perhaps the somewhat lower priority and salience of specifically "women's" work), it was nearly inevitable that the secretary of the Women's Council be female. The Women's Labor Council was involved in a variety of activities, but the major emphasis was on vocational training for the hundreds of young women who were arriving in Palestine without any relevant job or agricultural skills, at a time "when the idea that women should be trained for anything, let alone agriculture, was still considered absurd by most people" (Meir, 1975, p. 113).

Golda succeeded at the job and gained a reputation for effectiveness because the position gave her an opportunity to tackle problems that required her particular skills: concentrating on "practical" rather than theoretical issues, persuasively representing her organization within the emerging elite in Palestine, and traveling abroad as a persuasive representative of Jews in Palestine. Her sheer physical stamina and capacity for long hours of sustained work were obviously important ingredients in her success.

Throughout her autobiography, Golda Meir portrays herself as someone who simply did what was needed and accepted jobs as they were offered. She does not reflect on her motives deeply and does not even hint at ambition. It is impossible to determine whether she saw this position as a potential first step to something bigger and better. On the face of it, this was not a position of great power or opportunity for national prominence. If someone other than Golda Meir had become responsible for "women's" matters within Histadrut, there is no reason to assume that person would have become a member of the elite, let alone cabinet minister or prime minister. But, consciously or not, Golda made the job into a launching platform.

Golda's First Public Career

Golda Meir's career in national politics can be divided into two logical segments. Her first career ran from 1928 to 1968 and includes her entry into the political elite, role in the struggle for independence, critical contribution as fund-raiser abroad, service as ambassador and then cabinet minister, and nongovernmental role as party elder and coalition builder. The first period ends with her presumptive retirement from public life at age 70 in 1968. It includes the creation of the State of Israel and three wars. Rather than attempt a comprehensive review of the events and achievements of 40 tumultuous years, I will highlight those that illustrate the impact of gender, Jewish identity, and commitment to a political life on Golda Meir's life and career.

Golda had been suspect in the eyes of some members of her kibbutz because she was "the American girl." In her new role in the Histadrut, her years in Milwaukee and command of English were distinct advantages. She spent a substantial amount of time in the 1930s traveling in the United States and Great Britain, building support and raising funds for the Jewish settlers in Palestine in general and Histadrut programs in particular. Golda was, in many ways, an obvious choice for a person to send abroad. She had well-developed speaking skills and considerable experience in persuading groups and public meetings, and had been involved in successful fund-raising even before she came to Palestine. She was quite willing to travel, even when that meant leaving her two youngsters with her sister. Although the language of her early childhood was Yiddish, she had a native speaker's fluency in English as well. At the same time, it may not be completely off the mark to speculate that she was "available" for extensive foreign travel that would take her out of Palestine for months at a time because she was a woman and responsible for "women's issues" within the Histadrut, and hence perceived as more easily spared. The pattern was to be repeated in 1948.

In addition to direct responsibility for the Women's Council and her foreign travels, Golda was active in the formation of the Mapai political party and began to move into the ranks of the political elite. Her work was rewarded with a series of promotions, culminating in a 1946 appointment as head of the Political Bureau of the Jewish Agency in Jerusalem.[8] During this period, Golda received national attention as a feisty and defiant witness in a British trial against two men accused of smuggling arms to the Haganah (the official military wing of the Jewish Agency) and as one of the few members of the elite who was neither arrested nor forced into hiding by the British crackdown in June 1946.[9]

By 1947 Golda was responsible for settling the new immigrants arriving from Europe (and deeply involved in the increasingly bitter conflict with British authorities over the entry of Jews, many survivors of Nazi concentration camps). Late in 1947 it was decided that the demands of military security for Jews in the face of violent local opposition to the United Nations partition plan and defense against Arab attacks on the Jewish state when it did emerge required raising a large amount of money rapidly. Previous appeals to foreign Jewish communities had been couched in terms of hundreds of thousands of dollars donated in the course of a year; now the leadership felt that millions were needed immediately.

Golda Meir was sent. (David Ben-Gurion, the overarching and, at times, overbearing figure in the creation of Israel, initially insisted that he was the only person who could carry out the project. But a meeting of the leadership declared it necessary that he stay in Palestine and readily accepted Golda's offer to leave for the United States.) It was a continuation of what she had been doing for several years, but at a much larger order of magnitude. In six weeks of nonstop touring and talking, Golda Meir raised $50 million.[10] After her return, she participated in negotiations surrounding the drafting of the Israeli constitution and the decision on when to declare the state. Clear evidence of her elite status is the fact that she was one of 200 people invited to participate in the signing of the proclamation of the State of Israel.

It was also in 1947 that Golda Meir was the Jewish Agency's secret emissary to King Abdullah of Transjordan (grandfather of the present King Hussein of Jordan). Abdullah, by no means secure on his throne, had little to gain from war with Israel when the British left, and the Israelis were certainly willing to explore any avenue to delete the well-armed and -trained Arab Legion from the military equation. The result was two almost surreal sessions, with Golda and a colleague disguised as an Arab couple slipping into Jordanian territory to meet with the king. In Golda's telling, there was a moment when Abdullah seemed to have agreed to refrain from joining an Egyptian-Syrian-Iraqi assault, but in the end he was unable to resist the call to join the Arab armies besieging Israel, and the midnight meetings were relegated to historical marginalia.

The Ambassador

No sooner had Golda's signature dried on the declaration of independence than she was leaving the country for a fund-raising tour of the United States. This time she raised $75 million in a matter of weeks. Instead of returning to Israel, Golda was notified that she had just been appointed the first Israeli ambassador to Moscow.

After a year in the Soviet Union she finally returned to Israel to begin a seven-year tenure as minister of labor. Two major factors underlay Golda's selection for the labor portfolio. Her previous career in the Histadrut meant that she was familiar with both the issues and the key players, and the developing pattern of relations between Israel and the USSR did not require a high-profile ambassador. Her first major challenge was the construction of housing and infrastructure for the hundreds of thousands of Jews from Europe and elsewhere in the Middle East who were flocking to Israel. Golda Meir was ideally suited to the challenge of designing and building cheap, simple housing that would allow the new immigrants rapidly to leave the transit camps, with their primitive facilities and multifamily tents. When the costs quickly grew far too large to be accommodated by the national budget, she had the skill and experience to take to the road and raise the money in the United States from private donations and bond sales.

During this period, Golda was a candidate in a contested election for the first time.[11] She ran for mayor of Jerusalem but was denied election by the votes of two representatives of religious parties on the town council, explicitly because of her gender. Twenty years later, Golda followed a rather matter-of-fact account of the incident in her autobiography (even noting that it was fortunate for her because she could then stay in the Labor Ministry) with a sharp denunciation of the two individuals and a strong protest at the blatant injustice. She described herself as "enraged" at the time; the hurt was still very deeply felt (Meir, 1975, pp. 281-282).

From Labor to Foreign Affairs

In early 1956, David Ben-Gurion reshuffled his cabinet to remove Moshe Sharet from the Foreign Ministry and replace him with Golda Meir. In addition to a personal and political dispute between the two men, Sharet was too reluctant to strike back with military force after each guerrilla incursion from Egypt or Jordan and argued vigorously against what he felt was an overly rigid, hard-line policy toward Israel's neighbors. Golda was hardly open to that charge and was an active participant in the planning for the joint Israeli, French, and British attack on Egypt in October 1956. She quickly earned a reputation at the United Nations and elsewhere for taking uncompromising positions and for her resistance to any concessions in the negotiations for a cease-fire and disengagement agreement after Israel had pushed the Egyptians out of the Sinai peninsula. However, the British and French assault on Cairo and attempt to land at the canal were withdrawn under heavy pressure from the United States, the Soviet Union, and most of world opinion.

For the next nine years, Foreign Minister Golda Meir would be Israel's most public voice in world politics. She earned a reputation for two things in particular: a confrontational style and staunch line in dealing with the Arab-Israeli conflict, and an active campaign to develop close ties with the emerging nations of the Third World. She traveled extensively, particularly in Africa, and was the spearhead of a series of Israeli initiatives to transfer the lessons learned in nation building in Palestine to Africa and Asia. In addition to offers of technical assistance, she brought her no-nonsense, practical, and unassuming personal style to her hosts. She genuinely enjoyed meeting common people and seemed particularly adept at establishing rapport with the women and children of small villages.

In 1965 Golda could look back on a political career that featured increasingly important leadership positions, important contributions to settling hundreds of thousands of new Israelis, an extensive range of contacts and quiet cooperative efforts between Israel and the nonaligned states of Asia and Africa, a number of memorable confrontations with Arab and other delegations at the United Nations, and an important role in creating and maintaining a political party embodying the Labor Zionist principles she had first embraced as a young adult in Milwaukee. Her active life and frequent travels were taking a toll on her health and stamina, she felt she was missing the joys of quiet reflection and her grandchildren, and she decided the time had come to retire from active cabinet service.

On a speculative note, it may also be that Golda realized that the foreign ministry would be the summit of her political career. Ben-Gurion was clearly nearing the end of his remarkable role as the most dominant force in Israeli political life and had already anointed Levi Eshkol as his successor, and there were several powerful figures waiting in the wings: Dayan, Allon, Gallili, et al. If Golda ever entertained thoughts of the top job, it was not a likely prospect any longer.[12]

Of course, as she put it, she did not intend to retire to a "political nunnery." After less than a year, she returned to public life at the request of Ben-Gurion and others to become head of the Mapai party and to rebuild the labor coalition.[13] Golda was available for the job for three primary reasons. Her absence from day-to-day political life meant she was not tied to any of the personalized factions that had formed around several powerful individuals jockeying for position in the cabinet. Her political philosophy was a rather uncomplicated embrace of the basic principles of socialist Zionism and with little concern for the nuances of philosophy and ideological distinctions that exerted a centrifugal force among the parties in the coalition. And, as she had repeatedly demonstrated, she could mount extremely persuasive appeals for cooperation and action.

As party head but without a cabinet portfolio, Golda Meir played a relatively modest role in the discussions and planning during early 1967 and was not directly involved in the central decisions surrounding the Six-Day War of June 1967 or the protracted negotiations at the United Nations, in Washington, and elsewhere in its aftermath. But she was clearly supportive of the decision to initiate military action once it appeared to Israel that war was inevitable, shared the exultation at the entry of Jews into East Jerusalem, and endorsed the decision to retain control of the West Bank, Gaza Strip, and Golan Heights, pending formal negotiations with Jordan, Syria, and Egypt.

By early 1968, Golda had completed the task of forging a workable coalition and creating the Labor Alignment and had turned 70.[14] This time she retired and meant it—or so she thought.

The Prime Minister

Golda Meir's retirement lasted slightly more than a year. In February 1970, Levi Eshkol, Israel's prime minister, suffered a fatal heart attack. Israel was in the midst of what had become known as the War of Attrition, with a constant low level of armed clashes between Israeli and Egyptian air and ground forces at the Suez canal and Syrian forces in the Golan. The Labor Alignment threatened to split along the lines of the personal and political rivalry between Moshe Dayan and Yigal Allon. Levi Eshkol had been forced to include the leadership of several key right-wing parties (including Menachem Begin) in his governing coalition. A number of individuals and factions settled on Golda as an interim prime minister until parliamentary elections could be held, with the potential of realigning the factional balance of power.

Golda became prime minister in March 1970, selected by a party caucus instead of national elections, saddled with the assumption that she was merely a caretaker, facing a cabinet representing an un-manageably diverse political constellation, with the level of violence between Israeli and Egyptian forces at Suez escalating, and the Israeli economy reeling under the strain of enormous defense expenditures and the continued mobilization of a sizable number of reservists. Her response was action: negotiations with the Nixon administration for direct aid, with the purchase of Phantom jets on concessionary terms as a first priority, and a high-profile visit to Washington; attempts to control the inflationary spiral by actively discouraging strikes and wage hikes; and continuing conflict with the Begin forces over the issue of making *any* concession to the United States for the sake of getting aid.

The actions and initiatives did not immediately solve the problems. The trip to Washington yielded private assurances but not public an-nouncement of Phantom jets or other weapons; the economy continued to worsen; the confrontation along the Suez continued to escalate and Russian advisers began to play a larger role.

As national elections approached in October 1970, the only obvious change in the Israeli political landscape was the fact that Golda Meir had become the central figure. She was no longer an interim figure selected by party leaders and slated to return to retirement as soon as the major contenders sorted things out; she was the prime minister and the unquestioned choice to lead her party into the elections. The elec-tions resulted, as usual, in a divided outcome, with Golda's party falling 5 seats short of an absolute majority in the 120-member Knesset. But between her personal popularity and prominence and the size of her parliamentary bloc, it was obvious that she would form the next gov-ernment. That government included representatives of the right wing, including Begin. A measure of Golda's political strength is the fact that when the Begin forces left the cabinet some months later after a confrontation over strategy in dealing with the Nixon administration, she was easily able to replace them with other parties and strengthen her support in the Knesset.

Israeli foreign policy under Golda Meir was marked by increasingly close ties with Washington;[15] a cease-fire along Suez that silenced the guns temporarily; a consistent demand that Egypt, Jordan, and Syria agree to face-to-face negotiations with Israel and rejection of any other mode of negotiations; and an end to most of Israel's ties to Africa and Asia.[16] In tone and content, it was little different from the policies earlier governments had adopted and Golda had pursued as foreign minister.

Domestic problems proved no more tractable. The economy did not improve, inflation soared (as it did in much of the world, although more steeply in Israel), and tensions between religious and secular Israelis and between "European" and "Oriental" Jews, and the more general tensions that ultimately were to lead to the replacement of the founding Zionist establishment by a deeply divided elite, continued to grow.[17]

The pivotal event of Golda Meir's career as head of the government was the war that erupted on October 6, 1973.[18] The Soviet Union had rearmed both Egypt and Syria after the Six-Day War and the Egyptians in particular had embarked on a massive training program to remedy the gross deficiencies of their combat units. Faced with Israeli fortification along the Suez canal (the Bar-Lev line), the Egyptians developed a plan to outflank the positions by launching an amphibious assault. Israeli intelligence was correct in May when it discounted data suggesting military conflict was imminent. But assessments in September ignored or misinterpreted evidence that political and military preparations for a major offensive were well under way. Egypt attacked across the Suez and drove up the Sinai peninsula; Syria simultaneously launched an attack from the Golan Heights that nearly broke through the second line of Israeli defenses. There was no triumphant six-day rout; Israeli forces retreated and suffered heavy casualties.[19] The tide of battle did not turn until an American resupply program took effect. The end of fighting led to a period of intense negotiations, brokered by Henry Kissinger and Richard Nixon, leading to the disengagement of the combatants and a partial Israeli withdrawal from Sinai.

The war was traumatic for Israelis. The myth of military invincibility was profoundly shaken. The Egyptian military showed a capacity for battlefield coordination and mastery of modern weaponry that was a sharp contrast to the ineptitude of 1967. The complacent trust that Israeli technological superiority would easily offset the huge difference in human resources was radically undermined. Not since 1948 had there been such a serious threat of military defeat.

There was an immediate search for understanding and responsibility. Attention and accusations focused on Moshe Dayan as minister of defense, the army's chief of staff and senior generals, and the intelligence establishment, who were blamed for allowing Israel to be surprised. Golda was not directly blamed. She was seen as a victim of the military and intelligence officers who failed to foresee the attack. Her decision not to mobilize the reserves and launch a preemptive strike on October 5 was attributed to tragically flawed advice. During the fighting itself, she followed the precedent of other prime ministers in wartime of allowing the military staff and field commanders to run the war.

Parliamentary elections in December produced little change in the Knesset and returned Golda to office, but the fallout from the war was only beginning. The pressure on Dayan to resign as defense minister and on key military and intelligence officers to step down was overwhelming. The public mood was bleak, the domestic dilemmas facing the country were even less tractable than before the war, and there were intense and difficult negotiations with the United States as Kissinger and Nixon became the key players in efforts to construct a postwar settlement that would meet Israeli needs for security and Arab demands for return of territory.

By April 1975, Golda had had enough and announced her irrevocable decision to resign. The disengagement agreement that Kissinger put together was in place and the immediate security problems seemed manageable. It was a good moment to leave. On June 4, as the disengagement agreement was being implemented and Israeli prisoners were coming home from Egypt and Syria, Golda Meir became a private citizen. The last three years of her life were spent in retirement with her grandchildren and family; she died in December 1978 of leukemia.

She was replaced as prime minister by Yitzhak Rabin, whose brief tenure was marked by the continuing demise of the labor alignment and the emergence of the right-wing Likud group headed by Menachem Begin, who came to power in 1976, effectively ending some 50 years of dominance by the Zionist left. The power of the Labor Zionist movement and the founding generation in Israeli politics had been eroding for some time. The original elite was aging and passing from the scene; the national agenda was changing, with new issues replacing the challenges of the first 25 years; and the old ideological consensus was not automatically shared by younger Israelis, particularly the

Sephardim.[20] The fact that Israel was caught by surprise by the Arabs
and suffered serious initial setbacks in the Yom Kippur War was traumatic for most Israelis and sharply underscored the image of Labor
politicians as a tired old elite that had lost the will and ability to lead.[21]

An Evaluation

As prime minister, Golda Meir dealt with essentially the same issues
with the same approaches that marked her entire career. Her record of
achievement in coping with domestic policy during her five years in
office is minimal. The economy worsened and continued to decline until
a combination of the changes instituted by the Begin government and
substantially increased U.S. aid in the late 1970s allowed inflation to
ease and growth to resume. With the advantage of historical perspective, it seems clear that there was little Golda or her government could
have done to make much difference at the time. The religious/secular
cleavage remains a fact of Israeli political life; if anything, it is today
a more prominent dimension than in the past. The gap in standards of
living, education, and political orientation between Ashkenazim (Jews
whose roots are in Europe) and Sephardim remains; the political gap
has grown even as the material differences have narrowed.

Conflict with the Arabs and war dominated the agenda during Golda's
tenure, just as they had throughout much of her earlier career. Her
position on the use of force and her understanding of the Arab-Israeli
conflict were not qualitatively different from the perspectives of her
peers. Some of the elite were a little more hawkish, some a little more
dovish and willing to search for compromise, but Golda fit solidly in
the mainstream.

Prime Minister Meir drew her political strength from her ability to
maintain a coalition of generally socialist parties in the Knesset. While
she was initially chosen as a caretaker prime minister until the next
election, Golda was able to use the skills and political relationships
developed during her years of public service to build her own political
base. She had revitalized the Mapai party during her service as chair,
and many Knesset members owed their seats to her. Her long career in
government meant that she knew many parliamentarians personally and
could call in old debts. And her grandmotherly image and unpretentious
personal style proved immensely popular with Israelis (Peretz, 1979,
pp. 97-100).

Golda changed more than the traditional ban on smoking in cabinet meetings during her years as prime minister. She reorganized the work of the cabinet by assigning specific issues to subcommittees to work out the details and formulate recommendations. That left the full cabinet free to debate basic policy issues and deal with competing recommendations for action.

More important, she expanded the pattern of informal consultation and decision making that had been a prominent feature of every prior Israeli government. Golda would frequently invite a select group of cabinet members, her closest political allies and trusted advisers, to meet in her home to discuss and work out major issues. These meetings were often held on Saturday, the day before the regularly scheduled Sunday cabinet meeting and, more often than not, when the full cabinet met it was to ratify what had been decided the night before. The participants in the informal meetings were quickly dubbed the "kitchen cabinet," which was often literally true, as they gathered around the kitchen table. Golda would contribute to the informal domesticity by making and pouring the coffee or tea and, perhaps, baking cookies. But the tone and setting did not obscure the fact that this was Golda Meir's meeting. She set the agenda, she invited the participants, she decided when a consensus had emerged, and she announced the decisions.[22]

Golda Meir was a strong, self-confident person with few doubts about her abilities or the correctness of her positions. She had a high tolerance for discussion but a very low tolerance for explicit disagreement (Elizur & Salpeter, 1973, p. 34).

Golda Meir and Gender

Golda Meir's career seems to have been shaped primarily by the interaction between her personal attributes—high energy, preference for concrete problem solving over reflection or ideology, skills as speaker and fund-raiser—and the political environment. Aside from the mayoral election lost because of explicit bias on the part of religious parties, gender appears to have played a secondary role in shaping Golda's public career. There are two major considerations supporting this conclusion.

First of all, Golda Meir's public career took place in extraordinary times: the pioneering Zionist period, then the struggle for statehood, followed by life in a political system in which all other concerns were periodically swept aside in the face of a direct military threat. The recurrent crisis periods, when the question of physical survival was overwhelming, led to a powerful sense of shared experience and common purpose that helped override personal differences. In the aftermath of the Six-Day War, the grip of socialist-inspired Zionists on Israeli political life seriously weakened and the more conservative opposition, led by Menachem Begin, began to close in on power. Several profound divisions emerged, and Israel has not enjoyed sustained periods of consensus since. But by the time the founding generation began to lose its unquestioned authority, Golda was already at the peak of her career. Her membership in the generation of pioneers and heroes and her distinguished public career left her poised (although she did not know it) for accession to the ultimate position.

Second, the situation and experiences of Golda's generation were reinforced by an explicit commitment to equality on the part of the early Zionist movement. The members of Golda's generation were people who came to a new country from old lands and old societies. They certainly brought a great deal of cultural baggage along, but the shared consciousness of creating a new society and becoming new people reduced the impact of preexisting biases and unexamined assumptions. From the self-conscious discussions and debates of the kibbutz movement to the self-proclaimed principles of government,[23] the normative goal was equality. That by itself was probably not enough to overcome bias, but it likely inhibited overtly biased actions.[24]

As foreign minister, Golda Meir was quite ready to use force against Egypt in 1956, with or without the cooperation of the French and English; she was strongly supportive of Israel's actions in the Six-Day War of June 1967, although she was not then in the government. When she left retirement to become prime minister she was faced with the challenges of the traumatic Yom Kippur War of October 1973. The decision not to preempt reflected calculations of the reactions from the United States and other sources of support for Israel, as well as intelligence estimates. It was not a generalized reluctance to resort to military means. Golda was an outspoken and assertive defender of Israel's positions in the United Nations, and was consistently unwilling to make the first concession.

As she wrote her autobiography in 1975, Golda tried to understand Arab motives for the 1948 assault on Israel and the subsequent enduring conflict and recurrent wars. She found her enemies unfathomable. This passage is worth quoting at length, not only because it illustrates the conceptual framework she applied to the central foreign policy facing Israel, but because it captures the style and flavor of her approach.

> It has never ceased to astonish me that the Arab states have been so eager to go to war against us. Almost from the very beginning of Zionist settlement until today they have been consumed by hatred for us. The only possible explanation—and it is a ridiculous one—is that they simply cannot bear our presence or forgive us for existing, and I find it hard to believe that the leaders of *all* the Arab states are and always have been so hopelessly primitive in their thinking.
>
> On the other hand, what have we ever done to threaten the Arab states? True, we have not stood in line to return territory we won in wars they started, but territory, after all, has never been what Arab aggression is all about—and in 1948 it was certainly not a need for more land that drove the Egyptians northward in hope of reaching and destroying Tel Aviv and Jewish Jerusalem. So what was it? An overpowering irrational urge to eliminate us physically? Fear of the progress we might introduce in the Middle East? A distaste for Western Civilization? Who knows? Whatever it was, it has lasted—but then so have we—and the solution will probably not be found for many years, although I have no doubt that the time will come when the Arab states will accept us—as we are and for what we are. In a nutshell, peace is—and always has been—dependent entirely on only one thing: The Arab leaders must acquiesce in our being here. (Meir, 1975, p. 232)

There may be a temptation to attribute "toughness" and "intransigence" to the real or imagined pressure on a woman to overcome suspicions that she is "too soft." [25] It is impossible to rule that hypothesis out completely, but there is compelling evidence for a more straightforward hypothesis that Golda Meir's stance toward Israel's Arab adversaries was born out of her understanding that Jews lived in a dangerous world and must rely on themselves alone for survival, and a rather simplistic cognitive style that saw issues in stark good versus evil terms. [26]

That Golda's account of her childhood in Russia begins with two frightening incidents—a near-miss encounter with cossacks galloping down an alleyway over the heads of small children, and the fearful preparations her father tried to make against violence from his Gentile neighbors—seems to underline her own sense that Jews are threatened. She returns to the theme at the very end of her memoir, reflecting on the trials of a small state in a "harsh, selfish, materialistic" world in which great powers are susceptible to "blackmail" and survival ultimately depends on self-defense (Meir, 1975, p. 460).

Golda's autobiography and published speeches reflect a relatively uncomplicated view of the world. The autobiography has few purely reflective passages and little speculation on alternative explanations. Her writing is devoid of rhetorical flourishes, nuances, or asides; the judgments of people and events are clear and unambiguous. She notes the contrast between her approach to issues with that of the professional diplomats she inherited when she became foreign minister. "Many of the more senior ambassadors and officials had been educated at British universities, and their particular brand of intellectual sophistication . . . was not always my cup of tea" (Meir, 1975, p. 292). The passage seems to reflect both a preference for a less complex approach to questions and the self-consciousness of a Wisconsin Teachers' College dropout in the presence of graduates of Oxford or Cambridge. In sum, it appears more reasonable to attribute Golda Meir's attitude toward the Arab-Israeli conflict in general, and the use of force in that arena in particular, to her individual history and development than to any major causal impact of her gender.

In her own reflection on her life and career, Golda appears to assign gender a minor role:

I am not a great admirer of the kind of feminism that gives rise to bra burning, hatred of men or a campaign against motherhood, but I have had very great regard for those energetic hard-working women within the ranks of the labor movement . . . who succeeded in equipping dozens of city-bred girls with the sort of knowledge and training that made it possible for them to do their share . . . in agricultural settlements throughout Palestine. That kind of constructive feminism really does women credit and matters much more than who sweeps the house or sets the table.

About the position of women generally, of course, there is very much to say . . . but I can put my own thoughts on the subject into a nutshell. Naturally women should be treated as the equals of men in all respects, but, as is true also of the Jewish people, they shouldn't have to be better than anyone else . . . or feel that they must accomplish wonders all the time to be accepted by all. . . .

The fact is that I have lived and worked with men all my life, but being a woman has never hindered me in any way at all. It has never caused me unease or given me an inferiority complex or made me think that men are better off than women—or that it is a disaster to give birth to children. Not at all. Nor have men ever given me preferential treatment. But what is true, I think, is that women who want and need a life outside as well as inside the home have a much, much harder time than men because they carry such a heavy double burden . . . and the life of a working mother who lives without the constant presence and support of the father of her children is three times harder than that of any man I have ever met. (Meir, 1975, pp. 113-115)

Three aspects of these reflections on gender, the only point in her autobiography where Golda comments at any length on the question, deserve mention. First, her juxtaposition of "bad" feminism with "good" practical work is quite consistent with Golda's preference for the concrete over the abstract and the immediate problem over the larger question. It also sounds like the reaction of a woman whose perceptions of gender issues were set in the very different time and society of the post-World War I United States, when the issues and expressions of the commitment to equality were quite different.

Second, Golda clearly did not think that gender affected her political career or relationships with colleagues. In keeping with her general aversion to broad issues or social analysis not directly related to the struggle for a Jewish state, she did not ask whether her experience was typical or unique. The question of whether the larger society had lived up to the egalitarian goals of the founders of the state, or whether even in Israel there was bias and discrimination, was simply ignored.

Third, the comments about the double or treble burden of the woman who seeks a public career clearly reflect Golda's life history. They are followed by her comments on the way in which she raised her two children, including her overwhelming guilt at leaving them to travel abroad (Meir, 1975, p. 115). But the discussion is rooted at the personal level and tacitly accepts the social order that necessitates the extra burden on women. There is no comment on the fairness of social arrangements or her own acceptance of some critical assumptions about what women were supposed to do.

Several aspects of Golda Meir's life seem to have mitigated the impact of gender. While she was born into a quite traditional culture, the fact that her father left the family to seek a better life forced and allowed her mother to assume the role of head of the household.[27] Even when the family was reunited in Milwaukee, it was her mother's ability to cope with the practical business of opening and running a store that was the critical factor in moving from poverty to modest wealth. Her older sister's involvement in politics both in Russia and among emigré intellectuals in the United States gave her another example of a strong woman in a leadership role.

As a young adult, Golda embraced a highly egalitarian form of Zionism. She was impelled not just to go to Palestine but to join the explicitly utopian communal society of the kibbutz. Her sense of herself as strong and capable was reinforced by her ability to meet the rigorous physical and social demands of the community and to exert her skills in organizing portions of the daily routine.

Thus, by the time she was forced (as she saw it) to make a choice between the demands of her private role as wife and mother and her public role as participant in the creation of a new society, she was accustomed to acting independently and deeply committed to the necessity of life in the public sphere. Gender was hardly irrelevant; Golda's assumptions about what a woman should do and her responsibilities to her husband and children caused her years of personal suffering, but she was sufficiently free of traditional constraints to opt for the public over the private life.

Gender did have an obvious direct effect on the early stages of her political career through her position with the Women's Council of Histadrut. Her personal and political skills enabled her to transcend the potential constraints of "women's issues" and move increasingly into other roles, most critically as representative of Jews in Palestine and fund-raiser in the United States. While gender may have had some impact on Golda's selection for the various fund-raising campaigns, her background in America, flair for blunt and persuasive speech, and linguistic skills were clearly the primary factors.

But her subsequent career, in both foreign and domestic policy arenas, would appear to support her assertion that she did not experience to a great extent the direct effects of whatever gender bias existed. Her positions on issues did not distinguish her from her male colleagues. Her toughness as a negotiator was often noted, but Golda Meir is hardly the only Israeli politician or prime minister to be accused of "intransigence" by opponents. It was her political history and the accident of Levi Eshkol's untimely death that propelled her into the prime ministership.

At the outer edge of relevance are matters of personal style. Other Israeli prime ministers had informal sessions with advisers; Golda's "kitchen cabinet" met in the kitchen, and she would often make coffee or set out something to eat. When it was her turn in the communal kitchen on the kibbutz, she saw to it that coffee and sandwiches were waiting for the sentries as they came off duty at midnight; she would do the same thing for her bodyguards as prime minister when she had a sleepless night. There are occasions on which she cried in public when some, if not all, of her male colleagues were dry-eyed. Some observers used "grandmotherly" as a descriptor of her appearance and demeanor. Much of this is gender related. All of it is far more personal than political.

To the extent that a single case will allow generalization, Golda Meir's life suggests that gender is never irrelevant but that it is not necessarily the sole, or even major, determinant of political success. The traditional division of sex roles that assigns almost exclusive responsibility for the private sphere to women and by and large reserves the public sphere for men made it far more difficult for Golda Meir to choose a public life. The sense that she was somehow not meeting her obligations as wife and mother added guilt and anguish to her life; it did not deter her.

The life of a woman in the twentieth century cannot avoid being affected by her own understanding of her gender and the larger society's beliefs about women. But for Golda Meir the impact of negative aspects of gender stereotypes held by others was mitigated by the combination of a distinctive set of experiences early in life and the fact that her career paralleled the conscious creation of a new society.

Notes

1. Golda Meir was, throughout her life, a person of action rather than contemplation; an organizer, persuader and mover rather than a reflective thinker. Perhaps the clearest statement of her views is a speech she delivered at Dropsie College, a Jewish institution in Philadelphia (reprinted as "The Zionist Purpose" in Meir, 1973).

2. Despite her repeated protestations that she would have been happiest had she been able to remain a comparatively anonymous member of a small farming collective, it is hard to imagine Golda Meir restricted to such a small arena.

3. Throughout this chapter, Ms. Meir is referred to as Golda, in keeping with standard usage in both Israeli politics and much of the scholarly literature. Particularly at the height of her popularity, Israelis referred to the prime minister as Golda for many of the same reasons Americans had earlier called President Eisenhower Ike.

4. For the relevance of a political leader's initial success to later political style, see Barber (1972, p. 11).

5. Morris came, reluctantly, and at the last minute Golda convinced her older sister to come with them, leaving her husband behind to raise the money to bring himself and the children later—let no one underestimate Golda's powers of persuasion!

6. See the selections in Meir's 1973 book, *Golda Meir Speaks Out*. These are clearly speeches with a purpose, not philosophical or reflective discourses.

7. The Histadrut was the general organization for labor created by the Zionist movement in Palestine. It was (and is) far more than a labor union, serving as both owner of enterprises and representative of workers' interests. The Histadrut has always attempted to meet the personal and social needs of the labor movement.

8. The Jewish Agency was the quasi-state organization that coordinated the various groups and movements involved in Jewish life in Palestine under the British mandate. It was, and understood itself to be, a government in training. Note that although Golda's job now moved her from Tel Aviv to Jerusalem, where her husband still lived, they did not resume their life together.

9. Golda was clearly disappointed to be ignored by the British. The fact that her name was not on the list of those to be arrested was perhaps related to the fact that her official responsibilities were only indirectly related to the military dimension of the struggle for independence, perhaps a reflection of a belief that a woman could not be much of a danger.

10. She could not resist quoting, ostensibly for the sake of denying, Ben-Gurion's remark, "Someday when history will be written, it will be said that there was a Jewish woman who got the money which made the state possible."

11. In the Israeli system, members of the parliament, the Knesset, do not run as individuals from districts but as names on party lists. Seats are allocated to parties via proportional representation.

12. As noted earlier, Golda did not present herself as ambitious or even interested in a political career beyond being willing to serve and wanting to get the tasks at hand accomplished.

13. Israel uses a system of strict proportional representation and nationwide constituencies to allocate parliamentary seats. The result is a multiparty system in which there are two broad tendencies: parties whose ideological positions are marked by Zionism, secularism, and some degree of socialism; and parties marked by varying degrees of free-market economics, more traditional nationalism, or commitment to transforming Israel into an explicitly religious state. From the early 1920s through Menachem Begin's election in 1975, the Labor Coalition of the relatively leftist parties dominated Israeli political life. Both the Labor and Likud (rightist) coalitions have been marked by uneasy alliances among relatively independent parties who vigorously preserve their ideological and doctrinal distinctions even as they reach agreement on lines of policy.

14. She commented, "It is not a sin to be seventy but it is also no joke" (Meir, 1975, p. 374).

15. For an account of the evolution of the U.S.-Israeli relationship during Golda's tenure, see Safran (1978, pp. 448-475).

16. The relationships that Golda had been instrumental in developing as foreign minister were casualties of the Six-Day War.

17. For a thorough discussion of the dynamics of domestic problems and their political implications, see Perlmutter (1985, pp. 220-230).

18. Often referred to in Israel as the Yom Kippur War, with the accompanying connotations of a sneak attack launched on a solemn religious holiday, it is consistently labeled the October War by the Arabs. Safran (1978, pp. 278-316) describes the course of the war itself and deals with the controversies surrounding the Meir government's handling of the situation (pp. 180-187). See also Perlmutter (1985, pp. 232-237) for a succinct discussion. Heikal (1975) and al Shazly (1975) present insider accounts of the Egyptian war effort.

19. In roughly two weeks of fighting, 2,500 Israelis were killed. As a proportion of the population, this is roughly double the losses the United States suffered during the entire Vietnam War.

20. The Sephardim are the so-called Oriental Jews, who are descended from the Jewish communities expelled from Spain in 1492 and who settled in various areas of the Middle East.

21. See, for example, the discussion in Perlmutter (1985, p. 230) or the far more critical assessment in Avishai (1990, pp. 29-41) titled "Golda Meir's Last Hurrah."

22. The kitchen cabinet sessions are discussed in detail in Elizur and Salpeter (1973, chap. 3) and Golda's style as prime minister is described in Shimshoni (1982, pp. 203-204).

23. Note, for example, that the second of the 14 points defining the purpose and policies of the new government of the new State of Israel, issued by David Ben-Gurion in May 1948, was equality of men and women.

24. For a contemporary evaluation of the status of women in Israeli political life, see Swirski and Safir (1991), particularly the chapters in Section 3, "Golda Notwithstanding: Participation and Powerlessness."

25. See the discussion at several points in Fraser (1989, especially chap. 17).

26. See, for example, Amos Perlmutter's (1985, pp. 204-208) characterization of her worldview as "narrow and simple" and his discussion of how broadly shared the basic tenets were among the Israeli elite.

27. In Golda's memory, her father's action was necessitated by his lack of practical business sense and the pervasive anti-Semitism of Czarist Russia.

References

al Shazly, S. (1975). *The crossing of the Suez.* San Francisco: American Mideast Research.
Avishai, B. (1990). *A new Israel.* New York: Ticknor & Fields.
Barber, J. D. (1972). *Presidential character.* Englewood Cliffs, NJ: Prentice-Hall.
Elizur, Y., & Salpeter, E. (1973). *Who rules Israel?* New York: Harper & Row.
Fraser, A. (1989). *The warrior queens.* New York: Alfred E. Knopf.
Heikal, M. (1975). *The road to Ramadan.* New York: Quadrangle.
Meir, G. (1973). *Golda Meir speaks out.* London: Weidenfeld & Nicolson.
Meir, G. (1975). *My life.* New York: G. P. Putnam.
Peretz, D. (1979). *Government and politics of Israel.* Boulder, CO: Westview.
Perlmutter, A. (1985). *Israel: The partitioned state.* New York: Charles Scribner's Sons.
Safran, N. (1978). *Israel: The embattled ally.* Cambridge, MA: Harvard University Press.
Shimshoni, D. (1982). *Israeli democracy.* New York: Free Press.
Swirski, B., & Safir, M. (Eds.). (1991). *Calling the equality bluff.* New York: Macmillan.

7

Perónisma

Isabel Perón and
the Politics of Argentina

SARA J. WEIR

On July 1, 1974, María Estela (Isabel) Martínez de Perón became the first woman chief executive of an American republic. Only nine months before, she was elected vice president of Argentina as the running mate of her famous husband, Juan Domingo Perón. Isabel assumed the presidency upon his death.

By all accounts, the 18-month presidency of Mrs. Perón was a disaster. On March 24, 1976, the armed forces removed her from office, again taking over the government of Argentina (see, e.g., Hodges, 1976; Smith, 1983). After nearly 6 years of house arrest, Isabel was freed by a federal court and she returned to Spain, where she had lived with Juan during his 18 years of exile (1955-1973) from Argentina.[1] Mrs. Perón continues to reside in Madrid. She has returned to Argentina on several occasions, including the 1989 inauguration of Carlos Saúl Menem, a Perónist, as president of Argentina.

Isabel is not nearly as well known as Eva, Juan Perón's second wife, and her presidency has received universally poor ratings, but an in-depth analysis of her political career reveals a complicated picture of a

AUTHOR'S NOTE: My thanks to Stephen Trinkaus for his research support and translation of materials from the Spanish, and the Bureau of Faculty Research, Western Washington University, for financial support of this project..

woman who was more successful politically before and after her presidency than she was during it. The political career of Isabel Perón—as spokesperson for her exiled husband, as president of Argentina, and as, at least, the symbolic leader of the Perónist party until 1985—raises fundamental questions about women in leadership positions. How did she come to power in a country that has traditionally viewed politics as the domain of men? Was she simply the "inept and inexperienced wife" of Juan Perón (Smith, 1983, p. 128)? Or did she have a leadership style of her own—independent of the men who guided her politically? Finally, how did attitudes toward women shape her experience as an elected official?

The Political Culture of Argentina

The place of Isabel Perón in Argentine political life can be understood only in the context of the political culture and economic development of Argentina and the role of Perónism in the post-World War II era.[2] Argentina was a Spanish colony before gaining its independence in the 1820s. While much of its early political culture can be traced to the *conquistadores,* later waves of immigration from southern Europe (and especially Italy) shaped contemporary Argentine culture and contributed to continuing tensions over national identity. During the period 1857-1930, Argentina experienced a net immigration of 3.5 million people (net immigration equals immigrants minus emigrants). By 1914, 30% of the population was foreign-born (Skidmore & Smith, 1984, p. 71).

A rural peasantry such as has developed in many Latin American countries colonized by the Spanish never developed in Argentina. Instead, an urban proletariat emerged, made up of immigrants working in agro-export-related industries. While there was movement between the city and the country, Buenos Aires always attracted "a large share of the foreigners" (Skidmore & Smith, 1984, p. 71). It was these workers, along with powerful sectors of the military, who brought Juan Perón to power in 1946 and again in 1973 (after 18 years in exile).

Perón used a combination of personal charisma, collective political ritual, and economic policies that redistributed income in favor of the workers to forge a social movement. Its "extreme dependence on one man" (*verticalismo*) made Juan Perón indispensable. This loyalty and absolute belief in Perónism was "enhanced in considerable part through the personal devotion and activities of his second wife, Evita" (Turner

& Miguens, 1983, p. 4). Although Evita died in 1952, Juan Perón continued to use her image when he returned from exile in 1973. Perónism and the "cult of Evita" remained as powerful symbols of the past, but years of "bureaucratic authoritarian" rule by the military and shifting international markets weakened the working classes politically and led to divisions in the Perónist movement (Dominguez, 1987).

Perón was in poor health and was unable to provide the economic rewards that had successfully united the proletariat during his earlier terms of office. Major divisions within the movement emerged, and upon Perón's death this turmoil surfaced.

As previously mentioned, Isabelita was elected vice president of Argentina in September 1973 and upon Juan's death in 1974 she became president. She entered office with little political experience and without the charismatic appeal and natural leadership skills of Evita. She also took office in a country that was strongly antifeminist and opposed women's exercising power in public life. Eva Perón had used these attitudes to help build support for Juan Perón and to strengthen her own position in Argentine society: "I felt that the women's movement in my country and all over the world had a sublime mission to fulfill. . . . everything I knew about feminism seemed to me ridiculous. . . . it ceased to be womanly and was nothing" (Perón, 1953; cited in Carlson, 1988, p. 183).

Evita was the model of selflessness in her support for her husband and in her exhaustive work for the poor through the Fundacion Eva Perón, a private charitable institution she founded. She "made politics a legitimate activity for women," but as an extension of women's traditional family responsibilities (Navarro, 1983, p. 30). Isabel Perón benefited from the legacy of Evita and, at the same time, was limited by this legacy in her efforts to exercise formal political power. In this context of economic instability (and in the shadows of Juan and Evita Perón), the story of the presidency of Isabel Perón is told. That her presidency was unsuccessful and damaging to Argentina seems almost a foregone conclusion.

Overview of Isabel Perón's Career

As with the accounts of the early life of Eva Duarte de Perón, the exact nature of Isabel Martínez de Perón's childhood and adolescence is not known. Official and unofficial accounts differ greatly—particularly in their interpretation of Isabel's career as a dancer before she met

Juan Perón—but certain events are common among several biographical sources.[3]

Maria Estela Martínez Cartas was born February 4, 1931, in La Rioja, a provincial capital in northwestern Argentina. Her father was an official of the National Mortgage Bank. The family moved to Buenos Aires when she was 2 years old, and her father died four years later. As a child she was called Estelita, taking her confirmation name, Isabel, as a professional name around the time she began her career as a dancer.

There is no evidence from her childhood of an interest in politics on Isabel's part. We also know very little about her relationship with her mother or her siblings, except that she was the middle child, with two older sisters and two younger brothers. According to Current Biography (1975), Isabel showed little aptitude for academic studies, leaving school after the sixth grade, but "she reportedly studied ballet and Spanish dancing, acquiring some proficiency in French, developed a taste for romantic Spanish poetry, and qualified as a piano teacher" (p. 313).

She joined the Cervantes Theatre's dance troupe in 1955, but apparently did not stay long with the well-known group. When she met Juan Perón in 1956, she was dancing with Joe Herald's Ballet in Panama City (Current Biography, 1975, p. 313; Times [London], March 13, 1980). According to accounts, Isabel was ill and away from her native country and Perón, in exile from Argentina, was asked to visit her in her dressing room. Soon after their meeting, Juan hired Isabel as his personal secretary.

This seems to be the beginning of Isabel's political education. She is quoted as saying of her early relationship with Juan: "We talked about politics the day we first met, and afterwards he trained me to be his political representative" (Current Biography, 1975, p. 313). In 1961, Isabel and Juan were married in a secret ceremony in Madrid. Juan Perón continued to be the head of the Perónist movement during this time, and it was feared that knowledge of his marriage to Isabel might anger supporters at home, who continued to revere Evita.

Isabel learned about Perónism and began to develop the skills that would allow her to represent Juan in Europe and later on several occasions in Argentina. She lived in the shadow of Evita, becoming a blonde and taking up the emotional style of speaking that Evita was so famous for, yet the London Times (March 30, 1980) noted that the parallels between the two went only so far, pointing out that although, like Isabel, Evita was an actress, blonde, intelligent, and ambitious, "she was also an extremely adroit politician. . . . Isabelita, the understudy, lacked Evita's brains, charisma and raw, driving energy" (p. 15).

What does all of this tell us about Isabel Perón as an emerging leader? Nothing in her early life suggests that she would become a political leader; unlike some other women, who have moved into powerful positions because of the positions of their fathers or husbands, Isabel seemed to lack political ambition. Virtually all that she knew of politics was learned from Juan Perón or from their adviser and astrologer, the mysterious Jose López Rega. "It was Perón himself who brought Jose López Rega, that infamous Rasputin of the notorious Argentine Anti-Communist Alliance, into the government house" (Ratliff, 1988, p. xx).

After Juan's death, López Rega was a powerful force, personally and politically, in the government of Isabel Perón.[4] Little is written about her personal views or ideology, although she seems to have favored the most conservative elements within the Perónist movement.

Events leading to the presidency of Isabel Perón began in the 1960s. It must be remembered that Juan Perón was not formally overthrown— in 1955, after two serious challenges to his power from the military, he slipped into exile. In 1960, after moving from country to country, he settled in Spain, with the support of his friend General Francisco ("el Caudillo") Franco. Perón continued to head the Perónist movement, "estimated at having the support of about one-third of the nation" (Chaffee, 1976, p. 3).

"The armed forces were anxious to 'cleanse the nation of Perónism' and ousted President Frondizi in 1962 when he allowed the Perónists to put forward candidates for elections" (*Current Biography,* 1975, p. 313), but Perónism did not go away. Increasingly, Isabel represented her exiled husband in Argentine politics.

Path to Power

Perónism was far from dead during the 1960s and early 1970s, but clear divisions in the movement were emerging. A new generation of labor leaders (the traditional base of Juan Perón's support) were calling for "Perónism without Perón" (Smith, 1983, p. 129). Isabel traveled to Argentina several times during this period to serve "as Perón's stand-in, successfully promoting his chosen candidates in provincial elections," and to keep attention on Juan rather than those who called for Perónist policies under other leadership (*Current Biography,* 1975, p. 314). By 1971, the military dictatorship of General Alejandro Lanusse agreed to a return to civilian rule. Isabel again represented Juan in discussions with the government concerning the possible participation of Juan Perón in the elections scheduled for 1973. After more than 17 years in exile, Juan Perón returned to Argentina on November 17, 1972, but he remained in the country only one month. On March 11, 1973, Héctor Cámpora, Perón's handpicked candidate, won the presidential election with 49.6% of the vote (Smith, 1983, p. 134).

Cámpora was unable to reunite the factions of the Perónist movement. The breakdown was apparent when Juan and Isabel formally returned to Argentina in 1973 and were greeted at the airport by some 400,000 followers: "Left-wing and right-wing Perónists were determined to control the event and to plant their respective banners in the area around the platform. . . . A full-scale battle broke out . . . with automatic weapons being fired at close range in a packed crowd" ("Thousands Cheer," 1973, p. 4). An estimated 200 people were killed and thousands were injured. Whether it was part of a plan or a response to events is unclear, but in the months that followed Cámpora resigned, paving the way for Juan Perón to run for president once again.

The choice of a running mate was very important. This decision was a turning point in the political career of Isabel Perón. Juan Perón was in poor health, making a presidential succession likely. Only those closest to him knew the extent of his health problems—he performed the public duties required to keep his image alive, but increasingly Isabel traveled for him. Ricardo Balbín, leader of the Radical party, was considered as a possible vice presidential candidate, but in the end Isabel was nominated. Many reasons for the selection of Isabel have been given, but for her it brought the continuation of her growth politically. Historically, the vice presidency in Argentina has not been a powerful position, but given Juan Perón's health it was clear to some that Isabel would very likely ascend to the presidency. Following the official announcement of the all-Perón ticket, Isabel told the delegates, "I cannot offer you great things, I am only a disciple of Perón" (*Current Biography,* 1975, p. 314). But while it was Isabel who did most of the campaigning (and she was successful in winning the support of left-wing Perónists), there were few who considered her qualified to serve as president. Wayne S. Smith (1983) concludes: "Whatever the considerations behind Perón's decision, the result was the same. Isabel Perón was probably as incompetent a candidate as could have been found. A year later, she would become president and bring the country to the brink of disaster" (p. 134).

Juan Perón was elected with 61.85% of the votes, and Isabel Martínez de Perón became the first woman vice president in Latin America.

Isabel moved from spokesperson and political representative to elected official—a position the politically ambitious Evita Perón wanted, but was denied. During the months before Juan Perón's death, Isabel "worked long hours, behaved with quiet dignity and won the country's grudging respect" (*Current Biography,* 1975, p. 314). Like Evita, she took a special interest in women's issues, but she was never able to translate Eva's popularity with women into support for her own leadership. In June 1974, she made a state visit to Europe during which she had an audience with the pope and spoke before the International Labor Organization in Geneva, Switzerland (Sobel, 1975).

On July 1, 1974, Juan Perón died of heart failure. The new president of Argentina made the announcement to the public: "With great pain I must transmit to the people the death of a true apostle of peace and nonviolence" ("A Man on Horseback," 1974, p. 36).

The Presidency of Isabel Perón

> Verticality was Perón's. Now that the leader has died, this verticality is exercised by the person the people elected with him, the president herself. (Page, 1983, p. 496)

Some believed that Isabel would step aside and call for new elections, but she assumed the presidency. President Isabelita, as she was called by some, lacked the experience to rule effectively, and from the beginning of her presidency took the advice of Jose López Rega. "The commander-in-chief of the army came to her with a decree providing for certain security measures to take effect until after the funeral. She called López Rega and asked him what to do. He told her to sign and she signed" (Page, 1983, p. 495).

Isabel inherited a country with deep economic problems, where terrorism and violence were increasingly commonplace and the Perónist movement was at war with itself. According to Donald Hodges (1976), "The economic crisis compounded the political crisis, thus resulting in Isabelita's inability to rule" (p. 167). Isabel set out to continue the policies of Juan Perón, but her inner circle of advisers was much narrower than his, drawn increasingly from the "ultraright" sectors of the Perónist movement.

Conflict grew, not only with the General Labor Federation (CGT), the traditional base of support for Perónism, but also with more moderate factions of the military, who feared the effects of continuing violence and political repression. For some in the military the problem was not with repressive policies, but that these policies were directed by the government rather than the military. The political crisis led to a military crisis that was aggravated by economic mismanagement (Hodges, 1976, pp. 167-175).

The political problems began before Juan Perón's death, but they grew more serious during Isabel Perón's presidency. It is impossible to know how much of the resistance to her rule among certain sectors of the Perónist movement was because she is a woman, but there is certainly evidence that her abilities were questioned even by those who were ready to accept a woman in a leadership position.

The conflict within Perónism had three important elements. The left was virtually eliminated from the broader movement. The ultraleft People's Revolutionary Army (ERP) had already split with the rest of the movement and was engaged in armed conflict with the military. The economic benefits of Perón's earlier presidency were no longer available to leftist groups, and the military was increasingly free to engage in government-sanctioned acts of violence and repression against popular movements. Politically, Juan Perón had made the split certain when he tried to "compel the governor of Buenos Aires to resign because of alleged sympathies for the guerrillas" (Hodges, 1976, p. 168). The chasm deepened after Juan's death when the "moderate left, led by the Montoneros, followed in the footsteps of the ultra-left by denouncing the 'legitimacy' of Isabelita's 'inner circle' and then returning underground . . . to wage war on the government" (p. 168). Guerrilla warfare raged in the provinces and was increasingly directed at military targets. As the legitimacy of Isabel Perón's government declined, the left became popular among traditional Perón loyalists.

The elimination of the left from the Perónist movement led to a second area of conflict. With the left now working against the Perónists, the relationship between the remaining factions was destabilized. The new split centered on differences between the major trade union, CGT, which was controlled by the moderate right, and the government, which was controlled by the ultraright (Hodges, 1976, p. 168).

Finally, the Perónist movement was divided between verticalists and antiverticalists. The verticalists viewed the Perónist movement as focusing largely on Juan Perón personally. Isabelita was Juan's choice to succeed him as the leader of the movement—to question this choice was to be disloyal to Perón. Antiverticalists, on the other hand, saw the possibility of "Perónism without Perón."

In December 1975 the final split occurred between the "verticalists" in the CGT bureaucracy, backed by labor supporters in congress, and an emerging force of "antiverticalists" within both the labor and political branches of the movement. The "verticalists" supported Isabelita as head of the government, whereas the "antiverticalists" accepted only her role as head of the Party and the movement. (Hodges, 1976, p. 168)

Ripples from the split were felt in Congress and within the governing bodies of the Perónist (Justicial) party.[5] In the end, elements of the Justicialist party formed a coalition in support of Isabel at the National Party Congress. This brought an end to any hope of removing her from office constitutionally.

Political problems were intensified by the central role played by the unpopular, ultraright-wing (sometimes referred to as "fascist") cabinet minister and adviser Jose López Rega. Stories abound of the influence of López Rega over presidential decisions—his relationship with Isabel was "the subject of endless speculation and formed an integral part of the backdrop of Isabel's presidency" (Page, 1983, p. 497).

López Rega was influential in the 1973 presidency of Juan Perón, but his power was greatly increased upon Perón's death. As mentioned, Isabel depended on him from the beginning of her presidency. He attempted to keep support for the government among the masses by appealing to their emotions,[6] while consolidating his power within the government through the elimination of rival ministers from the cabinet.

The role of Isabel in these events is unclear, but one must assume that she was in agreement with these activities. In mid-1975, the military forced López Rega out of the government and "after the president made him a 'special ambassador' without assignment," he went into exile in Madrid. Had Isabel been "under the spell" of this "modern-day Rasputin," one might expect that her close affiliation with the far right and her policy orientation would change in his absence, but, according to Joseph Page (1983), "the elimination of López Rega turned out to have no perceptible impact upon the economy or internal security" (p. 499).

The economic problems Isabel Perón inherited were aggravated by her government's mismanagement of the economy. In 1975, the rate of inflation was as high as 350%. Isabel continued the policies of her husband with few exceptions—this meant keeping wages and subsidies high. The combination of high wages, which encourage domestic consumption, declining agricultural exports, and capital flight in search of more stable investment opportunities led to a deteriorating balance of trade and an intractable economic crisis.

In October 1974, the "new economic minister, veteran Perónist Alfredo Gomez Morales, utilized more traditional measures to stem the inflation, but to no avail. With wage contracts up for renewal in mid-1975, a crisis of major proportions loomed" (Page, 1983, p. 498). By 1975, a Perónist government faced a general strike for the first time. "Isabel had to give in and approve wage contracts with substantial increases. Inflation soared" (Page, 1983, p. 498). Guerrilla warfare in the provinces, combined with the deteriorating economy and labor unrest, strengthened the position of those in the military who called for Isabel's removal.

On March 25, 1976, the final coup came:

> A helicopter that was taking Isabel from the Casa Rosada to the Olivos residence developed "engine trouble" and diverted to the military section of the downtown airport. When it landed, armed soldiers stepped aboard, took her into custody and put her on an air force plane bound for the Andean lake country, where she was placed under house arrest. (Page, 1983, p. 499)

Isabel Perón was charged with fraud and corruption and held under house arrest, without trial or conviction, until 1981. But, as with so many others in politics—from Juan Perón to Richard Nixon—her career was not over. In 1981 she was convicted of two charges of corruption but acquitted of several counts of misuse of executive funds. On July 6, following the flurry of trials, Isabel was ordered freed on parole by a federal court. Three days later she boarded a plane bound for Spain (Schumacher, 1981a, 1981b). The former president lives in Madrid and has returned to Argentina many times since the end of military rule. She remained the head of the Perónist movement until she gave up that position in 1985.

What do these events tell us about Isabel Martínez de Perón as chief executive? The short answer is, Not much. But the absence of positive action is telling. Isabel Perón served as president for only 18 months. She faced political, economic, and military instability—much of which was inherited from her husband, Juan Perón. The broad-based populist coalition that Perón forged in the 1940s and 1952 was dissolving, and the urban proletariat, which had been the social base of Perónism, could no longer be counted on to give unqualified support—especially to the government of Isabel Perón.

Isabel Perón was not successful at crisis management. She did not possess the political skills, nor did she have the levels of public support necessary, to impose an austerity plan that might have reduced consumer demand and brought inflation down. Her government attempted to do this under the financial leadership of Dr. Alfredo Gomez Morales.

> The first austerity plan imposed by Gomez Morales became bogged down, however, owing to resistance from organized labor. With Perón's death there was literally nobody within the official sector of the movement with the authority to impose on its labor branch the type of austerity plan launched by him in 1952. Only Perón could do that because only he, by virtue of his deeds, had earned the confidence of organized labor. (Hodges, 1976, p. 173)

These attempts to reduce inflation in the domestic economy were coupled with efforts "to meet the demands of the multinational corporations and the international monetary agencies" (Hodges, 1976, p. 171). This is the only area of economic policy in which Isabel Perón's government took an independent position, attempting to impose policies that were inconsistent with the traditional populist distrust of multinational firms. Again, the proposed debt reduction plans were resisted by the Perónist-controlled congress and the labor sectors.

With regard to foreign policy, the United States and Argentina enjoyed "warm relations" during this period, as evidenced by "the signing of a $756 million loan pact with Inter-American Development Bank, in late 1973" (Sobel, 1975, p. 128). In 1974, López Rega, then minister of social welfare, headed a trade delegation to Libya, where a series of agreements were signed involving the exchange of Libyan oil for Argentine agricultural products and motor vehicles.

During the second presidency of Juan Perón, Cuba became "Argentina's principal trading partner in Latin America" (Sobel, 1975, p. 130). The government of Isabel Perón continued the relationship, exporting to Cuba motor vehicles produced in Argentine plants.

Leadership Style

Isabel Perón surrounded herself with representatives of the most right-wing elements of the Perónist movement. While most were not fascist in the strictest sense, many were authoritarian and willing to use the most brutal means to suppress domestic opposition. Increasingly, through legal and illegal means, acts of violence were committed against those on the left—many of whom had been supporters of Juan Perón during his first two terms of office (1946-1955). Violence was met with violence. In the months following Juan Perón's death,

> alleged Perónist rightists July 6 raped and beat to death a pregnant woman who belonged to the left-wing Perónist Youth (JP). . . . Unidentified gunmen fired on an army convoy outside Buenos Aires July 16, wounding a junior officer and a soldier. . . . A powerful bomb exploded in a Buenos Aires building housing offices of the Lawyers Guild July 17, wounding at least four persons. The Guild was well-known for its defense of leftist political prisoners and its lawsuits against right-wing labor unions. (Sobel, 1975, p. 118)

Isabel Perón responded by giving the military greater authority to suppress rebellion and by restructuring her cabinet (several times) to include those who favored more conservative policies. She banned "the last two newspapers representing the Perónist left, *Noticias* and *La Causa Perónista*" (Sobel, 1975, pp. 120-121). Her government was under siege, but Isabel Perón showed no willingness to seek negotiated settlements. Her responses were antidemocratic and repressive.

The Political Career of Isabel Perón in Perspective

Evaluations of Isabel Perón's performance as president are universally poor. Some accounts are sympathetic, arguing that she was a victim of circumstances. Others hold Isabel Perón responsible, at least in part, for the political violence that eventually led to the death or "disappearance" of more than 6,000 Argentine citizens. It is commonly understood that Isabel Perón was not qualified to serve as president of Argentina—under less difficult circumstances she might have completed her term of office and perhaps gained the political skills to remain an active force in Argentine politics, but given the economic and political crises she faced, there was no time for "on-the-job" training.

Criticisms of the presidency of Isabel Perón have softened over time. When she was paroled in 1981, ending nearly six years of house arrest, comments on the streets of Buenos Aires were not nearly as critical as they once had been. The *New York Times* (July 4, 1981) quoted a student: "The first Perón government did many good things, and Mrs. Perón was not so bad" (p. 2). In general, there was a feeling that Isabel Perón had inherited an impossible situation.

Isabel Perón remained leader of the Perónist party until 1985. She was not a unifying force; she spent most of those years in exile, returning to Argentina only for very brief stays. The verticalist wing of the party continued to support Isabel as the rightful heir to Juan Perón, but this support was never based on judgments about her ability to govern. More democratic elements within the movement wished to see reforms that would lead to a social democratic style of party.[7]

In the mid-1980s she considered running for office and pressure was put on the military government to restore Mrs. Perón's full political rights (*New York Times*, July 26, 1983). The question of Isabel's candidacy halted the Perónist party convention in 1983. Dissident factions in the party "demanded that the convention make no decisions until former President Isabel Martínez de Perón returns from exile in Spain" (*New York Times*, September 3, 1983, p. 3). It was not until Isabel removed herself as head of the party that the Perónist movement began to unify, electing the Perónist candidate, Carlos Menem, to the presidency in 1989.

Isabel Perón was most successful politically as a representative of Juan Perón. Although we know little of her private meetings on Juan Perón's behalf, she was able to pave the way for his return to Argentina. Her success as his representative and her ability to campaign successfully on his behalf may at least in part explain why he selected her as his running mate in 1973.

In sum, Isabel Perón played three critical roles in the politics of Argentina: chief executive, party leader, and political representative. In the private, informal negotiations that paved the way for Juan Perón's return to power, she played her most important and successful political role. The evaluation of her role as president is not nearly so positive. She inherited the presidency at a very difficult time, but there is no evidence to suggest that she struggled against the repressive forces of the ultraright; she seems, instead, to have supported them. A period of extreme repression and state-sponsored terror followed her overthrow. Although the evidence is inconclusive, she must bear some responsibility for the collapse of civil authority in Argentina.

Did Gender Matter for Isabel Perón?

In Argentina, where women were not given the right to vote until 1947, there continue to be high levels of discrimination against women's active participation in public life.[8] Marysa Navarro (1977) reminds us of the extent to which scholarship about women's activities and experiences is shaped by gender and class discrimination. Much, if not all, that has been written about Isabel Perón has been by men. To find an assessment of Isabel Perón's political career by feminists, we must look to the popular press.

"The predominant view of Latin American feminists is that while they want a woman for vice-president, they don't particularly like Isabel to hold that office." Noting that if women are qualified, they should be allowed to hold any office, women's rights activist Margot de Bottome of Caracas, Venezuela, went on to criticize the selection of Isabel Perón "because she is not qualified for the post. . . . Of course, there must be a first in history, but this is not a happy cause" ("Thousands Cheer," 1973, p. 5). Other feminists, such as Ana Avalos de Rangle, took a more positive view of Isabel Perón's vice presidential candidacy: "Obviously it demonstrates the importance of a woman's role in society and particularly in Latin America" ("Thousands Cheer," 1973, p. 5).

It must be remembered that, as undemocratic as Perónism may have been, it was Juan and Eva Perón who gave Argentine women the right to vote in 1947 and who founded the Feminist Perónist party in 1949. As Marifran Carlson (1988) observes, Perónism was antifeminist—the franchise came without the support of Argentine feminists. Yet, as Navarro (1977, 1983) observes, Perónism opened the door to women politically. The organizing skills women learned working with the Feminist Perónist party were later used by women (the Mothers of the Disappeared) against the brutality and violence of the military government that followed Isabel Perón's overthrow.

Unlike Eva Perón, Isabel was not a leader of women—she was not a feminist, nor was she successful at mobilizing women through appeals to traditional family (women's) values, such as nurturance and submissiveness to male authority figures. The other avenue that might have been open to her—to exercise political power as a public figure, using power and authority in more traditional (male) ways—was closed to women in Argentine society. Under these circumstances, no woman could have succeeded as president—but it is also unlikely that Isabel

Perón would have been successful in the presidency even if the political system had been more open to women. Unlike Golda Meir, Margaret Thatcher, and many other women who have held elected positions, she lacked the political skills necessary to govern.

Notes

1. Before going to Spain, Juan Perón lived briefly in the Dominican Republic and Panama. Isabel Perón's release was, in part, a result of pressure from General Franco of Spain and General Raphael Leonidas Trujillo of Panama.

2. Marysa Navarro notes that "Evita" is the name that Eva Perón was called by supporters—her political name. Isabel Perón was also called Isabelita by some, but without the same positive feeling or success politically.

3. Gender and class bias are common in many accounts of the lives of Eva Duarte Perón and Isabel Martínez Perón. For alternative views of the life and work of Eva Perón, see Fraser and Navarro (1985) and Flores (1952). Less scholarly discussion exists about Isabel Perón.

4. Accounts from the most scholarly to the most sensational repeat the continuing influence of Jose López Rega on Isabel Perón.

5. This is the formal name of the Perónist party, given to it by Juan Perón when the Constitution of 1853 was amended in 1949, allowing him to serve a second term as president.

6. For example, López Rega flew secretly to Madrid and brought back the body of Eva Perón to be displayed next to Juan's closed casket.

7. Carlos Saúl Menem, the current president of Argentina, is the first Perónist party candidate to be selected through a more democratic process.

8. This is not to suggest that women's participation, particularly election of women to high offices, is somehow greater in this country.

References

A man on horseback. (1974, July 15). *Newsweek,* pp. 36-37.

Carlson, M. (1988). *Feminismo! The women's movement in Argentina from its beginning to Eva Perón.* Chicago: Academy.

Chaffee, L. (1976). Coup finishes Perónismo era. *Latin American Digest, 10*(3), 1-6.

Current Biography. (1975). New York: H. W. Wilson.

Dominguez, J. I. (1987). Political change: Central America, South America and the Caribbean. In M. Weiner & S. P. Huntington (Eds.), *Understanding political development* (pp. 65-99). Boston: Little, Brown.

Flores, M. (1952). *The woman with the whip: Eva Perón.* Garden City, NY: Doubleday.

Fraser, N., & Navarro, M. (1985). *Eva Perón.* New York: W. W. Norton.

Hodges, D. C. (1976). *Argentina, 1943-1976: The national revolution and resistance.* Albuquerque: University of New Mexico Press.

Navarro, M. (1977). The case of Eva Perón. *Signs: Journal of Women in Culture and Society, 3*, 229-240.

Navarro, M. (1983). Evita and Perónism. In F. C. Turner & J. E. Miguens (Eds.), *Juan Perón and the reshaping of Argentina* (pp. 15-32). Pittsburgh, PA: University of Pittsburgh Press.

Page, J. A. (1983). *Perón: A biography.* New York: Random House.

Perón, E. D. (1953). *Evita by Evita.* New York: Proteus.

Ratliff, W. (1988). Introduction. In L. Horvath (Ed.), *Perónism and the three Peróns* (pp. ix-xx). Stanford, CA: Hoover Institution.

Schumacher, E. (1981a, July 7). Argentine court frees Mrs. Perón after five years. *New York Times,* p. 1.

Schumacher, E. (1981b, July 11). Freedom for Mrs. Perón reflects Perónist power. *New York Times,* p. 2.

Smith, W. S. (1983). The return of Perónism. In F. C. Turner & J. E. Miguens (Eds.), *Juan Perón and the reshaping of Argentina* (pp. 97-146). Pittsburgh, PA: University of Pittsburgh Press.

Sobel, L. A. (Ed.). (1975). *Argentina and Perón 1970-75.* New York: Facts on File.

Thousands cheer triumphant return of Perón. *Latin American Digest, 8*(1), 4-6.

Turner, F. C., & Miguens, J. E. (Eds.). (1983). *Juan Perón and the reshaping of Argentina.* Pittsburgh, PA: University of Pittsburgh Press.

8

Margaret Thatcher and the Politics of Conviction Leadership

MICHAEL A. GENOVESE

In many ways, Margaret Thatcher is a political phenomenon. Not only was she England's first woman prime minister, but she served in that capacity longer than anyone in this century, won three consecutive elections, reshaped much of the British political landscape, ranks as one of the most important prime ministers in British history, has been compared with Clement Attlee and Winston Churchill, *and* is the only British prime minister with an "ism" named after her: Thatcherism! There can be no doubt that Margaret Thatcher has stamped her imprint on British politics and life.

How did she do it? How did so seemingly unlikely a character rise to the top of a male world in the most suffocatingly traditional bastion of male supremacy, the British Conservative party? And how did she so thoroughly dominate her party and political scene as to transform British politics from the old Churchill/Attlee postwar consensus to a new, different political and economic orientation? It is indeed no exaggeration to say that Margaret Thatcher transformed British politics, making *her* mark on government and society. The unlikelihood of achieving such a transformation is matched only by the even greater surface unlikelihood that this would be achieved by a woman, and one such as Margaret Thatcher. What did she do, and how did she do it?

The Context

Before Thatcher's rise to power, events of the twentieth century had been very unkind to the British Empire. At the turn of the century, Britain ruled one-fifth of the globe; was widely recognized as hegemon of the West; exerted vast economic, political, and diplomatic leverage throughout the world; possessed a mighty military machine; and basked in the glory and rewards of empire. But in less than a generation, Britain was stripped of empire, might, and glory. Starting with World War I, extending to the depression of the 1930s, and culminating in World War II, Great Britain's rapid decline in economic, military, and geopolitical power led from *Pax Britannica* to *Pax Americana*.

In the period immediately following World War II, Britain was forced to accept a world role dramatically reduced from the days of empire, as the nation became a peripheral power to the American core. "British decline" became a phrase of common usage. Recovering from the devastation of the war proved a formidable task, but Britain and Europe began the slow climb back. Living standards improved, growth and development proceeded apace, and, as a result of military and economic alliance with the United States and the development of a postwar consensus at home, Great Britain slowly regained a sense of economic security and social advancement.

The postwar "consensus" (or settlement) that came to so utterly dominate British politics emerged out of Churchill's wartime consensus government and postwar recovery plans, but came to full fruition under the prime ministership of Clement Attlee. The consensus consisted of an agreement on the part of both Labour and the Conservatives over how postwar Britain should be governed. Its elements included agreement on both the foreign policy and domestic/economic components of British politics. The foreign policy elements included a bipartisan approach to problem solving, support for NATO, decolonization (in the 30 years after World War II, more than 30 nations achieved independence from British rule), and Britain as a nuclear power. The domestic/economic elements of the consensus consisted of a bipartisan commitment to full employment, greater acceptance of trade unions in the political arena, more public ownership of industry, the pursuit of a mixed economy of public and market orientation, active economic management of the economy by the government, and the rise of the social welfare state. This required an active government, significant public expenditures, and high taxation.

This consensus was remarkably durable. It resulted in a striking continuity between governments and parties, and resulted in a marriage of sorts between modern capitalism and social democracy (Kavanaugh, 1990, pp. 26-62). But the great successes of the consensus, and the economic and political recovery it engendered, did not last forever. As economic and political problems rose in the 1970s, cracks in the consensus began to emerge.

The solidity of the postwar consensus was jeopardized by a combination of factors, none more menacing than the economic and trade union problems that beset England in the early 1970s. The promise of the postwar consensus—full employment, economic growth, security—was undermined as OPEC oil embargoes, strikes by trade unions, rising joblessness, inflation, and overall economic malaise challenged the legitimacy of the consensus. The center could not hold. As Peter Jenkins (1988) notes, "Economic failure had gradually taken its toll on the social cohesion and stability which had made Britain for so long one of the political wonders of the world" (p. 30). England's postwar recovery, sluggish by European standards, went into a tailspin, and the consensus began to unravel. Britain began to be seen, and to see itself, as being in a state of decline and deindustrialization. The British governing class was being challenged. Decline threatened to continue beyond the nation's ability to arrest its extension.

It was not until the mid-1970s that the consensus came to be seen as the enemy of economic growth. Britain came to be seen as "ungovernable" and an "overloaded" state. The government seemed on the verge of economic bankruptcy and political insolvency. Britain was seen as "the sick man of Europe"; trade union strikes increased in number and severity and came to be seen as "the British disease." Big government was not working. High inflation, low economic growth, high unemployment, strikes, and weak government conspired against the consensus.

By the mid- to late 1970s, a window of political opportunity opened for those wishing to challenge the consensus. The economic downturn exposed a weakness in the consensus as the government's performance could not match public expectations. All that was missing was a viable challenger with a salable alternative. At first, that person *did not* appear to be Margaret Thatcher, for, up until her prime ministership, Thatcher was an unlikely rebel: a woman, a traditional Tory conservative, a team player.

Thatcher's Early Life, or
"Why Can't You Be More Like Margaret Roberts?"[1]

If Margaret (Roberts) Thatcher had been a man, biographers would have insisted that she was "born to be a politician." [2] But if anyone in her day had seriously thought that a girl born to middle-class British parents in Lincolnshire in 1925 could one day become leader of the Conservative party and prime minister, they would have been thought mad. With all the political schooling Margaret Roberts received at the feet of her father, the England of 1925 and beyond was distinctly a "man's world." The social expectations of middle-class women when Margaret was growing up were centered almost exclusively on home and family. Thus Margaret Thatcher's political career looms all the more remarkable given the odds against her.

Margaret Roberts, second daughter of Alfred and Beatrice Roberts, grew up in the small town of Grantham, Lincolnshire. The daughter of a grocer, she lived with her family above their shop. Alfred Roberts was a successful small businessman, and was very active in civic affairs. He was, beyond question, the biggest influence on Margaret's life.

Alfred Roberts, who had only minimal formal education but was a voracious reader, instilled in his youngest daughter a need to win, an ethic of work, a drive to succeed. Alfred Roberts dominates Margaret Thatcher's recollections of childhood. He is seen by his daughter as teacher, mentor, guru, and guide. No other figure in her life comes close to the influence of Alf. When she became Britain's first woman prime minister, she spoke of her father:

> He brought me up to believe all the things I do believe and they are the values on which I have fought the election. It is passionately interesting to me that the things I learned in a small town, in a very modest home, are just the things that I believe have won the election. I owe almost everything to my father. (quoted in Webster, 1990, p. 3)

Such tributes to her father were not unusual. He overwhelms her memory and is seen as the force that shaped her and moves her.

To Alf, Margaret was more than a daughter; she was "pupil, protégée, and potential *alter ego,* the offspring who could and would achieve the greater, wider life which circumstances and the accident of birth had denied him" (Harris, 1989, p. 59). Alf was very active in the affairs of his community, serving as lay preacher in the local Methodist church and as a school governor, borough councillor, alderman, and, finally, mayor of Grantham. Margaret was thus reared on a life of public affairs and learned about politics at her father's knee.

As for shaping her character, Margaret recalls two lessons she learned from her father that stand out: First, "You must make your own decisions. You don't do something because your friends are doing it. You do it because you think it's the best thing to do"; and second, "Don't follow the crowd; don't be afraid of being different. You decide what you ought to do, and if necessary you lead the crowd. But you never just follow" (quoted in Harris, 1989, p. 66). During her prime ministership, these two traits would be borne out time after time. Biographer Kenneth Harris (1989) asked the prime minister what she had learned from her father, and she responded:

> His simple conviction that some things are right, and some are wrong. His belief that life is ultimately about character, that character comes from what you make of yourself. You must work hard to earn money to support yourself, but hard work was even more important in the formation of character. You must learn to stand on your own feet. There was great emphasis on learning to stand on your own feet. There are many things which ought never to be done for money—marriage, for instance. Money was only a means to an end. Ends never justified means. (p. 60)

The contrast between Margaret's relationship to her father—so close, so influential—and her relationship to her mother is absolutely striking. Where she identified with and tried to emulate her father, she seems intent on erasing the memory of her mother from her life. Hugo Young (1989) notes that in Thatcher's "adult mind, Alfred was as prominent as her mother was obscure" (p. 4). Thatcher mentions Beatrice rarely, and whenever an interviewer attempts to draw her out on the subject of her mother, she almost always turns the answer into a reference to her father. This obsessive avoidance of discussion of her mother relegates Beatrice to a mere footnote in Margaret Thatcher's life. In fact, there is no mention of her mother in Thatcher's *Who's Who* entry, where Thatcher is listed simply as her father's daughter.

Beatrice Roberts was a quiet, house-centered wife, a subordinate figure within the family dominated by Alfred. In a 1975 interview, Thatcher said of her mother, "I loved my mother dearly, but after I was fifteen we had nothing more to say to each other. It wasn't her fault. She was weighed down by the home, always being in the home" (*Daily*

Telegraph, February 5, 1975). Margaret Thatcher seems to feel she owes almost everything to her father, and practically nothing to her mother. As Young (1990) notes, "There is scarcely an aspect of Alfred that has failed to find its way into the politics of his daughter. Rarely in the history of political leadership could one find an example of such extravagant filial tribute" (p. 4). As an interesting note, many strong male leaders had strong or dominant mothers. In Thatcher's case, she had a strong father to guide her.

If the impact of Alfred overwhelms, the impact of religion on Margaret Thatcher seems negligible. She was raised as a strict Methodist and regularly attended Sunday services, but one finds very few clues that this had anything but a peripheral impact. One is also hard-pressed to find many clues into the makeup of Margaret Thatcher from her school days. She had few close friends and (at her father's insistence) spurned almost all social activities. She was in school, as in all other things, very serious, officious, and hardworking. Even in her days at Oxford, where she began to emerge as a social being, she remained aloof and withdrawn from most of her contemporaries. Home, not school, not church, not community, shaped Margaret Thatcher. And in the home, Alfred dominated (Webster, 1990, p. 6).

Margaret entered Somerville College, Oxford, in 1943 to study chemistry. In college she became active in the Oxford University Conservative Association, eventually becoming its president. She was, according to her tutors, "able but not noticeably imaginative, studious but not creative" (Little, 1988, p. 94). She completed her degree with upper second-class honors.

What are we to make of this childhood and upbringing? Several characteristics stand out as shaping the development of Margaret Roberts (Thatcher). She was driven to achieve by a father who seemed to be all things to young Margaret. She absorbed as her own the goals, ideas, and aspirations of the father. Hard work, individualism, Victorian values, discipline, combativeness, single-mindedness, frugality, and duty were stressed. Her mother is mere footnote in all of this, a memory to be overcome, not an influence to be admired. It was Alfred Roberts whom young Margaret aspired to emulate.

After college, Margaret's first job was with British Xylonite as a research chemist at their Manningtree, Essex, plant. The work was mundane, and Margaret's real interest, politics, always came first. But how to pursue a career in politics while working for a living? At this point in life, Margaret began her search for a safe parliamentary seat.

Margaret Roberts, young, a woman, of limited means, did not find her early efforts at breaking into politics very easy. In 1949, at the age of 24, she was selected as conservative candidate in Dartford. She changed jobs, joining the research department at J. Lyons and Co., moved into the district, and began to campaign feverishly. But in the 1950 election, while the Conservative party trimmed Labour's House of Commons majority from 150 to 5, Margaret Roberts lost her election.

During the campaign, Margaret met Denis Thatcher. He was then the managing director of his family's paint and chemical business and, at 36, was 10 years older than Margaret. Denis had been married several years earlier (a fact that, to this day, Margaret Thatcher seems unable to accept or even admit), but was divorced at the time he met Margaret. They were married in 1951. In that same year, another general election took place, and while once again Margaret lost, she cut into the lead of her opponent's majority. But Margaret Thatcher, at the ripe young age of 26, was a two-time loser, newly married, and groping for a political future.

For Thatcher, marriage meant financial freedom. She was free to pursue a political career unencumbered by the demands of job or paycheck. It freed her time and freed her from worry. It also freed her from the traditional demands of housekeeping. Margaret Thatcher did not have to choose between career and marriage; her marriage freed her to pursue her career.

She began to study for the bar, and specialized in tax law. Her studies were interrupted in 1953—but only temporarily—by the birth of twins, Carol and Mark. How could Margaret have children, a home life, *and* a career? Hire a nanny/housekeeper, educate the children in private and boarding schools, and continue the pursuit of power. She would not be a traditional homemaker, like her mother. Denis's financial position allowed Margaret to return to the study of law, and in 1954 she was called to the bar. The children were not a great burden on Margaret Thatcher, and she managed to soothe whatever guilty feelings may have emerged by assuring everyone that no matter what, she was only 20 minutes away from the children, "if I was needed" (Little, 1988, p. 106). As Wendy Webster (1990) writes about the tug between home/children and career for Thatcher, "She made few, if any, concessions to the dual role model then, and its requirement that family needs were women's first responsibility and working life subordinate to this" (p. 38).

In the space of a few short years, Margaret Roberts had married into wealth and security, passed the bar, had twins, and *finally* found a safe parliamentary seat. Jenkins (1988) writes of this meteoric rise: "The idea that the family is the true centre of her moral universe, that she was a paragon of motherhood and wifely virtue, does not fit easily with the speed and determination with which the Grantham girl made good" (p. 85).

If Margaret Thatcher appeared to be overly ambitious it is because she was. There is a compulsive, driven quality about her determination to succeed. She seemed unfulfilled by home and family, and, with an almost desperate determination, sought a safe seat in Parliament. As her past efforts prove, this was not an easy task. A safe seat is prime political real estate, and the battle to be accepted by the party leaders as a candidate for such a seat is a competitive, often bloody, venture. Finally, in 1957, she was accepted by Finchley, a safe Conservative district near London. In the next election, in October of 1959, Margaret Thatcher, at the age of 34, was elected to Parliament.

The 1959 Parliament would last five years, and it was not long before Margaret Thatcher, one of the few women in the Conservative cadre, began to rise in the party leadership. In 1961 she received her first ministerial assignment as joint parliamentary secretary to the Ministry of Pensions and National Insurance.

The Conservatives lost the 1964 general election, and Thatcher began a string of shadow offices. In 1965, when Edward Heath took over leadership of the Conservative party, Thatcher moved to Housing and Land, and after the Conservative 1966 defeat, she was promoted to the number-two spokesperson on Treasury matters under shadow chancellor Ian Macleod. Later she became shadow minister for fuel and power, then shadow minister for transport. In 1969, Heath appointed her shadow minister of education.

When the Conservatives won the general election of 1970, Heath made Thatcher minister of education and science. It was in this capacity she received the appellation "Thatcher the Milk Snatcher" for her cuts in a school milk program (Young, 1990, chap. 6). Her tenure in this office was controversial, and earned her the dubious distinction of being dubbed by the *Sun* "the most unpopular woman in Britain" (Ogden, 1990, chap. 5).

At this stage in her career, Margaret Thatcher was greatly aided by the fact of her gender. The Conservative party was overwhelmingly male, and in these early days of the women's liberation movement, Heath felt compelled to appoint women to shadow roles. But if gender opened doors for Thatcher, there can be no mistake that, once in office, she performed tirelessly and credibly. If gender got her the job, hard work, determination, and skill kept her there.

The early 1970s were a time of trouble and turmoil for the Heath government. Economic downturns, union problems, and general malaise plagued Britain. Strikes became known as "the British disease," and Britain became known as "the sick man of Europe." As is usually the case in politics, the "in" party was blamed for the problems, and in the general election of 1974, the conservatives, unable to form a government, fell from power, and Labour took control of the government. Once again, Margaret Thatcher was in opposition. But she would not sit idly by. Thatcher quickly began a move to capture control of the Conservative party.

Margaret Thatcher was one step away from the pinnacle. But who was Margaret Thatcher? Clearly the small-town virtues and Victorian values she absorbed from her father guided her. As John Vincent (1987) has written:

> Yet this is perhaps the essential Thatcher, the suburban professional woman of the 1950s living in a period of naively moral anti-totalitarianism, of declining taxes, in a state whose frontiers could, it seemed, be rolled back. Putting aside the symbolism (later to be electorally useful) of Grantham, the fifties were her real formative decade; and what her efforts in the eighties proved was that the fifties could not be brought back. (p. 276)

But she was more than this, for Margaret Thatcher was equally determined to rid Britain of the evils of the 1960 and 1970s: socialism, state power, centralization of authority, welfarism. If Thatcher wanted to restore small-town virtues, this meant the destruction of socialism. It was a return to small-town Britain and a return to a vision of nineteenth-century economic liberalism, a free-market economy, that Thatcher sought.

Her character was shaped by life with father, but her public life and her views on politics and policy were also shaped by her times. As Jenkins (1988) has written, "Her crucial political experiences were gained under socialism at home and communism abroad; she was a daughter of the age of austerity, a child of the Cold War" (p. 82). She wanted change, radical change, social transformation—a revolution.

As Margaret Thatcher prepared herself for the exercise of power, she seemed quite ready to lead. She benefited from the aid of mentors such as her father and, later, such figures as Sir Keith Joseph, Airey Neave, William Whitelaw, and Gordon Reece. Thatcher was willing to sit at the foot of a wise man from time to time, she was a good student of the art and science of politics, but when the lesson was over, she resumed control. Was she, as Young claims, "born to be a politician"? Perhaps so, but one would be hard-pressed to say that one such as Margaret Thatcher was born to be prime minister, because she was born before women were given the vote (Webster, 1990, p. 8). Clearly, the tectonic plates of gender politics were shifting. If Margaret Thatcher was reared to be a politician, she certainly was not born to be one. For that to take place, the social changes inspired (insisted upon) by the nascent women's movement created the opportunity for Margaret Thatcher to be a politician. It was a debt Thatcher would not repay.

Path to Power

After the Conservatives' defeats in two general elections of 1974, the party was prepared to jettison Ted Heath and embrace a new leader. But Heath did not give up power easily. After a good deal of political maneuvering, after several of Heath's most likely challengers withdrew from the contest, Thatcher entered the leadership battle. While Thatcher charted a course to the political right of Ted Heath, it was not yet clear just how far right or how much of a conviction, or ideological, leader Thatcher was to become.

After losing three of four elections in a 10-year period, the Conservatives were ready for a change of leadership. In the party's first ballot for leader, held on February 4, 1975, Thatcher outpolled Heath 130 to 119. While this was not enough for her to be elected on the first ballot, it was clear that Heath was out. In the scramble to fill the second-ballot void left by Heath's withdrawal, several people offered themselves, but it was too little, too late. On the second ballot, held on February 11, Thatcher got 146 votes. The next-closest candidate, Willie Whitelaw, got only 79 votes. In what was essentially an anti-Heath leadership battle, Margaret Thatcher emerged as head of the Conservative party. The party had chosen an outsider, a dissident, and a woman as its new leader.

Thatcher was, as Chris Ogden (1990) notes, "no one's first choice" (p. 119), but she was the only truly conservative challenger to emerge, and in a time when the centrist consensus politics of Ted Heath were held up to ridicule, even as unlikely a candidate as Margaret Thatcher became viable. Harris (1989) argues that Thatcher became head of the party "as the result of a series of accidents" (p. 48), and Ogden (1990) suggests that she led a "coup" against the party regulars (p. 115). Young

(1990) says she was "a mistake that should never have happened" (p. 100). Thatcher herself had told a newspaper reporter six months earlier, "It will be years before a woman either leads the party or becomes prime minister. I don't see it happening in my time" (Ogden, 1990, p. 119).

While there were some early indications that Thatcher was a radical conservative, her years as leader in opposition belied this. Her shadow cabinet was dominated by unreconstructed Heathites, and her policy advocacy seemed moderate and cautious. Thatcher's caution reflected the precariously fragile perch upon which her leadership rested. But public appearances aside, Thatcher was determined to chart a new, more radical brand of conservatism for Britain.

In the late 1970s, the new right, or the more radical right, gained ground within the Conservative party. Rejecting the policies and politics of the old consensus-oriented wing of the party, the intellectual center of the Conservatives began to drift slowly to the right. Thatcher, always skating on political thin ice as party leader, slowly and cautiously moved the party right. She knew her hold on the party was precarious and a major blunder could cause her demise. She repeatedly said, "I shall have only one chance" (Vincent, 1987, p. 278), for there were always political sharks waiting to depose her.

While in opposition, Thatcher witnessed the collapse of yet another government, as Labour was unable to solve the economic and trade union problems that plagued Britain. Thatcher began to develop economic policies in sharp contrast to the consensus model, and, as economic conditions worsened, this new economic philosophy gained adherents—not so much because it was convincing, but because it was an alternative to the status quo. Margaret Thatcher was again winning by default.

In the general election of 1979, the in party was thrown out, and the out party was put in. Owing her election more to the failure of the Callaghan Labour government than to the attractiveness of her policies or her personality, Thatcher was once again a leader on shaky ground. But she was the leader. She was the prime minister.

In the 1979 election, the Conservatives won a majority of 43 seats. This marked the largest shift from one party to another since 1945. At the time, however, the 1979 election appeared to be anything but a watershed election. While the Conservatives outpolled Labour, Thatcher always ran behind Callaghan in personal popularity and was consistently less popular than her party. While her proposals of tight control of the money supply, lower taxes, trade union bashing, anti-immigration, and racial divisiveness had some appeal, Thatcher's goal of a consensus-shattering social revolution would have to wait. At age 53, she was a prime minister who headed her party but did not yet control or dominate it. Nor did she capture the imagination of the British public.

How did Thatcher win? First and foremost, Labour lost. The 1979 election was a "throw 'em out" election. Second, the ideas that animated Thatcher's drastic social revolution were not yet fully formed, and thus the election was about change, but it was always unclear just how much change was involved. Third, the 1970s were a time of international economic malaise, and Britain suffered more from this than most. Worldwide, ruling parties were thrown out, and Thatcher benefited from this trend. Fourth, while gender mattered, other factors dominated the election, and gender—while important—was overshadowed by the failure of Labour and the desperation of Britain's economic condition. All these factors, and many more, coalesced to bring an unlikely person to power. As Young (1990) points out, Thatcher was "a cluster of paradoxes" (p. 140).

After the results of the 1979 election were announced, Thatcher went straight to her new home at Number 10 Downing Street. The new prime minister stood in front of the black door of Number 10 and said to the crowd of gathered reporters, "I just owe everything to my own father, I really do" (Ogden, 1990, p. 152). While Alfred Roberts had been dead for nine years, it was still to him that she turned at her moment of triumph.

The Thatcher Agenda

Margaret Thatcher seemed an unlikely rebel. How could this small-town girl grow up to be a radical, anticonsensus revolutionary? How did she change Britain? Margaret Thatcher's policies—if not her politics—were conservative, perhaps radically so. She attributed her policy formation not to any abstract philosophical principles, but to the everyday lessons she learned from her father.

Thatcher's goal was to break down the postwar consensus and revitalize Britain with a free-market, entrepreneurial public philosophy. The fact that the old consensus was seen as a failure created a window of opportunity through which Thatcher was determined to take Britain. In economic policy primarily, but also in defense, domestic, and social policy, Great Britain would be recast from top to bottom.

Economic Policy

At the center of the Thatcher revolution was her determination to change economic relations and attitudes radically. As Thatcher often said, "economics are the method. The object is to change the soul" (Ogden, 1990, p. 173). Thatcher's goal was to reverse Britain's economic decline, overthrow the postwar consensus, bury socialism, and change the way the British people thought about politics and economics. In short, she sought a revolution.

In economic terms, the revolution was to be accomplished by curbing public spending, lowering taxes, liberating the entrepreneurial spirit, tightly controlling money, lowering inflation, reducing government regulations, moving toward privatization of publicly owned industries, and busting the unions.[3] It was, of course, an amazingly ambitious plan, but one that Thatcher was driven to put into place.

How successful was the Thatcher government in accomplishing its myriad goals in economic policy? On inflation, the government had some early success. Aided by an international recession in the early 1980s, the inflation rate fell dramatically. But by the late 1980s and early 1990s, Britain's price index increased to the point that by 1990, the nation's double-digit inflation was one of the highest in the European Community. Inflation was linked to the control of the money supply, a vital strategy for Thatcher. While there was a fairly rigid control of the money supply in the first Thatcher term, as time went by, strict money control was jettisoned in favor of growth policies.

In the area of public spending, Thatcher sought to control growth, but was only marginally successful. The rate of growth was reduced, but total spending did increase, albeit at a slightly lower rate. What has been clear is that there has been a marked shift in spending between government programs: Defense and law-and-order spending increased, housing and industry money was cut, and education and transportation remained about the same.

Thatcher also sought to rid the public sector of the nationalized industries. This effort at privatization continued apace in the 1980s as the assets of several key industries were sold. Many industries, including British Petroleum, British Aerospace, Rolls Royce, British Steel, British Telecom, Jaguar, British Airways, and British Gas, were privatized under Thatcher.

There was, as promised, a cut in the top tax rate (from 83% to 60%) as well as in the standard rate of income tax (from 33% to 30%). But the value added tax (VAT) rose from 8% to 15%, and employers' national insurance contributions also rose. In 1988 taxes were cut even further, with the top rate dropping to 40% and the standard rate going down to 25%. Overall, however, taxes did not go down. There was a shift from direct to indirect taxes, but not a cut.

As the 1980s drew to a close, Thatcher proposed, and passed into law, a poll tax aimed at shifting the burden of taxes away from the wealthy and onto the middle and lower classes. This tax, the level of which was determined in large part by local authorities, and in which almost everyone had to pay an equal tax total, was presented as a tax reform, but was really a way to try to dump the tax blame onto the local (or liberal) governments. The poll tax was highly unpopular, and proved to be short-lived.

Due in part to increased revenues from North Sea oil that offset declines in manufacturing, Britain experienced economic growth during the 1980s. While this growth was not dramatic, approximately 2%, it did mark an increase over the very sluggish (less than 2%) growth of the 1970s; however, it was lower than the growth of the 1960s.

Union-busting efforts were designed to eliminate what Thatcher saw as the stranglehold that trade unions had over the government. Thatcher was determined to bring the trade unions down, and proved to be unrelenting in this goal. She was very successful. As Dennis Kavanaugh (1990) writes:

> In many respects the Thatcher years have been depressing for the trade unions. The setbacks include mass unemployment, decline of Labour, loss of members, privatization of parts of the public sector, cash limits in much of the public sector, which limited opportunities for bargaining, government initiated incursions into their internal affairs, and minimal access to Whitehall. (p. 237)

Strikes, which had so often crippled Britain, were met with firm resolution, and eventually became politically insignificant. Thatcher succeeded in busting union power in Britain.

Linked to the decline in union power was a dramatic rise in unemployment. Upon taking office, Thatcher faced an unemployment rate of 5.4%. This doubled under Thatcher. High unemployment, which may have been a policy goal linked to lowering wages, lowering inflation, *and* busting unions, did have the effect of weakening labor's bargaining power, and, as long as high unemployment did not create significant social repercussions, could be tolerated by the Thatcher government.

Thatcher's policies raise questions about winners and losers. Clearly labor and the underclass were losers. Under Thatcher, the tax system became less progressive, social services were cut, and unemployment rose. The number of homeless skyrocketed, government support for housing dropped. The disabled, the weak, the poor, and the elderly all suffered under Thatcher's policies. Under Thatcher, inequality and poverty rose, adding to what Neil Kinnock has called the "archipelago of poverty" in Britain. There was no measurable "trickle down." The big winners were those in the upper class. In short, under Thatcher, the rich got richer and the poor got poorer, and, according to Ogden (1990), "a meaner and greedier society" was created (p. 335).

Thatcher's goal of freeing the economy came at a high cost in human terms. It also required a strong state to implement these goals. That a free economy would go along with a strong, centralized, more intrusive state runs counter to traditional conservative goals. But that is precisely what took place in Britain. Thatcher, more of an authoritarian conservative than a libertarian conservative, gave lip service to the rhetoric of the minimalist state, but her activist government expanded the power of the central state and pursued what one of her ministers called "the smack of firm government" (Kavanaugh, 1990, pp. 284, 294). Thatcher attempted to enforce a "moral" code of competitive capitalism. This required government rulemaking as well as a good deal of persuasion. The government's education policy serves as an excellent example of the contradictions in a system of heightened government control in a less controlled economy. The state intruded more often as guide and rule enforcer as Thatcher divested the government of nationalized industries and attempted to create a new model of economic man for Britain.

Military and Defense Policy

When Margaret Thatcher took office in 1979, Britain's international standing was quite low. The heady days of empire had ended, and the "sick man of Europe" had limited power and little prestige. On top of that, Thatcher herself had no prior experience in foreign affairs.

Thatcher's early foreign policy goals were clear: Increase defense spending, maintain a nuclear arms deterrent, support the United States, oppose the Soviet Union and communism, support NATO, but maintain cool relations regarding Britain's membership in the European Economic Community (EEC). But Thatcher's policy goals were very quickly overshadowed by her style in foreign affairs: resolute, unyielding, nationalistic, rigid. It was not long before the sobriquet "the Iron Lady," given to Thatcher by the Soviet news agency, TASS, became both a fitting appellation and a description of her style of governing.

After 11 years in office, Thatcher faced several seemingly intractable foreign policy problems. She was unable to make headway with the problems of Northern Ireland (Ogden, 1990, chap. 13), faced severe criticism for her support of the white minority government in South Africa, and stubbornly fought the move to a more truly united European Community, leaving Britain outside the inner circle as Europe moved toward unity in 1992.

On the more positive side of the foreign policy ledger, Thatcher was successful at strengthening the already strong ties between Britain and the United States. In fact, so close was Margaret Thatcher to Ronald Reagan that the mutual fawning society between the two leaders, while it helped both leaders in their respective countries, actually masked a deeper unease that Thatcher felt toward Reagan. While Thatcher and Reagan competed in public to see who could heap higher praise on the other, in private Thatcher had grave doubts about Reagan's ability. "Poor dear," she once said, "there's nothing between his ears." After a meeting with Reagan, Thatcher remarked, "Not much gray matter, is there?" (Ogden, 1990, chap. 14).

Thatcher's relationship with Mikhail Gorbachev and the Soviet Union represents one of the few cases in which she actually changed her mind. Beginning her term as a rabid anti-Communist, Thatcher was captivated by Gorbachev, concluding, "We can do business together," and indeed Thatcher helped persuade Ronald Reagan that he too could do business with Gorbachev (Ogden, 1990, chap. 18).

On other foreign policy issues, Thatcher faced significant problems, especially in her handling of the transition to black rule in Rhodesia/Zimbabwe, for which she was given high marks (Young, 1990, pp. 181-183), and her handling of transition of British control of Hong Kong to China (pp. 291-292). But no foreign policy issue loomed larger, or had a greater impact on Thatcher's power, than the 1982 Falkland Islands war. This war, more than any other event, "created" and cemented Thatcher and Thatcherism in the hearts, minds, and politics of Great Britain.

On March 19, 1982, a small group of Argentineans landed on the Falkland Islands. These islands, just off the coast of Argentina (which the Argentineans called the Malvinas), were claimed by Argentina but had been controlled by Britain since 1833. The Thatcher government responded swiftly and forcefully, sending British forces to the islands to recapture them.

The war itself was in part the result of gross errors of judgment and policy by the Thatcher government. Several steps were taken just prior to the Argentinean invasion that served as indications that Britain was unwilling to fight for or defend the Falklands. This led Young (1990) to conclude that "the war to reclaim the Falkland Islands from Argentinean occupation was the result of a great failure in the conduct of government: arguably the most disastrous lapse by any British government since 1945" (p. 258).

But the errors in judgment ended up being the best thing that ever happened for Margaret Thatcher's leadership. In the aftermath of Britain's Falkland victory, Thatcher emerged in a stronger position than she had ever had before. After victory was assured, Thatcher emerged from seclusion and announced, "Today has put the Great back in Britain," and, indeed, that is the way many in England saw it. The Falkland victory proved to be the seminal event in Thatcher's years in power. She was now seen as *the* leader of Britain, with virtually no challengers. And from that point on, Thatcher acted with a bolder, more self-confident style. She was virtually unstoppable. Almost overnight, her hold on power was solidified. Thatcher was now a world figure who halted Britain's retreat and brought victory. Her popularity skyrocketed. Her style, seen as abrasive and strident before the war, was now applauded as firm and resolute. The Falkland victory dramatically transformed Thatcher's leadership and power, and from that point on she dominated, even overwhelmed, the political scene.

Domestic and Social Policy

While Margaret Thatcher was determined to transform Britain through a new economic policy, the domestic and social policy agenda was to contribute to and complement the "Thatcher revolution" (Clayton & Thompson, 1989). Thatcher opposed increases in welfare, hoping instead to shrink the welfare state, reduce its costs, and break the chain of dependency that she felt it created. The problem, however, was not merely economic, but also political, for the social welfare programs were extremely popular, and therefore Thatcher was able to make only marginal changes in funding and policy.

In education, while no drastic cuts took place, Thatcher so politicized the issue that morale plummeted, resulting in a crisis in the educational system. As part of her effort to discredit the leftist-leaning Greater London Council (which eventually she disbanded), which controlled local policy, Thatcher also disbanded the Inner London Education Authority, which controlled local schools. Thatcher was upset that too much social engineering was taking place in the London school system (e.g., each school was required to implement an antiracism program) and was determined to purge the schools of liberal content, regardless of the cost in educational quality. This led Thatcher—in spite of her public statements honoring local control—to centralize education policy further by establishing a national curriculum and national assessment program. Public pronouncements about local control aside, this was centralization on a massive scale. Thatcher thus displayed her willingness to violate her own philosophy (conservative, local control) in an effort to gain her desired political ends (control of the schools).

Thatcher's policy toward British higher education was even more devastating. In both rhetoric and action, Thatcher made it clear that the university system was a political enemy, and her harsh rhetoric and frugal policies created a crisis in higher education. The result has been a "brain drain" (especially in the sciences, but in other academic areas as well), with the very best British scholars leaving England for greener and more welcoming academic pastures abroad.

On the environment, Thatcher's record began with benign neglect, but by the end of the 1980s she discovered environmental protection as an issue, and began to increase government activity modestly. Britain, however, long considered the dumping ground for European refuse (toxic and otherwise), has serious environmental problems that were addressed in only the most peripheral manner (Robenson, 1989, p. 38).

Thatcher's efforts at union busting, mentioned earlier, led to some severe domestic repercussions, but ultimately Thatcher outlasted and won out over the unions. In confrontations with Arthur Scargill (who headed the National Union of Mineworkers), the most radical of the union leaders, Thatcher outlasted the union strikes and forced the unions to back down. By remaining tough, Thatcher won another victory over her "enemies." But other strikes plagued Britain, and as Thatcher dug in, with her "never surrender" approach, violence erupted. In 1981, in the south London Brixton area, a racially mixed community, riots broke out in which 279 police and an estimated 200 members of the community were injured. Nearly 30 buildings were damaged. No one was killed. How did the prime minister respond? Young (1990) writes:

From Margaret Thatcher . . . this epochal event elicited a response that hardly did justice to its complexity, still less to the hazards it apparently portended as a consequence of her economic policy. It touched her on one of her least sensitive nerves. As she had sometimes shown before, she possessed no delicacy, such as other politicians of all parties had learned to cultivate, when dealing with black or brown people. Rather the reverse. Permanently on her record, and permanently lodged in the memories of leaders of the ethnic minorities, was the remark she had made on television in January 1978 about the legitimate fears of the white community that it was being "swamped" by non-whites. On immigration she had always belonged instinctively, without effort or much apparent thought, on the hard right of the party. (pp. 233-234)

On seeing pictures of the violence and rioting, Thatcher responded, "Oh, those poor shopkeepers" (Young, 1990, p. 239). Such callousness and insensitivity cemented in the minds of the left and underclass an image of Margaret Thatcher as cold, uncaring, and cruel. This conception was not completely off the mark, for Thatcher could be a blind ideologue, more concerned with property than human suffering.

The Thatcher revolution had only marginal impact on health policy. In the late 1980s, the Thatcher government began an attempt to place a conservative hue onto the health services system, but the health system was highly popular and nearly immune to deep budget cuts. On crime, the government's policy had little impact; crime and violence remained major problems.

A government in office for a dozen years is bound to face ethical problems from time to time. How did Margaret Thatcher handle such crises? Her first significant ethical challenge came in 1983, when a *Daily Mirror* headline blared "Tory Chief's Love Child." Thatcher's valued cabinet minister and campaign manager, Cecil Parkinson, had been having an affair with his secretary, Sara Keays, who was pregnant. How did Thatcher, the strident advocate and protector of Victorian values, respond? She supported Parkinson. But as events unfolded, and as the political heat was turned up, it became clear that Parkinson had to go. The messy scandal, however, revealed that the prime minister was willing to overlook scandal when it suited her; however, when self-interest dictated, she would jettison even her most trusted aides.

In early 1986, the Thatcher government faced a much more serious political scandal: the Westland affair. This scandal was to reflect very poorly on Margaret Thatcher's credibility and her character. Due to carelessness, poor management, and the desire to cover up wrongdoing, Thatcher engaged in what Young (1990) calls "the darker political arts" (p. 427).

Westland p/c was a small helicopter company, the only British company, in fact, that made helicopters. It was facing bankruptcy, and went to the government for assistance. Thatcher was a devout opponent of public money going to save businesses, but since Westland was defense related, it merited a second look. Michael Haseltine, a member of Thatcher's cabinet, but seen as a rival for power, was at the time minister of defense. He opposed a buyout deal by the Sikorsky Company, a U.S. firm, and instead favored purchase by a European consortium.

From this point on, the affair took a variety of twists, turns, and back-stabs. Thatcher, in part to take a slap at rival Haseltine, sided with Trade and Industry Minister Leon Brittan in favor of the Sikorsky sale. What followed were a series of behind-the-scenes promises and deals, press leaks and lies, accusations and deceits. Thatcher claimed ignorance of all wrongdoing, a claim unconvincing to even the staunchest Thatcherites. At the height of the scandal, Thatcher told one associate, "I may not be prime minister by six o'clock tonight."[4] But amazingly, the opposition could not strike the fatal blow—Thatcher was blessed from the beginning with a weak, divided opposition—and the prime minister weathered yet another political storm. While Thatcher's reputation suffered, she hung on to power and soon the Westland scandal was forgotten.

Margaret Thatcher always had as her stated goal in domestic and social policy to provide less government and promote more individual responsibility. The individual and the entrepreneur were her heroes; the group, the society, the community were secondary. She told an interviewer in 1987, "There is no such thing as society. There are individual men and women and there are families" (Webster, 1990, p. 57). Hardly the comment of a Burkean conservative! As was the case with education and local government control, the goal of less government was often superseded by a narrower, more partisan question of whose ox was being gored. Thatcher was not immune to violating principle when that meant hurting political opponents.

But Thatcher made only very limited headway in these policy areas. By overpoliticizing many of these issues, she ended up having limited impact and few successes. Most social and domestic problems worsened under Thatcher, and after her nearly 12 years in power, the intellectual cupboard on conservative social policy seemed bare.

Thatcher's Leadership Style

How did Margaret Thatcher exercise power? What was her style of political leadership? In many ways—not solely because she is a woman—Thatcher was a different type of British political leader. Margaret Thatcher was a bold, innovative, ideological leader, a populist radical who relied on a strong sense of self, a warrior image, self-confidence, determination, and "conviction." In fact, she called herself a conviction leader. "I am not a consensus politician," she once said, "I'm a conviction politician" (Jenkins, 1988, p. 3). At another time she said, "The Old Testament prophets did not say 'Brothers, I want a consensus.' They said: 'This is my faith. This is what I passionately believe. If you believe it too, then come with me' " (Rose, 1984, p. 4).

Thatcher came to power determined to end the era of consensus politics that had characterized British politics for more than 30 years. Consensus was, to her, the problem (Harris, 1989, chap. 3). Thatcher was an outsider bent on breaking the consensus. There was thus a crusading zeal about her, a strong sense of belief or conviction that harbored few doubts and allowed little dissent. On taking office, she said, "It must be a conviction government. As Prime Minister I could not waste time with any internal arguments" (quoted in the *Observer*, February 25, 1979).

The sense of moral rigidity and mission led Thatcher continually to ask of subordinates, "Is he one of us?" meaning, Is he ideologically pure and temperamentally strong enough? This question was the test that, after the first two or three years, all would-be ministers had to answer before being allowed into the corridors of power. This led Thatcher to develop a highly (perhaps overly) personalized, somewhat imperious style of leadership. Inside the executive office, one had to either submit to the cult of her leadership or be dismissed. Few felt free to tell the emperor she had no clothes.

Thatcher's leadership traits demonstrate a paradoxical quality, and could be seen as a series of dichotomies: Her single-mindedness was often dogmatic; conviction was often rigidity; strength was often an aggressive drive for control; her determination was often contentiousness; her forcefulness was combative; her moralism was often quarrelsome.

Thatcher was a true believer determined to lead a moral crusade. Her messianic spirit was captured in her pre-prime ministerial comment,

"You can only get other people in tune with you by being a little evangelical about it" (Harris, 1989, p. 126). Her messianism fit comfortably with her warrior style, in which she set policy by full frontal assaults on her cabinet, party, and political system. She saw governing as an adversarial, not a collegial, process. Getting her way was everything, and she used fear, threat, intimidation, and all other means of persuasion to win. There may have been a type of method to this madness, in that since Thatcher had not won the hearts of the British people (public opinion polls reflected only lukewarm support for Thatcher and her policies; see Skidelsky, 1989, p. 45), she tried to get her way by bullying the cabinet and party.

Thatcher's jarring personality and sheer force of will, coupled with her Churchillian rhetoric, were formidable political tools. Where others sought to build a consensus, Thatcher attempted to dominate allies and adversaries into submission. "I am not ruthless," she once said, "but some things have to be done, and I know when they are done one will be accused of all sorts of things" (Young, 1990, pp. 104-105).

Thatcher's style of leadership was unique when compared with the styles of her predecessors. Thatcher was generally more ambitious, more of a centralizer, more autocratic, less collegial, more confrontational, and more ideological than her predecessors. As Anthony King (1986) notes, Thatcher "leads from the front. She stamps her foot, she raises her voice. For a British prime minister, she is extraordinarily assertive" (p. 118). This assertive style was essential to Thatcher's success. Not only did she take her cabinet and party by storm, she also took them by surprise. Thatcher was different, and the difference often worked.

Leading in the Cabinet

Thatcher's aggressive style was very evident in her dealings with her cabinet. The tradition of collegial decision making gave way to prime ministerial rule. Thatcher's vision of collegiality saw her cabinet falling into line behind her. With her early cabinet, Thatcher moved cautiously but later adopted a bullying style when the cabinet was "hers" (Harris, 1989, p. 109). And after she solidified her power, Thatcher chose her cabinet more on the basis of loyalty and obedience than on ability and experience. It was to be a *conviction cabinet.*

Her first cabinet was a mixture of old traditional Tory conservatives sprinkled with a few true believers. But over time Thatcher replaced the traditionalists with a cabinet more loyal to her. "Is he one of us?" was the question often asked by Thatcher; or, Is he "wet" or "dry"? (Harris, 1989, p. 128; Young, 1990, pref.). It was *her* cabinet, *her* party, *her* government. Decisions were not generally agreed to after debate and discussion. Often, Thatcher would tell her cabinet what she wanted, then try to bully them into submission. She was frequently successful.

Cabinet meetings were often tense and conflictual. Former cabinet minister David Howell remembered that "some arguments just left such acrimony and ill-feeling. . . . I think the general atmosphere in the government of which I was a member was that everything should start as an argument, continue as an argument and end as an argument" (quoted in Young & Sloman, 1986, p. 14). Thatcher controlled her cabinet through fear and intimidation, by controlling the agenda, by sheer force of personality and conviction, and by creatively using cabinet committees for her purposes. But even with her formidable skills, when matters reached the cabinet level for decisions, Thatcher was on the losing end of the cabinet vote "on more numerous occasions than any other post-war prime minister" (Jenkins, 1988, p. 184). Thus Thatcher's bullying style proved a two-edged sword. She was sometimes able to force her will upon her cabinet, but, when given the opportunity, the cabinet often struck back.

Thatcher often seemed an outsider in her own cabinet. She once referred to herself as "the cabinet rebel." This allowed or compelled her to over-personalize everything, and to look upon cabinet meetings as contests to be won. And how was one to win in cabinet? Usually by bullying. Thatcher saw the cabinet as a group organized to endorse her policies, not as a collegial body designed to discuss issues and arrive at decisions.

While Thatcher has not significantly altered the machinery of cabinet government, she did succeed in bending it to her will. She increasingly surrounded herself with weak men, to the point where Denis Healey called the cabinet "neutered zombies." And Shirley Williams remarked after one of Thatcher's periodic cabinet reshuffles, "She has replaced the Cabinet with an echo chamber" (Ogden, 1990, pp. 176, 197).

Thatcher and Parliament

In general, when the cabinet collectively decides, the Parliament usually follows. As leader of her cabinet *and* party, Thatcher commanded a good deal of power. This was heightened by the inability of the opposition, Labour, to mount any sustained challenges to Thatcher's leadership. Being able to bully her cabinet, dominate her party, and usually ignore or scoff at her opposition made Thatcher the preeminent force in government. While she did not structurally alter the government, she dominated it. All of this adds up to a style of leadership more *presidential* than prime ministerial in nature, and while one is cautioned against stretching the analogy too far (British power is "fused" or "unified;" U.S. power is separate and often divided), Thatcher clearly preferred the presidential operating style.

For both the style and the ideological substance of what Thatcher accomplished, an *ism* has been created: Thatcherism. It refers to force of will, depth of conviction, and personal drive. It is also about bullying, rigidity, and closed-mindedness. Thatcherism includes dogged determination, clarity of theme, Victorian values, and a crusading approach; it is also about a combative style and a rejection of consensus, about radical economic conservatism and jingoistic patriotism, about promoting inequality and rough justice (Riddell, 1985, chap. 1). Thatcher earned a variety of caustic nicknames, from "the Iron Lady" to "Leaderene," from "Her Malignancy" to "Attila the Hen," from "Boadicea" to "Virago Intacta." But regardless of how one views her, no one can doubt that she made an enormous difference.

The Fall

The fall of Thatcher came, as falls so often do, not as the result of a single dramatic event, but from a culmination of a series of smaller acts that, one by one, opened the political window of opportunity for Thatcher's critics, and eventually pulled her down.

Thatcher had been vulnerable before, but she always managed to fight off potential challenges and retain power. This was partly a function of her being blessed with a weak and divided opposition party, but was also a function of Thatcher's political skill and savvy. By 1989, however, time and good fortune seemed to be running out for Thatcher. She had been in office nearly a dozen years, and many were tiring of her bullying style of leadership. The economy, which during the 1980s was one of her claims to fame, worsened as unemployment and inflation were rising, and economic growth was declining. In this atmosphere, a series of blows to Thatcher's power occurred that led to her downfall.

One can trace the beginning of the end to the resignation in protest of Nigel Lawson, chancellor of the exchequer, in October of 1989. From that point on, criticism of Thatcher became harsher and more biting, especially relating to the widely unpopular poll tax and Thatcher's intransigence over European unity. When, on November 1, 1989, former Thatcher loyalist and Deputy Prime Minister Sir Geoffrey Howe resigned from the cabinet and, on November 13, made a devastating House of Commons speech in which he attacked Thatcher, saying that her style of leadership was leading to "a very real tragedy" for herself and "running increasingly serious risks for the future of our nation," and accusing her of a failed policy toward European unity, the floodgates of Thatcher busting broke loose. In resigning, Howe invited "others to consider their response" to his "conflict of loyalty." This invitation to insurrection was not lost on Michael Haseltine, who saw this as his opening to challenge Thatcher for leadership of the Conservative party.

The flamboyant Haseltine (referred to as Tarzan), a former defense minister under Thatcher, sensed the rumblings of discontent within the Conservative party, and after five years of quietly but unceasingly campaigning for Thatcher's job, made his move, and openly challenged Thatcher for control of the party. Thatcher accepted the challenge. Haseltine's challenge proved viable not merely on policy differences (which were rather insignificant), but on political grounds. Increasingly, Conservatives came to believe, and their opinion polls verified this, that the Conservative party was likely to lose the next general election with Thatcher at the helm.

After a very brief leadership campaign, the party voted. Of the 372 votes, Haseltine won 152 to Thatcher's 204. Under the party's leadership selection formula, Thatcher did not receive enough votes for a win (falling 2 votes short), and was forced into a runoff. Vowing that she would "fight on. I fight to win," Thatcher retreated and prepared for the next battle. But the momentum was shifting, and Thatcher soon found her top ministers deserting her sinking ship.

In spite of her pronounced intent to "fight on," it soon became clear that the party was deserting Thatcher. Minister after minister met with Thatcher and finally persuaded her that the only way to stop Haseltine, whom she detested, was to pull out of the race and allow a cabinet ally to enter. She reluctantly did so, announcing, "Having consulted widely among colleagues, I have concluded that the unity of the party and the prospect of victory in a general election would be better served if I stood down to enable Cabinet colleagues to enter the ballot for leadership." Two did: Douglas Hurd and John Major. Thatcher let it be known that she supported Major, who eventually won.

Major, Thatcher's 47-year-old chancellor of the exchequer, became the youngest British prime minister since 1894. He was, in many ways, a Thatcher clone. He was not born to privilege, but worked his way up. This self-made man appeared to be a true believer in the Thatcherite creed. But it was not long before Major began to undo some of the more extremist of Thatcher's policies, including an abandonment of the poll tax in March of 1991.

Thatcher's Performance

It is especially difficult to evaluate Thatcher's performance in office because (a) she is so controversial, (b) her style was so abrasive, and (c) she has only recently left office and the long-term consequences of many of her actions are as yet unknown. Few people are neutral about Margaret Thatcher. She evokes strong emotions. One thing, however, is quite clear. Thatcher is, as King (1986) has noted, a person of "extraordinary personal force." She has gotten her way. She has imposed her will. She has won.

But how deep is Thatcher's success? Was she good, or merely important? By almost all accounts, Thatcher's victories were personal victories, not party or ideological victories, and some were quite ephemeral. She changed Britain's policies, but did not win the hearts and minds of the people. As Ivor Crewe (1989) notes, "She is *both* intensely admired and deeply loathed" (p. 45). People respect Thatcher, but do not like her. In short, the electorate *has not* become Thatcherite. She has won few converts with her missionary style. Her effort to transform the British people from a dependency culture to an enterprise culture has not succeeded in any deep sense. There was no revolution in social values.

One can examine Thatcher's success in political, policy, and personal terms. Politically, Thatcher was in office nearly 12 years, won three general elections, and utterly humiliated the opposition. In policy terms, the record is mixed, but she did elevate Britain's international reputation, moderate the pace of British decline, and establish the conservative agenda in the political sphere. In personal terms the record is also mixed. It is true she has won, but she has not sold Thatcherism to the British people. She was powerful, but there was a shallowness in many of her victories. She was respected, but unloved; powerful, but a temporary force.

Thatcher was one of the most powerful prime ministers in this century, and she succeeded in implementing almost all of her agenda. She changed Great Britain, remaking it in her image. As Harris (1989) writes, "Only Gladstone, perhaps, has had such a profound personal effect on government and politics, on shaping society according to a vision" (pp. 288-289). There has indeed been a "Thatcher revolution," and while her contemporaries are mixed (generally along partisan lines) regarding its long-term impact, it is clear that the revolution has changed Britain.

The nation is more prosperous, but the prosperity is not evenly spread. The rich are richer, the poor poorer; the south of England is strong, the north weak. The unions have been weakened, and a sense of "acquisitive individualism" has spread. Market liberalism has been increased; so too have poverty and unemployment. Inflation is down; inequality is up. Local governments have become less powerful, the central state more powerful. Whatever the long-term results, one knows whom to praise or blame: It has indeed been a Thatcher revolution.

The Gender Factor

To what extent did gender matter in Thatcher's rise to power and in the way she exercised power? How did this nonfeminist (many would say antifeminist) woman rise in a male society, male party, male political system, to govern a nation? Thatcher is, in Webster's (1990) words, "a conspicuous figure in the world of sexual politics." She adds:

> Gender has been central to the way in which she has been seen and understood, to the images and narratives which have been shaped around her, and to the cult which surrounded her for much of the 1980s. Her presence at the centre of the national stage has raised in a dramatic form questions and meanings about masculinity and femininity, public and private life. In the discussions which have circulated around these, what it is to be a "real woman" and a "real man" has been a prominent theme, reflected in two paradoxical and common judgments: that "she isn't really a woman", and that "she is the best man in the country." (p. 1)

Feminists are torn when it comes to Thatcher. After all, Thatcher benefited from the repercussions of the women's movement, without which she could never have achieved the prime ministership. But at the same time, Thatcher rejected, even vilified, the women's movement. Webster (1990) writes of Thatcher:

> For women Mrs. Thatcher has often been an ambivalent figure. Some feminists have found little difficulty in reaching a verdict: she is an ardent servant of patriarchy, colluding with male power and male violence. She is not, and never has been, one of us. Others have felt the problems of attacking her, the dangers of a slide into misogyny, the need to disassociate themselves from sexist slogans like "Ditch the Bitch." Those who have written about her from a feminist perspective have often felt a need to recognize that she has proved that a woman can be Prime Minister, that she is capable, well-organized, articulate and courageous, that she has coped extremely effectively with the demands of the job, and in that sense has not "blown it for women." (pp. 1-2)

Thatcher's rise was made possible by the strides of the women's movement, but she often chided and denigrated that movement. Two representative quotes from Thatcher illustrate:

> The battle for women's rights has been largely won. The days when they were demanded and discussed in strident tones should be gone forever. And I hope they are. I hated those strident tones you hear from some "women's libbers." (from a speech to the Institution of Electrical Engineers, July 26, 1982)

> The feminists have become far too strident and have done damage to the cause of women by making us out to be something we're not. You get on because you have the right talents. (quoted in the [London] *Times,* May 10, 1978)

Thatcher used her femaleness when it suited her interests, but women were not a part of the Thatcher revolution. Thatcher's political agenda was decidedly lacking in proposals designed to advance the cause of women's rights in Britain. In fact, Thatcher often enjoined women to stay at home, to raise families, to assume traditional roles—Do as I say, not as I do. There is, in the Thatcher revolution, room for no more women.

Gender is important to Thatcher, and she has used it repeatedly and in a variety of ways. As Barbara Castle has noted:

> She's . . . shown almost a contempt for her own sex in the way she has used her power as Prime Minister. Of course she has sex consciousness . . . she wouldn't bother so much about her appearance, her grooming . . . if she weren't sexually conscious. But that's different from what I mean. Her treatment of the services that matter so much to women, that liberate them

from the domestic servitudes, all the social services . . . these don't arouse her interest at all. (quoted in Little, 1988, pp. 110-111)

She surrounded herself with men, but rarely strong, independent men. Thatcher's cabinet, and even her closest advisers, were usually fairly weak men, willing not only to take orders, but to suffer blistering public humiliation at the hands of Thatcher. Throughout her public life there seems to be only one woman whom Thatcher admired: India's Indira Gandhi (Young, 1990, p. 120).

Throughout her career, Thatcher was very adept at sexual style flexing, using a variety of different approaches to her femaleness as circumstances dictated. Early in her career she assumed the public role of devoted housewife and mother, though in fact she spent little time at either task (Young, 1990, pp. 306-312). Later, she assumed the roles of mother to the nation, firm nanny, wartime dominatrix, and, still later, androgynous leader. This style flexing allowed Thatcher to pick and choose sexual roles to fit perceived needs. "I don't notice that I'm a woman," she once remarked, "I regard myself as the Prime Minister" (Daily Mirror, March 1, 1980).

How did Thatcher's gender affect her sense of self? Some argue that she "discarded most of the significant gender traits and became for all practical purposes, an honorary man" (Young, 1990, p. 304). Governing in a "man's world" of politics, it is argued, forced her to jettison all aspects of femininity and "act like a man." In fact, her style of leadership, domination and bullying, is often characterized as a male style. As prime minister she led almost a womanless existence. Practically no one on her staff or in her cabinet was female, and she spent her time in the company of men. She was almost always the lone woman, surrounded by men.

Thatcher was a "gender bender," floating back and forth between what are conventionally seen as male and female roles, producing a synthesis, or a type of political cross-dressing. But if Thatcher's career was a tribute to the "manly qualities" of toughness, aggressiveness, and power, how did she escaped the scorn of society for being "unfeminine"? The fact of the matter is that by her style flexing, Thatcher was seen as different things at different times.

Often, Thatcher used gender differences as a political tool. In a way, being a woman proved to be one of her greatest advantages. Women have a great deal of experience dealing with men who hold positions of power, but men have virtually no experience dealing with women who are in positions of political power. Men were not accustomed to being in subordinate positions politically, and Thatcher exploited this situation. Melanie Philips has noted, "If she'd been a man, she would never have got away with half of it; she understood this and played it for all she was worth." She continued:

> Mrs. Thatcher simply didn't behave as men thought a woman should behave. She was rude, she shouted, she interrupted, she was tough, she was ruthless— male qualities that she used more effectively than the men who thought all this just wasn't cricket. If a male Prime Minister had behaved like this, it would have been thought entirely normal and his colleagues and opponents would have had no difficulty in using the same tactics against him. (quoted in Harris, 1989, p. 66)

Just as being a woman helped Thatcher gain some early political appointments (the Conservative party had few women in Parliament, and thus Thatcher was tabbed for ministerial appointments prior to proving her ability), it also helped her in dealing with the men in her government. Many of the men in her cabinet simply did not know how to deal with an assertive woman, especially one in a position of political superiority. Thatcher's bullying style got the best of a number of her cabinet appointees. One, Jim Prior (1988), wrote an almost apologetic biography, in which he confesses his inability to stand up to an aggressive woman. Even opposition leader Neil Kinnock noted that "Mrs. Thatcher is more difficult for me to oppose. . . . I've got, however much I try to shrug it off, an innate courtesy towards women that I simply don't have towards men" (quoted in Little, 1988, p. 109).

Thatcher often showed men up and, by all indications, derived a great deal of pleasure from such encounters. Webster (1990) notes that Thatcher enjoyed demonstrating to an audience "what they [men] really were—the weaker sex. Conventional sex roles were reversed as men were lumped together as feeble and fumbling, a gang of 'wets' and craven yes-men, while Mrs. Thatcher alone carried the banner of masculine virtues—strong, decisive, determined, courageous" (p. 117).

In dominating her cabinet and colleagues, Thatcher would, and could, engage in a variety of different styles and roles depending upon her approach to the situation. She thus kept her cabinet off balance, and often at her mercy. She was indeed different, and the men around her did not know how to deal with her. Even the few skilled and strong men who would sometimes fly into the Thatcher orbit (e.g., Michael Haseltine) had trouble dealing with the prime minister. As Webster (1990) notes of the men in Thatcher's cabinet, "They simply did not know how to handle her" (p. 118).

Overall, the gender factor helped Margaret Thatcher. From her early political rise, when the Conservatives needed "a woman," to her tenure as prime minister, Thatcher used gender issues with skill and cunning. She used her gender, sometimes relying on feminine wiles, sometimes as nanny, sometimes as bully, sometimes to coax, cajole, and flatter, but always calculatedly. As Young (1990) notes, "Without discarding womanhood, she has transcended it" (p. 312).

But Thatcher's success and her style of governing were not merely a result of gender. Clearly, she was driven by unbending ideological conviction. She was a crusader whose forcefulness mixed with the gender issue to produce a truly unusual politician. As she noted, "If a woman is strong, she is strident. If a man is strong, gosh, he's a good guy" (quoted in Young, 1990, p. 543). This represents a paradox of women in power. If they are strong, they are criticized for not being "womanly"; if they are weak, they "prove" that women simply cannot govern. It is a no-win proposition.

Conclusion

Margaret Thatcher came to power with the cards stacked against her. She had limited experience, did not have the support of a majority of her party's leaders, promoted a new and radical agenda, *and* she was a woman. But while her level of political opportunity was not high upon assuming office, a dozen years later one is struck by just how many of her key agenda items have been implemented. Historians, looking back on the Thatcher years, will note that, more than most prime ministers, she left her mark. She was powerful and purposeful, a force for change, a woman who dominated the political landscape of Britain. There is no question that Thatcher made a difference. She won. But were Thatcher's victories also Britain's victories? She won, but did Britain?

Long-term evaluations must be left to historians, but from the vantage point of 1992, Thatcher's record seems decidedly mixed. She left Britain more prosperous, but it is a prosperity not evenly shared. Britain is today in social disrepair, divided and unequal. The social cohesion and harmony that resulted from the welfare state have deteriorated. The wealthy, who were poised to profit from Thatcher's vision of an opportunity society, have benefited greatly. As Peter A. Hall (1989) has written:

> Nagging doubts remain. There is something ignoble about a regime that preaches the virtues of personal initiative and equality of opportunity while cutting back on the social and educational programs that generally extend such opportunities to those at the bottom of the ladder. If all revolutions have their shadows, this is the shadow that still hangs over Mrs. Thatcher's moral revolution. (p. 14)

Thatcher's philosophy of rugged individualism has opened entrepreneurial doors for the British, but it has also closed other doors. Britain is less a community, is more divided, has less that binds it together. Thatcher saw the choice as either self-interest *or* society; she chose the former. But clearly self-interest is not enough. The search for community must also be a part of the national quest. However, for Thatcher, the invisible hand guides, the trickle-down theory determines.

Thatcher was the first woman to head the government of a major Western nation, served longer continuously than any modern prime minister, tamed the trade unions, revived Britain's pride and economy, led her country to victory in war, and overwhelmed her opposition. But, as the *Financial Times* wrote as she departed in 1989, "Her flaws were as large as her virtues." She turned a blind eye to the poor and dispossessed, was overbearing and domineering, and left Britain a harsher, nastier place than she found it. She was a woman of firm conviction and great strength, but she had been running against the "socialist past" for so long, many in Britain wondered if, toward the end, she had a proactive vision. Thatcherism, it appears, may have reached its limits.

Clearly, Thatcher changed Great Britain. She accomplished a great deal through the force of her will and the power of her ideas. Where most British governments ground to a halt because of failed policies, scandals, lack of leadership, or electoral shifts, Thatcher managed not only to stay in power for a dozen years, but also to dominate her party thoroughly and to demoralize her opposition.

Can Thatcherism survive after Thatcher's departure? It is unlikely. While Thatcher did implement a variety of changes, much of her power was built on her persona. It is unlikely that Thatcherism as a style of governing can survive her. It was too dependent on Thatcher's unique style and drive. But what of Thatcherism as a policy approach? Robert Skidelsky (1988) has doubts:

Thatcherism may have been necessary to break out of the corporatist and bureaucratic impasse of the late 1970s; but the analysis was over simple, the means crude and mean. More fundamentally, Thatcherism as an economic and social philosophy—as a basis for the long-term government of Britain—is seriously one-sided. (p. 23)

One senses that Thatcher herself knows that Thatcherism is coming to an end. Her importance to the revolution is not lost in modesty. Thatcher once remarked, "I think I have become a bit of an institution," and "The place wouldn't be quite the same without this old institution" (quoted in Young, 1990, p. 543). Her handpicked successor, John Major, while a true believer, is up against formidable odds in attempting to reinject Britain with another dose of Thatcherism, not the least of which is Thatcher's apparent reluctance truly to step down from power. After all, shortly after announcing her resignation, Thatcher publicly stated that she would make a "good back-seat driver," leading a Labour critic to charge, when noting that Major's first cabinet contained no women (the only cabinet in all of Western Europe *not* to have a woman minister), "Is the only woman in the Cabinet the back-seat driver?" and other opposition politicians took to calling Major "Mrs. Thatcher's poodle." This prompted Major to fire back, "I am my own man."

Less than two years after assuming office, John Major was required to call a national election. In the midst of the worst recession in Britain since the Second World War, but facing weak opposition in Neil Kinnock and the Labour party, Major and the Conservatives, while losing approximately 40 seats, managed to maintain a slim majority in the Parliament. It was the fourth consecutive national election victory for the Conservatives, and in some ways it served as vindication for Margaret Thatcher. In June 1992, upon the recommendation of John Major, Queen Elizabeth II named Thatcher a "peer of the realm," and she became Baroness Thatcher, a life member of the House of Lords.

Margaret Thatcher was a revolutionary leader, not simply because she was a woman, not simply because she was a powerful woman, but because she was these things and more. She governed for a dozen years, won almost all of her major policy goals, and vanquished her opposition. Unusually, Thatcher was the beneficiary of the gender issue. She used her opportunities wisely and well, and seized power. As Webster (1990) says, there was "not a man to match her."

Notes

1. This quote is from the mother of one of Margaret Roberts's (Thatcher's) schoolmates to her daughter. Quoted in Harris (1989, p. 66).
2. As indeed Hugo Young (1990, p. 3) claims in the opening sentence of *One of Us*.
3. For reviews of the Thatcher economic policy, see Kavanaugh (1990, chap. 8) and Menford (1989).
4. This was confirmed by Thatcher in a June 7, 1987, television interview with David Frost.

References

Clayton, D. H., & Thompson, R. J. (1988, Summer). Reagan, Thatcher, and social welfare. *Presidential Studies Quarterly, 3,* 565-581.

Crewe, I. (1987). Has the electorate become Thatcherite? In P. Hennessy & A. Seldon (Eds.), *Ruling performance: British governments from Attlee to Thatcher* (pp. 25-49). Oxford: Basil Blackwell.

Hall, P. A. (1989, October 2). The smack of firm government. *New York Times Book Review,* p. 8.

Harris, K. (1989). *Thatcher.* London: Fontana.

Hennessy, P., & Seldon, A. (Eds.). (1987). *Ruling performance: British governments from Attlee to Thatcher.* Oxford: Basil Blackwell.

Jenkins, P. (1988). *Mrs. Thatcher's revolution.* Cambridge, MA: Harvard University Press.

Kavanaugh, D. (1990). *Thatcherism and British politics.* Oxford: Oxford University Press.

King, A. (Ed.). (1986). *The British prime minister.* London: Macmillan.

Little, G. (1988). *Strong leadership.* Melbourne: Oxford University Press.

Menford, P. (1989). Mrs. Thatcher's economic reform programme. In R. Skidelsky (Ed.), *Thatcherism* (pp. 93-106). Oxford: Basil Blackwell.

Ogden, C. (1990). *Maggie.* New York: Simon & Schuster.

Prior, J. (1988). *A balance of power.* London: Hamish Hamilton.

Riddell, P. (1985). *The Thatcher government.* Oxford: Basil Blackwell.

Robenson, M. (1989). *Mother country.* London: Farrar, Straus & Giroux.

Rose, R. (1984). *Do parties make a difference?* Chatham, NJ: Chatham House.

Skidelsky, R. (Ed.). (1989). *Thatcherism.* Oxford: Basil Blackwell.

Vincent, J. (1987). The Thatcher government, 1979-1987. In P. Hennessy & A. Seldon, A. (Eds.). (1987). *Ruling performance: British governments from Attlee to Thatcher* (pp. 274-300). Oxford: Basil Blackwell.

Webster, W. (1990). *Not a man to match her.* London: Women's Press.

Young, H. (1990). *One of us.* London: Pan.

Young, H., & Sloman, A. (1986). *The Thatcher phenomenon.* London: BBC.

9

Women as National Leaders

What Do We Know?

MICHAEL A. GENOVESE

Having examined the lives and careers of the seven leaders discussed in this volume, what patterns or lessons can we draw? What can we learn from these cases, these stories of lives lived in the private world of the family and the public world of politics? Can we draw preparadigmatic or pretheoretical conclusions about women and leadership? Can we bring these seemingly disparate stories together to form patterns and make generalizations about women as national leaders?

From this study, a number of patterns appear to be especially noteworthy.[1] Several patterns stand out when we examine the contexts in which women have emerged as national leaders. Most female national leaders have held office in less developed nations (8 of 11: Aquino, Bandaranaike, Bhutto, Chamorro, Charles, Gandhi, Pascal-Trouillot, and Perón); most rose in nations that maintained some form of democracy; few rose in "stable" times, meaning that most have come to power in times of social or political distress; and most have come to power in secular political regimes (see Table 9.1).

Table 9.1 Women as National Leaders

Name/Nation	Education	Political Family?	Previous Political Experience	Years of Rule	Age on Taking Office	National Development
Maria Corazon Aquino, Philippines	graduate of Mt. Vernon College	*yes*; husband was slain opposition leader; father and grandfather in politics	none	1986-1992	53	developing
Sirimavo Bandaranaike, Sri Lanka	Catholic school education	*yes*; husband was former prime minister	none	1960-1965; 1970-1977	44	developing
Benazir Bhutto, Pakistan	graduate of Radcliffe and Oxford	*yes*; father was former prime minister	limited	1988-1990	35	developing
Gro Harlem Brundtland, Norway	M.D. from Harvard	*yes*; father and husband active in politics	extensive	1981; 1986-1989	42	advanced
Violeta Chamorro, Nicaragua	some college	*yes*; husband prominent political activist and newspaper editor	limited	1990-	61	developing
Mary Eugenia Charles, Dominica	law degree from London School of Economics and Politics	*no*	extensive	1966-1977; 1980-	61	developing
Indira Gandhi, India	attended Oxford	*yes*; father was India's first prime minister	extensive	1980-1984	61	developing

Golda Meir, Israel	attended Milwaukee Teacher's Training College	*no*	extensive	1969-1974	71	new nation
Ertha Pascal-Trouillot, Haiti	law degree	*yes*; family very active politically	extensive	1990	46	developing
Isabel Perón, Argentina	sixth grade	*yes*; husband was president	limited	1974-1976	43	developing
Margaret Thatcher, England	graduate of Oxford	*yes*; father was mayor of city	extensive	1979-1990	54	advanced

Rise to Power

Why did *these women,* above all others, rise to power in their political systems? What distinguishes their career paths from those of other women? In an examination of the career patterns of the women who have become national leaders one characteristic stands out above all others: Very few of the women rose to power "on their own." Most of the women who have become leaders came to power in periods of social or political turmoil, and "inherited" power from family, father, or husband. Many of these women had precious little independent political experience on their own. Aquino, wife of the slain opposition leader; Bhutto, daughter of the ousted (and later executed) prime minister; Chamorro, wife of the opposition leader and *La Prensa* editor; Gandhi, daughter of India's first prime minister; and Perón, wife of the deceased president—all came to power as a direct result of family status. Unusual is the woman (e.g., Thatcher and Meir) who can rise to power on her own without the aid of powerful family connections. Also, the route to political power varies with level of development: Women in less developed societies are more dependent on spousal or family position than are women in more developed societies.

This trait is linked to another curious familial factor. Just as many forceful male political figures have had strong identification with their mothers (e.g., Lyndon Johnson), so too have most women leaders had very strong bonds to their fathers.[2] They have tended to come from families where much was expected, where opportunities for personal development abounded, and where the male figure encouraged or pushed the daughter to move beyond role limitations and social stereotypes.

Leadership Style

Are there "male" and "female" styles of leadership? Many researchers, such as Astin and Leland (1991), see men and women as exercising very different styles of leadership, with males using a hard style of leadership that stresses hierarchy, dominance, and order. Women, on the other hand, exercise leadership characterized by a soft style of cooperation, influence, and empowerment. In this sense, have the women who have headed national governments exercised more "male" or "female" styles of leadership?

No one would ever accuse Margaret Thatcher, the Iron Lady, of exercising a "soft" style of leadership, nor could such a thing be said of Golda Meir. On the other hand, Violeta Chamorro and Corazon Aquino are often criticized as being weak or soft. When examining the styles of leadership exercised by the women who have headed governments, no clear pattern (certainly no distinctively "feminine" leadership style) emerges. Some of the leaders have exercised a hard style, while others exercised a softer style of leadership. This of course raises the question: Is there an *androgynous style* of leadership, one that combines elements of what are seen as the male and female styles of exercising power and leadership? Or, rather than choose one or another style of leadership, should the goal be for the leader to exhibit *style flexing?* Different situations require different styles of leadership. The leader adept at recognizing what the situation requires and adapting his or her style of leadership to fit that situation stands a better chance of achieving success than the leader who rigidly adheres to one style of leadership in all situations.

Policy Consequences

Do women leaders pursue policy agendas that are different from those of their male counterparts? Are women in power more likely to promote a feminist political agenda? To promote family issues? To promote a leftist agenda? In short, speaking in policy terms, does it make a difference that a ruler is a woman?

In general, the research on women who hold political office reveals a tendency for women to be slightly more liberal than men (see Thomas, 1987; Welch, 1985). Is this also true of women who lead nations? In examining the policy preferences of the women who have served as national leaders, no clear pattern emerges. None of these women has been a "revolutionary" leader, and overall they have tended to be spread across the ideological spectrum.

The concern for "women's issues" likewise has varied from leader to leader, with Margaret Thatcher promoting what many referred to as policies that were hostile to women's interests, and other leaders pursuing a more profeminist agenda.

All leaders face enormous constraints that must be overcome if they are to achieve policy and political success. It is not unreasonable to presume that one of the reasons women leaders have not been more demonstrably profeminist is because such a policy agenda might be considered radically anti-status quo, and pushing these issues would be too politically risky.

Performance in Office

By what standards are women judged? What are the assessments of their tenures in office? How well—or poorly—have these women played the political hands they were dealt? Under what circumstances have these women left office? And to what extent did gender matter?

Overall, the performance of women who have headed national governments has not been ranked very highly. While some female leaders have achieved a great deal (e.g., Thatcher), many others have not been thought of as political successes (e.g., Perón, Aquino, Bhutto). This is so for a variety of reasons, not the least of which relate to gender. Even under the best of circumstances leaders have a difficult time overcoming the barriers to rulership, but when one remembers that most women leaders have risen at times of great societal hardship and systemic stress, and that they have had to confront the great barrier of gender, it is not surprising that their efforts at leadership have often been rebuked.

Very few leaders are considered "great" to begin with; the circumstances under which most women national leaders have risen have clearly contributed to the failure of most to overcome the barriers of gender and prejudice to achieve greatness. A woman in power is unusual; only when it is seen as unremarkable that a woman holds power will we be able to judge women's performance in office adequately.

Characteristics

The average age at the time the woman leaders assumed office was 51, with Bhutto the youngest at 35 and Meir the oldest at 71. Approximately half of the leaders had extensive political experience; four (Aquino, Bandaranaike, Chamorro, and Perón) had very little.

Most of the women leaders were highly educated; only Isabel Perón had a low level of educational achievement. A key finding relating to gender and leadership in general focuses on educational experience. A disproportionate number of accomplished women in both the public and private sectors are graduates of women's colleges (Astin & Leland, 1991, pp. 55-58), where it is argued that leadership opportunities are greater, expectations are heightened, and experiential confidence is built. It is thus clear that opportunity and experience are key factors in women's pursuit of leadership roles in society.

Conclusion

There is no question that opportunities for women have opened up in the past 25 years. The women's movement, the spread of democracy, and other factors have coalesced to open doors that have historically been closed to women. But the basic structure and legacy of male domination remains intact and virtually unchallenged. The women who have headed national governments, while a varied lot, do have one thing in common: None of them has challenged, in any fundamental way, the patriarchal power structure of her society. To do so would have been political suicide.

If doors have opened for women, enormous barriers still exist. Women remain outsiders and second-class citizens. The hurdles that inhibit the emergence of women in the public sphere are formidable, but, as Alexis de Tocqueville reminds us, "evils which are patiently endured when they seem inevitable become intolerable when once the idea of escape from them is suggested" (quoted in Tauris & Wade, 1984, p. 362). That there is increasingly believed to be an escape from the bondage of patrimony is the essential ingredient in the creation of a just and equal society that liberates both men and women (Cantor & Bernay, 1992).

Notes

1. In many of the categories to be examined, we can include the other women who have headed governments but whose cases are not presented in this book: Sirimavo Bandaranaike of Sri Lanka, Gro Harlem Brundtland of Norway, Mary Eugenia Charles of Dominica, and Ertha Pascal-Trouillot of Haiti. See Table 9.1 for further details.

2. This is true of most women who have achieved political success at the subnational level as well. See Astin and Leland (1991, pp. 42-47).

References

Astin, H. S., & Leland, C. (1991). *Women of influence, women of vision.* San Francisco: Jossey-Bass.

Cantor, D. W., & Bernay, T. (1992). *Women in power: The secrets of leadership.* Boston: Houghton Mifflin.

Tauris, C., & Wade, C. (1984). *The longest war: Sex differences in perspective.* San Diego, CA: Harcourt Brace Jovanovich.

Thomas, S. (1987). *Explaining legislative support for women's issues.* Paper presented at the annual meeting of the Midwest Political Science Association.

Welch, S. (1985). Are women more liberal than men in the U.S. Congress? *Legislative Studies Quarterly, 10,* 125-134.

10

Women as National Leaders

Patterns and Prospects

PATRICIA LEE SYKES

Essays in this collection address several significant questions and identify important issues that can provide the basis for further research, but some aspects of the subject of "women as national leaders" remain unexplored and merit brief consideration here. Despite the diversity of cases presented, none reveals the potential for women executives to provide transformational, feminist leadership. (On the contrary, as "models," Margaret Thatcher, Indira Gandhi, and Isabel Perón offer little hope to those who wish to advance feminist issues and objectives.) Furthermore, this text demonstrates how traditional approaches can be applied to the study of women leaders. Yet the subject also invites an alternative perspective: Viewed through a feminist analytic lens, the experience of women leaders can reveal the limitations of traditional analysis. Finally, the central lessons learned from the study of women leaders can inform research on elite political behavior in general. The following discussion begins to develop each of these points, but these concluding remarks primarily serve to invite further investigation and attempt to influence future discourse.

Women as Transformational Leaders

Transformational leaders seek to change individual citizens, their states, their societies, and the relationships among these.[1] Many of the leaders examined in this study have brought about such fundamental change. Former Prime Minister Thatcher illustrates one type of transformational leadership: Her trade union reforms and privatization schemes reversed the collectivist trend in British politics and helped to restructure the state and society. Nevertheless, like the other leaders in this study, Thatcher declined to use her office to alter the place and perception of women in the state or society. The cases selected for study could create the misleading impression that women succeed as leaders only when they conform to the traditional female stereotype or behave as their male counterparts would: Either approach precludes the possibility of transforming the state and society in ways that advance feminism. Other cases of women leaders call that understanding into question.

Furthermore, the women discussed in this volume who have promoted fundamental change have done so within the framework of a conventional left-right dimension, by increasing or restricting the realm of state activity, but they have failed to advocate or advance new "dimensions."[2] Here again, additional cases can shed light on the capacity of women leaders to depart from tradition and break new ground.

Consider the case of Norway and its progressive prime minister, Gro Harlem Brundtland. She served as prime minister from February to October 1981 and from May 1986 to October 1989, and has been in that office again since November 1990. When she took office in 1981, she became the youngest and the first female prime minister of Norway. Brundtland started her political activity at the age of 7, in the youth movement of the Norwegian Labour party; she became its deputy in 1975 and continued until she assumed the party leadership in 1981.

Her early participation in the youth movement and her parents' involvement in the party[3] influenced Brundtland's career and commitments, but the feminist movement of the 1960s and 1970s provided her central inspiration. Brundtland has persistently championed feminist issues, campaigned for the liberalization of abortion laws, and promoted the increased political participation of women. As prime minister, she has consistently seized the opportunity to put into practice her feminist principles.

In 1986, Brundtland broke a world record when she appointed 8 women to her 18-member cabinet, and the impact of her appointments rippled throughout the government and the country. Women cabinet members aggressively worked to advance other women: Helen Bosterud as minister of justice increased the number of women judges in Norway; Kirsti Kolle Grondahl as minister of church and education appointed a record number of women ministers in the State Church of Norway. When Brundtland formed her third government in 1990, she appointed 9 women to her 19-member cabinet. By actively promoting the political careers of other women, Brundtland and her female ministers provide a sharp contrast to Margaret Thatcher and Indira Gandhi.

Brundtland's transformational leadership extends beyond the field of feminism. After she completed her training as a physician in Norway, she continued her graduate education at the Harvard University School of Public Health, where her study of pollution problems sparked an interest in environmental protection. (As a physician and a scholar, she wrote numerous articles on school health, preventive medicine, and human growth.) From 1974 to 1979, Brundtland served as minister of environmental affairs. She advanced a popular program to establish nature preserves, campaigned for environmental protection from damage by offshore oil drilling in the North Sea, and advocated safer working conditions in offshore drilling and other industries. As a result of her efforts, the daring young cabinet minister became known as the "green goddess."

Prime Minister Brundtland has pursued her commitment to green politics at home and abroad. In Parliament, she served as leader of the Committee on Foreign and Constitutional Affairs from 1980 to 1981, from 1981 to 1986, and again from 1989 to 1990. As prime minister, Brundtland has always supported NATO, but she has also worked for nuclear disarmament and consistently promoted a nuclear weapon-free zone in Scandinavia. After Brundtland served as a member of the Independent Commission on Disarmament and Security Issues (the Palme Commission), U.N. Secretary General Perez de Cuellar asked her to chair the World Commission on Environment and Development. For three years the committee gathered scientific evidence and expert advice, but it also held public hearings throughout the world before publishing its report, *Our Common Future,* in April 1987. By consulting ordinary people as well as environmental experts, Chair Brundtland introduced a new approach to global affairs, one that reflects her commitment to open, participatory politics. The international community has rewarded her efforts and acknowledged her accomplishments: In 1988, Brundtland won the Third World Prize and the Indira Gandhi Prize for Peace, Disarmament and Development.

Like other female "conviction politicians," Brundtland has confronted her share of critics, most of whom attack her leadership style.
A profile published by the *New York Times* (September 14, 1981)
summed up her detractors' depiction of the prime minister as "a bit of
a nit-picker and occasionally self-righteous." According to the *Times,*
"Her directness and aggressiveness have offended many of her Labour
colleagues in a country where confrontation is a dirty word." Generally,
her critics consider her "hot-tempered" and arrogant, and the prime
minister's fiery comments occasionally fuel the criticism. For example,
after her party suffered substantial losses in the 1991 local elections,
Brundtland threatened to resign, but added, "The only reason why I will
not throw [in] my cards now, is because no one else can take over"—
shades of Indira Gandhi and Margaret Thatcher, or so most of the
political elite view her leadership style.[4]
    Brundtland has encountered other difficulties. In 1981, the economic
downturn and the conservative wave that swept across many Western
democracies drove her party out of power. (A Conservative supply-sider
took her place as prime minister.) Furthermore, Labour initially selected Brundtland to provide decisive leadership, but disputes about
defense and leadership rivalry continued to plague the party. Nevertheless, despite the difficulties she has encountered and the criticism she
has received from the elite, Brundtland has consistently remained
popular with the public, who refer to her with great affection as "Gro."
    Admittedly, Norway provides an unusual case in many respects.
During its early history, women ran local politics in the fishing villages,
where adult males were often absent. Norwegian society has always
maintained a strong commitment to egalitarian values and social justice. The nation experiences high levels of political activity in general,
and the participatory structure of its electoral and party systems permits
the advancement of women. (Voters can delete or add names of candidates on the ballot, and the country has proportional representation in
multimember constituencies.)[5] Political parties and public authorities
finance electoral campaigns. Activity flourishes at the level of local
politics, which provides numerous opportunities for the recruitment
and training of women candidates. Furthermore, Norway has had a
successful, coalition-building women's movement since the late
1960s (Bystydzienski, 1988). Finally, and perhaps most significant,
several Norwegian political parties have set quotas of women to elect,
and Brundtland's own Labour party requires that women occupy 40%
of the seats on party committees. The parties' adoption of quotas both

reflects the advancement of women in Norway and ensures its continuation in the future.

Norway provides a national context conducive to feminist politics,
but another example of transformational, feminist leadership emerges
in the highly unlikely setting of Ireland. On December 3, 1990, Mary
Robinson secured election as president of Ireland, a largely ceremonial
post, but one that Robinson has used to signal and enhance reform.

Robinson's political career began after she obtained her law degree
in Ireland and returned from a one-year fellowship at Harvard Law
School in 1968. Her interest in the civil rights movement attracted her
to the United States, and she returned to Ireland an ardent defender of
human rights and civil liberties. In 1969, Robinson secured election to
the Senate as a candidate for Labour, Ireland's third-largest party. (She
represented Trinity College, where she had been the youngest professor
in the university's history.) One year after her election, she introduced
legislation to legalize the sale of contraceptives. (Nine years later, a
revised version of the bill passed.) Throughout her career as a politician
and as a barrister in Irish and European courts, Robinson has argued
against laws that make homosexuality a punishable offense and has
campaigned against a constitutional ban on divorce. At the same time,
she has promoted greater rights for women, reproductive freedom, and
reforms of family law. As president, Robinson has continued to stand
for greater civil liberties and social justice.

When Robinson initially campaigned for the presidency, her prospects appeared dim. According to one biographical sketch:

> The notion that an ardent feminist could prevail in a presidential election in
> a country whose government had alternated between two conservative, male-
> dominated parties for nearly three-quarters of a century was inconceivable.
> Dublin bookmakers listed her as a 1,000-to-one underdog. (*Current Biogra-
> phy,* 1991, p. 49)

Nevertheless, when news of a political scandal involving her main
opponent broke, the event reversed her fortunes and put Robinson in
the presidency.

To a great extent, luck accounts for her electoral victory, but the
nature of her campaign and its consequences prove significant for the
study of transformational, feminist leadership. Her campaign slogan—
"You have a voice, I will make it heard"—spoke to the interests and
aspirations of young Irish women. (Even her theme song, Simon and

Garfunkel's "Mrs. Robinson," appealed to the younger generation.) Her campaign strategy also marked a departure in Irish politics: For more than six months, she used a campaign bus to canvass the country at the grass roots. Following her election, she proudly proclaimed, "We have seen an example of people power." According to Robinson, "It was a great, great day for the women of Ireland" (quoted in the *Chicago Tribune,* December 16, 1990).

The response from the political elite came quickly. Prime Minister Haughey announced that his government would repeal the law that threatens homosexuals with life imprisonment and review the constitutional ban on divorce. A conservative senior member of Parliament described Robinson's victory as "a culture shock" and admitted, "It's significant and forces everyone to take a look at themselves. . . . Clearly, [it] gave us a message about change and about the way we did things" (quoted in the *New York Times,* December 27, 1990).

During her term of office (which lasts until 1997), Robinson would like to alter the "ceremonial" post of the presidency. The Constitution prevents the president from delivering partisan political statements, but Robinson has discovered ways to express her views and support progressive change within the constitutional constraints of her office. By frequently meeting with feminists and other reformers, she offers encouragement, and by nodding her head in agreement, she endorses their positions. Robinson need not speak to send a message to the public at home and abroad: Her presidency stands as a symbol that "clearly represents the new, modern version of what the republic stands for" (*Washington Post,* February 19, 1992).[6] As Robinson sees it, "The office of the president can be a resource and a catalyst and give leadership" (quoted in the *Chicago Tribune,* December 16, 1990). Occupied by Robinson, it might also become a place for transformational, feminist politics.

The Study of "Women as National Leaders"

Add Mary Robinson and Gro Harlem Brundtland to the list of leaders in this study, and the task of generalizing about "women as national leaders" constitutes an even greater challenge. Ultimately, it proves as difficult to generalize about women as it is to generalize about men when it comes to the subject of leadership. In the field of leadership studies, political scientists rarely reach the heights of grand theory.

Instead, they usually adopt an approach that attempts to isolate and examine one or more explanatory variables, a method that explores various dimensions of leadership without neglecting the unique features of individual leaders. (Several authors in this volume have emphasized the tendency of women leaders to personalize politics, but no area of politics proves more personal than political leadership.) The essays in this text follow the "multivariate" approach and demonstrate that many traditional notions about leadership (derived from the performance of men) apply to the experience of women leaders.

By following a similar outline and employing the same explanatory variables, the chapters in this book permit easy comparisons and contrasts. To adapt a traditional approach to a nontraditional subject, the authors add "the gender factor" to the usual list of variables: context, style, psychology, career, and agenda. Nevertheless, the subject of women as national leaders invites an alternative perspective, one that employs a feminist lens to view the experience of women. Broadly construed and pursued, any feminist analysis would find that the gender factor permeates all the others.

For example, consider leadership style and the case of the "Iron Ladies." Indira Gandhi, Margaret Thatcher, and Prime Minister Edith Cresson of France all fall within this category. (Even critics of Gro Harlem Brundtland allege that she appears self-righteous and "difficult" at times.) Indeed, a disproportionate number of "iron" rulers appear in the category of women as national leaders. How and why did these leaders acquire their reputations as Iron Ladies? Political analysts have suggested possible explanations: Women leaders feel compelled to cultivate a style that conveys strength in traditional male terms, or women who mimic men prove more likely to succeed as national political leaders. In either case, responsibility for their reputations rests with the women leaders.

Yet these explanations overlook the origin and source of the term *Iron Lady*. The women who wear the label did not coin the phrase or name themselves (though some have turned it to their advantage). The Soviet news agency Tass originally called Thatcher the Iron Lady, and more recently, *Business Week* ("An 'Iron Lady,' " 1991) and the *Economist* ("The Passion," 1991) have applied the term to others.[7] In short, news organizations (dominated by men) designed the label and continue to make it stick. The term transforms strength and determination (so admired in men) into rigidity and insensitivity (perceived as flaws in women): Women are supposed to be "soft," not hard as iron. Perceptions of leadership style prove more important than any "objective reality," and gender clearly colors both popular and elite perceptions of the Iron Ladies.

Consider a second example that illustrates how gender pervades other variables—in this case, context as well as style. Most accounts of Thatcher and her cabinet describe a leader who bullied her ministers, one who governed through fear and intimidation. Journalists and scholars describe her "strident" approach and "shrill" voice; they portray the woman as high strung, prone to overreaction, occasionally driven to hysteria. These secondary sources always draw on primary ones—the memoirs and exposés written by Thatcher's male ministers. As a result, most stories about Thatcher and her cabinet reveal more about their sources than about the subject of study.

Viewed through a feminist lens that puts gender into context, a different picture of Thatcher and her cabinet comes into focus. Admittedly, Thatcher possessed and expressed strong views, and she always completed her homework, which made her well prepared to argue her case. (Indeed, she often appeared better prepared than her cabinet colleagues.) Typically, she would voice her views at the start of cabinet meetings. The response from her male ministers became predictable: They simply sat in silence. No cabinet member wants to be banished to the back benches, but many of Thatcher's ministers had been quick to oppose her predecessors. Some of the most vocal ministers in Heath's cabinet sat in silence in Thatcher's presence. The source of their silence presents a puzzle, but feminist analysis can help to unravel it.

Gender might not be the only factor (the duration of Thatcher's leadership provides another), but it emerges as a significant force. During interviews that I conducted with dozens of Thatcher's ministers, cabinet members frequently and surprisingly turned to the subject of their mothers.[8] (I said nothing to prompt such remarks, although my gender could have been a factor.) In the minds of many ministers—educated in British public schools—Thatcher apparently evoked the image of the only other female authority figure they knew: mother (and perhaps nanny).

The example of Thatcher and her ministers illustrates how gender colors all the other factors. A feminist analysis finds gender in every variable: psychology, career, context, and style. (Indeed, when political scientists examine the factors that affect male leaders, they frequently find it difficult to isolate the impact of a single variable or to distinguish one factor from another.) In several respects, feminist analysis can enhance our understanding of political leadership: A feminist perspective paints an alternative picture of women as national leaders, but it also points to even larger lessons for the study of leadership in general.

The Study of National Leaders

As the examples above demonstrate, the experience of women as national leaders can provide a reminder that leadership must be studied in conjunction with followership, broadly construed. Followers include not only members of the electorate or the party, but also the elite in government and the media. To understand any leader, we must start by looking at and listening to the followers.

At the same time, the view through a feminist lens reveals that leadership studies require a skeptical eye. If political scientists accept at face value what followers say about leaders, they will learn more about the speakers than about the subjects. In sum, one need not be a feminist to heed the admonition, "Trust the tale, but not the teller."

The relationship between leadership and followership points to the most significant lesson revealed by the experience of women leaders, a lesson about power in general. Political theorists who study power understand its many dimensions, but empirical political scientists have been slow to employ and operationalize these concepts. Most empirical research continues to examine power at its most basic level—as persuasion or influence (Neustadt, 1990). According to this definition, a prime minister must often bully or intimidate (when bargaining fails) in order to get her way.

The essays in this study also examine power as it operates on a second level, as agenda setting (Bachrach & Baratz, 1962). Michael Genovese points out, for example, that Thatcher was quick to set the agenda and put her opponents at a disadvantage. Not all political actors operate on equal footing in the arena of power. Presidents and prime ministers who take advantage of the agenda-setting capacity of their offices can determine what issues their opponents will address and what battles they will fight.

Furthermore, power often operates at a third, more subtle, level, as consciousness (Lukes, 1974). Even when Thatcher failed to produce an agenda, her ministers sat in silence and waited for her to do so. One prominent member of her government declared that "cabinet ministers could have exercised collective decision making if they had wanted to."

Instead, they acquiesced and allowed her to dominate. In that case, gender figured prominently in their consciousness, and their consciousness influenced her exercise of power. In any context, political scientists must remain alert to power's several dimensions: Consider not only what leaders do, but what they often decline to do. Perhaps more significant, consider what followers frequently fail to do in the face of leadership and why.

Finally, the larger lesson about leadership and power rebounds, sending a message back to the feminist scholar who examines "women as national leaders." The nature of the subject and the discourse it invites threaten to place feminists in the position of adopting the language of patriarchy and phallocentrism (see Diamond & Quinby, 1988; Martin, 1988). The search for similarities among women as national leaders occurs in the context of fundamental contrasts between men and women, which places women in opposition as "the other." In a sense, failure to find hard-and-fast rules about women as national leaders could reflect a rejection of the identity that the state and society have assigned, and instead signal success for those who appreciate diversity and seek to develop their own identities.

Notes

1. See Burns (1978). In addition, two subfields in political science address the subject of transformational leadership. Renewed interest in political development has inspired research on the conditions conducive to systemic transformation. For examples, see Skowronek (1986, 1988). Even more recently, the subfield of transformational politics has been formed to focus on new ways to conceptualize and participate in politics. Studies in transformational politics add "self" to the subject of state and society and consider both institutional and noninstitutional forms of leadership. For example, see Fishel (in press).

2. Feminism cuts across the usual left-right dimension. Some feminists (on some issues) advocate a greater role for the state; others critique the state as patriarchal and wish to restrict its influence in many areas of "private" life.

3. Both of her parents engaged in Labour party politics, but her father also served as Norwegian minister of social affairs, 1955-1961, and minister of defense, 1961-1963 and 1963-1965.

4. In this chapter, the term *political elite* is used to signify elected and appointed officials and members of the media. Statements about the elite do not necessarily apply to the mass electorate. In this case, for example, the elite view Brundtland as aggressive and self-righteous, but ordinary citizens tend to respect her convictions, and their statements about her indicate affection as well as admiration, as noted below.

5. Women candidates fare much better in proportional elections. For more on this, see Rule (1981, especially pp. 73-76) and Sykes and Gonen (1991).

6. When the Irish courts barred a 14-year-old rape victim from obtaining an abortion in Britain, press reports portrayed Robinson's presidency as a sign that Ireland is a society in transition, albeit one that faces "conflicts over its future."

7. The latter of these cited works is a story about former Brazilian Economy Minister Zelia Cardoso de Mello.

8. I conducted these interviews in the United Kingdom during 1990 and 1991. Elite interviews supply much of the research for my upcoming book on U.S. presidents and British prime ministers, which is titled *Conviction Politics: Leaders in Pursuit of Change.*

References

An "Iron Lady" across the channel? France's new prime minister could heighten tensions in Europe. (1991, May 27). *Business Week,* pp. 58-59.

Bachrach, P., & Baratz, M. S.(1962). The two faces of power. *American Political Science Review, 56,* 947-952.

Burns, J. M. (1978). *Leadership.* New York: Harper & Row.

Bystydzienski, J. M. (1988). Women in politics in Norway. *Women & Politics, 8,* 73-95.

Current Biography. (1991). New York: H. W. Wilson.

Diamond, I., & Quinby, L. (Eds.). (1988). *Feminism and Foucault: Reflections on resistance.* Boston: Northeastern University Press.

Fishel, J. (in press). Leadership for social change: John Vasconcellos (D-CA) and the promise of humanistic psychology in public life. *Political Psychology.*

Lukes, S. (1974). *Power: A radical view.* London: Macmillan.

Martin, B. (1988). Feminism, criticism, and Foucault. In I. Diamond & L. Quinby (Eds.), *Feminism and Foucault: Reflections on resistance* (pp. 3-19). Boston: Northeastern University Press.

Neustadt, R. (1990). *Presidential power and the modern presidents: The politics of leadership from Roosevelt to Reagan.* New York: Free Press.

Rule, W. (1981). Why women don't run: The critical contextual factors in women's legislative recruitment. *Western Political Quarterly, 34,* 60-77.

Skowronek, S. (1986). Notes on the presidency in the political order. *Studies in American Political Development, 1,* 286-302.

Skowronek, S. (1988). Presidential leadership in political time. In M. Nelson (Ed.), *The presidency and the political system* (2nd ed. pp. 117-161). Washington, DC: Congressional Quarterly Press.

Sykes, P. L. (in press). *Conviction politics: Leaders in pursuit of change.* Lawrence: University Press of Kansas.

Sykes, P. L., & Gonen, J. S. (1991). *The semi-sovereign sex: U.S. parties as obstacles to the women's movement.* Paper presented at the annual meeting of the Midwest Political Science Association.

The passion of the (other) Iron Lady. (1991, November 9). *Economist,* p. 43.

Index